Pater Gaudentius

The Christian trumpet

about impending general calamities

Pater Gaudentius

The Christian trumpet

about impending general calamities

ISBN/EAN: 9783741156298

Manufactured in Europe, USA, Canada, Australia, Japa

Cover: Foto ©Lupo / pixelio.de

Manufactured and distributed by brebook publishing software (www.brebook.com)

Pater Gaudentius

The Christian trumpet

THE CHRISTIAN TRUMPET

OR,

PREVISIONS AND PREDICTIONS

ABOUT

IMPENDING GENERAL CALAMITIES,
THE UNIVERSAL TRIUMPH OF THE CHURCH,
THE COMING OF ANTICHRIST,
THE LAST JUDGMENT, AND THE END OF THE WORLD.

COMPILED
FROM THE WRITINGS OF THE SAINTS
AND EMINENT SERVANTS OF GOD, AND OTHER APPROVED
ANCIENT AND MODERN SOURCES,

BY A MISSIONARY PRIEST.

WITH SUPERIOR'S PERMISSION.

The testimony of Jesus is the spirit of prophecy.
Apoc. xix. 10.

LONDON:
THOMAS RICHARDSON AND SONS,
26, PATERNOSTER ROW; AND DERBY.
1875.

PREFACE.

Some writers have to begin their prefatory introduction with an apology in behalf of the publication of another book upon subjects already treated by previous authors in the same language. Catholic authors in these circumstances usually quote St. Augustine's trite aphorism, that it is advisable to write upon an important subject in different styles, varying diction and phraseology, in the hope of inducing more numerous readers with different tastes to peruse one at least of these works.

Whilst the humble compiler of the present volume approves this idea, he considers himself dispensed from using it as his apology. He has made some inquiries to discover whether any book has ever been published in the English language upon the subjects treated in this work. Though many books of the kind have at various times been printed in other languages in several European countries, yet he could not succeed in finding one published in the English tongue, spoken at the present time by so many millions of men spread over a wide surface of the globe. In the hope and expectation of seeing this want supplied, he has been awaiting for some years, but all in vain. He is not the only person who believes that the present work will prove both interesting and profitable to the general English reader. Hence, in spite of his deeply felt shortcomings, he ventures to send it to the press for publication.

It will cause no surprise if the compiler says a few words in behalf of his own work. It has cost some study and some labor. It has been written, as the variations of the style will show, amidst frequent unavoidable interruptions, and some occasional physical sufferings. He has been obliged to make translations for the First and Second Parts from different books in divers languages, of which he does not boast of being perfect master. With the aim of combining brevity consistent with order and clearness, he has found it necessary to give an entirely new form to this work. This book has been divided into three parts.

In the First Part it has been judged proper to collect and arrange those prophetical predictions, the main object of which evidently is to warn mankind about impending serious and more or less general calamities.

In the Second Part he is gratified by being able to give many prophecies of a more cheering and hopeful nature, announcing the fast-approaching universal triumph of the true faith and holy religion of Jesus Christ.

The Third Part, if more gloomy and saddening to worldlings, will prove very useful to the true believer, and full of solid hope for the virtuous Christian soul, with fervent aspirations for the end of sin, and the general resurrection to glory of the elect of God.

Though the writer of these lines is more than satisfied with the humble office and title of compiler, it will, however, in the perusal of this book, be found that it contains more than a simple translation or compilation. This is particularly the case with the Third Part. Each of the three parts is subdivided into chapters. The compiler has connected prophecies and statements made by the same person, which were found separated, not only in several books, written in divers languages, but also scattered in different portions of the same volume. In the French works in his possession he found their respective and respected authors too strongly biassed in their political opinions, and too much disposed to accommodate different predictions to their cherished theories of human government. Whilst he sincerely respects their good intentions, and praises their worthy motives, he felt that he should not imitate their example. As it will be obvious to every intelligent mind, the compiler's aim has been directed above and beyond the earthly limits of republics, kingdoms, and empires.

When practicable, he has added a short biography of the person whose prophetical previsions are published in this book. In the arrangement of the various prophecies he has, as much as possible, tried to preserve the chronological order, which plan was not much observed in the books he used. He has, likewise, thought proper occasionally to make some short comments, in order to facilitate the intelligence of some prophetical predictions. These comments or explanations will be found enclosed within brackets, when necessary to distinguish them from the text. After careful examination, the compiler has determined to omit a pretty good number of prophetical predictions, which, in his humble judgment, were not sufficiently authentic, or too obscure, or not essential to the perfection of this work. The contents of this sufficiently large volume will, for various good reasons, be found of the highest general interest to humanity. In fact, human society, the Church, dynasties, human governments, time and eternity, pass in review before these prophetical previsions. In point of time they embrace more than fifteen centuries. They have relation to popes and to bishops, to ecclesiastics and to religious, to the clergy and to the laity, to believers and unbelievers, to Catholics and to Protestants, to Turks and to Pagans, to Jews and Gentiles.

It seems very evident that God desires to have these prophetical warnings made known to the world at this present time. This conviction is grounded upon the remarkable fact, that in former centuries Divine revelations were almost exclusively confined to holy religious living in cloistered seclusion; during the present century, and more especially within the last thirty years, they have been almost without exception communicated to pious persons living in the midst of society, where it is morally very difficult, if not impossible, to conceal their extraordinary Divine gifts and lights. Moreover, these privileged persons are commanded by the Divine Spirit to publish the revelations which they have received, and some continue to this very day to receive, from God. It is in consequence of this fact and of repeated commands from God that different prophetical revelations have, of late years, been published in France and in Italy, where such Divine manifestations have been very frequent.

There is another stronger and more comprehensive reason why God wills the publication of menacing prophecies as soon as possible. The perusal of this work will show, to those who like to see, that we are on the eve of startling events over the whole earth. There shall soon be terrible punishments on account of manifold sins and crimes daily committed, and hourly increasing in number, malice, and enormity. More than at any other period of human history, the earth is filled with iniquity. Hence with the Prophet Osee we may say: *Hear the word of the Lord, ye children of Israel, for the Lord shall enter into judgment with the inhabitants of the land. For there is no truth, and there is no mercy, and there is no knowledge of God in the land. Cursing and lying and killing and theft and adultery have overflowed, and blood hath touched blood.* Good God! were these inspired words pronounced about 2,570 years ago, or in this very day? What a truthful picture do they give of the actual state of human society! *Therefore*, let us conclude with the holy prophet, — *therefore shall the land mourn.* (Osee iv. 1, 2.) The infinite goodness of God, however, before allowing his Divine justice to inflict the deserved punishment upon guilty humanity, previously invites, in mercy, sinners to repentance, and warns them in a clear and strong manner of the impending chastisements if they continue obstinate in their career of iniquity. Such has ever been the wise and merciful conduct of God's holy providence in the old and new dispensation.

If we believe in revelation and admit these principles, if we cannot deny that human society is corrupted and filled with iniquity, if we are convinced that voices of heavenly warning proclaim to a guilty and almost godless humanity terrible impending punishments, why should we systematically attempt to stifle these charitable voices into a forced silence by refusing to them the breath of translation and the public trumpet of the press? Can we suppose that our affected, if not guilty, silence will be able to keep back from us the punishments so solemnly and so frequently announced by hundreds of divinely inspired prophets of eminent sanctity? or do we, like the Pharisee of old, believe ourselves different from the rest of men? In this manner we may through our culpable connivance accelerate its stroke, and intensify its severity, but we cannot presume to stay the uplifted hand of Divine Justice from inflicting upon us the threatened scourges.

For the sake of the general good, in announcing salutary truths we should neither fear the sneer of the sceptic, the sarcasm of the infidel, nor the sickly condition of the effeminate and sensual Christian. O, peruse the letters of St. Francis di Paola, and the more recent revelations of Melanie de la Salette, and then let us nobly despise the adverse criticisms of a selfish generation of morbid sensibilities, and of infidel and impious scepticism! Let us bravely and wisely act upon the maxim of the great Pope St. Gregory, *Minus jacula feriunt, que previdentur,—Foreknowledge blunts the stroke.* Whether we like it or not, the threatened punishment shall soon fall upon a guilty world. It is then more wise to listen to words of information, and still more prudent to make a timely and suitable preparation before their infliction.

There is another important reflection which we wish to make in these prefatory remarks. It is a theological axiom, that God is more grievously offended by infidelity than by immorality. Sins against morality are indeed a violation of God's holy law, but infidelity not only refuses to admit any Divine sanction to law, but boldly denies the very existence of the Divine Legislator. We are now arrived evidently at the unhappy epoch foretold by St. Paul in the following words: *There shall be a time when they* (men) *will not bear sound doctrine, but according to their own desires they will heap to themselves teachers having itching ears; and will turn away indeed their hearing from the truth, and will be turned to fables.* (2 Tim. iv. 3, 4.)

Besides the *heaps* of heretical teachers so emphatically foretold by the Apostle, we have in these sad days crowds of lying prophets and of bewitching prophetesses, reckless apostles of Spiritualism, deluding spirit-rappers, greedy fortune-tellers, enchanting mesmerizers, presumptuous astrologers, and impious necromancers, all of whom are unhappily too much believed, admired, praised and patronized by effeminate men and silly women, and by many perverted Christians. All these and similar superstitious impieties are most injurious to the Christian faith, and most offensive to God's eternal truth. It is evident that God wishes to confound these lying prophets and their deluded abettors by manifesting to his truly humble and faithful servants real and true supernatural revelations of certain future events, which shall infallibly take place. Our Lord moreover desires that in atonement for the credulous superstition of their fellow Christians, all sincere and virtuous Catholics should believe those truths which his Holy Spirit vouchsafes to reveal to his favorite friends for our common good and edification. It is under this deeply seated conviction that this book has with some labor been prepared for publication.

It has been objected that at this age, and especially in those countries wherein the English language is spoken, human society is so wholly taken up with matters of fact, that it will not be interested in the perusal of predictions about the future. It might, however, be doubted whether this indifference be the effect of the Saxon character, Northern climate, national habits, and domestic training, or rather the consequence of the loss, during the last three hundred years, of the true light of supernatural faith in the fulness of Christian revelation and genuine Catholic tradition. Whatsoever the cause may be, history and experience sufficiently prove that people of Saxon origin have their periods of strong religious and political excitement. This has been the fact both in Europe and America. There is perhaps scarcely any other race of people more eager than the

Saxon to read the leading newspapers of the day, wherein the political and religious problems of the age and country are discussed in relation to the immediate future, particularly when material interests are at stake. How often the waning popularity of the Protestant preacher seeks to recruit the decreasing numbers of *his dearly beloved audience* by repeated vocal and printed announcements of prophetical predictions extorted through sectarian commentaries from their favorite Book of Revelations! And who is more ready and willing than the Saxon non-Catholic mind to believe their oracles of the press and of the pulpit, when these gravely announce their desired speedy downfall of the papacy and of all Catholic power and influence in mundane affairs! The probability of a change in the ministerial governments of England and Germany, the general or State elections in these United States, manifest very strongly the real nature of the Saxon character.

But we have just reasons to thank God that not all persons of Saxon blood are unbelievers or sceptics. Many millions of these, both in Europe and in America, are strong, sincere, and fervent Catholics. Those who can read an English book shall not be found unwilling to examine the authenticy, the nature and intended object of these prophetical predictions. Moreover, the majority of Catholics in America do not claim to be of Saxon origin, but they glory in being of Celtic race. There is no doubt that these also will be glad to have the opportunity of reading a book like the present, which is offered to the public.

Here, however, a second objection of an opposite tendency has been proposed. Some timid persons somewhat fear that the publication of a volume of previsions and predictions like those contained in this book may cause undue excitement and unwholesome dread in many Catholics. We cannot see any cause for this apprehension. In fact, a very large number of books of the same nature have, during the last twenty years and more abundantly during the last few years, been published in Germany, particularly in France, and in Italy. We possess some of these works, from which the present compilation has in great part been made. But it has to be heard yet that any undue or even special excitement has been produced in the mind of millions of attentive readers. On the contrary, to our edification we learn that the perusal of such books has revived in many thousands of persons their dormant Catholic faith, and has produced a salutary change in their moral conduct. Such is at present the case in France and in Italy.

Moreover, these prophetical predictions or other statements contained in this volume are not proposed as articles of Christian faith, except what has been declared as such by the Catholic Church. To the rest we attach no more credence than what human authority deserves. The compiler does not and cannot expect his readers to believe these statements more than he believes them. Experience shows that the generality of Catholics will rather undervalue than overvalue the importance of a book of this nature. Superstitious enthusiasm is not the child of true Catholic belief, but rather the offspring of a corrupted faith and of infidelity.

Lastly, the attentive perusal of the present work will soon convince the intelligent reader that the punishments prophetically announced in it are neither intended nor calculated to alarm the sincere and devout Catholic believer. These events are intended by a wise and just God, and announced by him through his inspired prophets, *as a purification for the just and for the punishment of the wicked.* They should indeed be dreaded by the bad Christian, by the obstinate sinner, by the impious unbeliever, by the tyrannical oppressor and cruel persecutor of Christ's Holy Church and of our saintly and venerated Pope of Rome. Why should we conceal these truths from our enemies?

This should be kept in mind in a more special manner in reading the different announcements of the three days' darkness, of the prophecies about future massacres of ecclesiastics, religious persons, and devout Catholics, and the predictions of the schism which will, *too soon, alas!* be attempted in the Church by powerful and wicked men through a clandestine election of some anti-pope. We should remember that, according to St. Paul's warning, *schisms and heresies must occasionally come, that they who are reprobates may be made manifest amongst us.* (1 Cor. xi. 9.) Again, let us reflect that the sacred blood of Christian martyrs will satisfy and appease Divine Justice in behalf of mankind, and produce more numerous and sounder children in the Catholic Church. Finally, future happy experience will show that the three days' darkness shall prove in their inevitable effects to be the three brightest days for the Catholic faith and the dismal shroud of death intended by God for the general funeral and unlamented burial of schism, heresy, infidelity, and sin. Then, on the following Holy Saturday, the Catholic Church will have an additional reason for jubilation in singing in her sublime *Exultet* those words: *The dreaded sanctity of that awful night has banished crime and cleansed with tears the stains of sin. It has restored innocence to the fallen and joy to the sad. It has extinguished hatred, humbled pride, and united regenerated humanity in the bond of harmony and peace.*

Finally, we beg the reader to reflect that in this book he will find more than forty prophetical predictions, made by persons of eminent holiness of life. The very nature and object of these prophecies are an internal evidence and guaranty of their sincerity. These prophetical previsions and predictions are not intended or calculated to flatter human passions or national ambition. If hope is given to the repenting sinner, terrible chastisements are fearlessly announced against the obstinate criminal. Many predictions found in this book announce great victories, glory, power, and prosperity for France; but these glorious promises are made to France of the future. To France, contemporaneous with several modern prophets, her infidelities to God, her crimes, her impieties, are reproached by them in such plain and strong expressions that could only be inspired by the true spirit of God. These inspired prophets, humanly speaking, could only expect derision, contempt, and persecution from an incredulous and perverse generation reproached so severely by them. It is only power from above that could sustain their natural timidity in announcing terrible impending calamities over an entire nation, and over all mankind. However, as to what degree of authority and credence these revelations may claim, the compiler fully adopts the golden maxim of the learned Cardinal Lambertini, afterwards Pope Benedict XIV., who writes thus: *Though an assent of Catholic faith be not due to such revelations, they, however, deserve a human assent, according to the rules of prudence, by which they are probable, and piously credible, as the revelations of blessed Hildegarde, St. Bridget, and St. Catherine of Sienna.* (De canoniz. sanctorum, Lib. II. chap. 32, No. 11.)

CONTENTS.

INTRODUCTION 1

FIRST PART.
WARNING PROPHECIES.

CHAPTER   PAGE
I. Prophetical Predictions of the Solitary D'Orval relative to the Present Condition and Future Destiny of France   11
II. Prophecy of St. Remigius 31
III. Prophecy of St. Bridget, of Sweden . . . 34
IV. Prophecy of Father Jerome Botin, a Holy Benedictine Monk 40
V. Prophecy of Father Neckton, a Jesuit, about France . 44
VI. Prophecy of Sister Marianne, an Ursuline Nun . 48
VII. Prophecy of a Franciscan Capuchin Friar . . . 54
VIII. Prophecy of George Michael Wittman . . . 57
IX. Our Lady of La Salette. — Revelations of the Blessed Virgin Mary to Melanie and Massimin . . . 59
     I. Preliminary Remarks 59
     II. Letter of Melanie, of La Salette . . . 63
     III. Letter of Melanie to a Sister of Providence . 70
     IV. Portion of Melanie's Letter to M. Gerard . 72
     V. Letter of Melanie to Victor C—— de Stenay 72
     VI. Letter to the Same 75
X. Manifestation of the Secret of La Salette made by Melanie to the Abbé Felician Bliard . . . 77
     I. Words of the Most Holy Virgin to Melanie . 77
     II. Words of Melanie, and Portions of some of her Letters 83
     III. Present Mode of Life of Melanie . . . 85
     IV. Secret of Massimin Girand 85
XI. Prophecy of the Venerable Abbé Viannay, Curé d'Ars, France 86

CONTENTS. xv

 XII. Prophecy of the Venerable Anna Maria Taigi . . 88
 XIII. Predictions of Sister Rose Colomba, a Dominican Nun 99
 XIV. Predictions of Palma Maria Addolorata Matarelli . 105
 XV. Prophecy of Jane le Royer, in Religion Sister of the
   Nativity 115
 XVI. Poetical Prediction, which exists in the Public Biblioteca of Piacenza, in Italy, with some Remarks
   about Republican Governments 117

SECOND PART.
TRIUMPH OF THE CATHOLIC CHURCH.

 I. Jesus Christ ever triumphs in and through his Church 132
 II. Prophecy of St. Cesarius 148
 III. Prophecy of St. Edward, King of England, and of St.
   Malachy, Archbishop of Armagh 150
 IV. Previsions and Predictions about England, of St. Paul
   of the Cross and of Domenico Savio . . . 153
 V. Letters of St. Francis di Paola 158
 VI. David Lazzaretti 168
 VII. Prophetical Previsions and Predictions of the Venerable Bartholomew Holzhauser 175
 VIII. Prophecy of Mary Lataste, a Religious of the Sacred
   Heart 178
 IX. Visions of Elizabeth Mora 183
 X. Prophecy of Blessed Bobôla, S. J. . . . 190
 XI. Prophecy of Rodolphus Gekner 192
 XII. Prophecy of Magdalene Porsat 193
 XIII. Prophetical Announcements about the Popes, attributed to St. Malachy, Archbishop of Armagh, Ireland 198
 XIV. Prophecy of the Abbot Merlin Joachim . . . 207
 XV. Address of the Catholics to his Holiness Pope Pius IX. 211

THIRD PART.
THE LAST JUDGMENT.

 I. Necessity of a General Judgment 217
 II. Nature of the General Judgment 223

III. Signs of the approaching General Judgment	230
IV. Remote Signs of the General Judgment	233
V. Two other Important Signs of the approaching General Judgment,—Apostasy from Faith, and the Abolition of the Roman Empire	241
VI. More Signs of the approaching General Judgment	247
VII. An Objection answered	253
VIII. Prophecy of an Olivetine Monk	259
IX. About Antichrist	262
X. The last Prophecies and recent Facts about Antichrist	268
XI. Concluding Remarks	276

THE CHRISTIAN TRUMPET.

INTRODUCTION.

"Extinguish not the spirit. Despise not prophecies. But prove all things, and hold that which is good." — 1 Thess. v. 19.

MAN, being composed of soul and body, has need of food for his existence. But as the sensible life of his body requires material food, so the intellectual life of his soul must be nourished with truth. Truth is eternal; thence it embraces all time, past, present, and future. In the past we search truth in history. We seize with eagerness present events, and we experience a strong innate impulse to explore the unknown future. This hankering for knowledge in man is the appetite of the soul for her natural food, which is truth. A desire to penetrate the future is therefore as innate to man as it is natural to him to seek after truth. Any undue interference tending to hinder man from this legitimate search is an attempt to extinguish his spirit. But St. Paul says, "Extinguish not the spirit."

These words of St. Paul possess, however, a higher import. The fact that man is composed of spirit and body, proves that he occupies a middle state in creation. As his body indicates the existence of mere material being, so his spirit demonstrates the separate existence of pure spiritual substance. In short, as there are stones, so there must be angels, because the works of

God must be perfect in every kind and in every part. If there were material beings, and also beings composed of body and spirit, but there were not likewise purer spiritual substances, then between man and God a certain void would exist, which every law of nature abhors; therefore, the perfection of this universe requires the existence of pure spiritual substances that we call angels.

Moreover, every creature is the expression of one or more of God's infinite attributes. Hence every creature bears some trait of likeness to the Divine Creator. Now God, who is the first cause of all beings, is a most pure Spirit, therefore in this universe there must be created agents, as St. Thomas says, who, as much as possible to a creature, are by nature like unto him, namely, *pure spiritual substances.*

All true Christian divines teach, that as God communicates his special lights to inferior angels, through the means of those higher and nearer to him, so God communicates supernatural lights to the soul of man through the ministry of his inferior angels. Thus, *Every good and perfect gift must come from above, from the Father of light.* How beautiful is this Catholic doctrine of divine economy in the government of this world! St. Paul, therefore, for graver reasons, says: *Extinguish not the spirit, despise not prophecies.* Because, as the human body could not naturally exist totally separated from contact with any other material being, so the human soul is necessarily degraded, and rendered miserable, if excluded from every intercourse with superior intelligences. Hence, in every age of the world, among Jews or Gentiles, in Christian and pagan nations, a most firm and universal belief in these spiritual intelligences has ever existed. Moreover, it is a general conviction in the human mind that these superior intelligences occasionally communicate to man the knowledge of hidden and future events.

Let us pass from reason to authority, and from theory to facts. Because the preceding reflections have been made for a special class of readers with a sceptical turn of mind about modern prophecies, so these persons will not dislike to hear the opinion upon this matter of the famous political philosopher, Nicolas Machiavelli. In the first book and fiftieth chapter of his lectures on Titus Livy, he writes what follows: —

"Before any extraordinary event takes place in any city or province, it is previously announced by mysterious signs, or by human prophetical predictions. I do not pretend to know the origin of this. But the examples of ancient and modern times demonstrate the fact that no grave event has ever transpired in any city or province, which has not been foretold by *auguries*, or by *revelations*, or by prodigies, or by other supernatural signs. In confirmation of this I might refer here to many examples; but for the sake of brevity I must forbear. I shall, however, mention a fact related by Titus Livy, which occurred a short time before the Franks came to Rome. A certain man, by name Marck Leditius, told the Roman senators that about midnight, whilst he was passing through Via Nova, New Street, in the city, he heard a superhuman voice commanding him to inform the Roman magistrates that the Franks were coming to attack Rome. The event soon verified the prediction. I should not go from home for proof of this truth. Every person among us is well aware how Friar Jerome Savonarola foretold beforehand the coming to Italy of Charles VIII., king of France. Besides, over all Tuscany, it was well known that visions of armed men were seen fighting in the air above the city of

Arezzo. The cause of these events should be searched and explained by those who possess the knowledge of natural and supernatural things, which I have not. However, as some philosophers assert, it may be that the *sky being full with spiritual intelligences*, who by their natural power can foresee future events, these, moved by compassion for men, give them a timely warning by supernatural signs, in order that they may be prepared for the impending calamities. Whatever the cause may be, the facts are certain that *before any extraordinary event transpires in any province or kingdom, preternatural signs always give the warning in anticipation*."

If Machiavelli believes that angels are moved by natural compassion to give men timely notice of impending calamities, how much more should we admit that God will admonish men before he is obliged to inflict any public chastisement! God punishes in mercy. He wills not the death, but the conversion of the sinner. If the obstinacy of the wicked forces the justice of God to chastise them publicly, yet in his divine mercy he always vouchsafes to warn men beforehand. These miraculous signs and predictions are a practical protest of his divine goodness, a sign of his predilection for the just, and a lesson for future generations. Hence the royal prophet says, *Thou, O Lord, hast given warning to them that fear thee, that they may flee from before the bow, that thy beloved may be delivered.* (Ps. l.)

Christians, who believe in the divine authority of the Bible, can find in that sacred book innumerable instances of prophetical predictions, and *signs and wonders* admonishing the Jewish people about impending calamity. The spirit of prophecy is not less remarkable in the Church of Jesus Christ. This fact is so evident throughout all the New Testament, that it would be a loss of time and labor to transcribe the proofs. This prophetic spirit will be more fully manifested in this last age of the world. "*It shall come to pass in the last days (saith the Lord) I will pour out my spirit upon all flesh, and your sons and your daughters shall prophesy, and your young men shall see visions, and your old men shall dream dreams. And upon my servants indeed, and upon my handmaids, will I pour out in those days of my spirit, and they shall prophesy. And I will show wonders in the heaven above, and signs on the earth beneath; blood and fire and vapor of smoke.*" (Acts ii. 17.) I have insisted longer than I intended or desired in bringing forward arguments and authorities in confirmation of the maxim laid down by Machiavelli, that, before any grave event takes place in any city, province, or kingdom, God always gives beforehand supernatural warnings to mankind. If this infidel age attempts to exclude the providence of God from the government of human society, it is the duty of every true believer to uphold on every suitable occasion this fundamental principle of our holy religion. We have now — and we Catholics shall have more in a few years — much need of these considerations.

I shall close this long and perhaps dry article with some practical illustrations. Many readers may remember to have perused in Robertson's "History of America" some facts adapted to our present subject. This Protestant English historian relates that the Spaniards, at their first discovery of America, found among those native savages a general tradition and certain expectation that formidable conquerors were to come from an easterly direction to take possession of their country. Again, at the arrival of the Spaniards with Cortez in

Mexico, Montezuma delivered a public address to the principal men of his empire, reminding them of the traditions and predictions of their forefathers, announcing the conquest of their country by a foreign nation.*

From America let us rapidly pass to Africa. In the year 1830, at the arrival of the French army in Algeria, the French learned from the conquered Algerines and Arabs the existence of a prophecy foretelling the conquest of their country by the Franks in punishment for their sins. Whilst we are with the Turks we may add, that in Palestine and Syria, and in other parts of the Ottoman Empire, there is a general expectation and presentiment that the Franks are destined by Providence to take possession of those countries. We shall have a future opportunity to read this prophecy, which cannot be far from its happy realization. Our circle round the earth will be complete if we travel to Europe and rest in Paris, whilst it enjoys *a short and stormy peace.*

Thirteen years before the first French Revolution of 1792, a venerable old priest, L'Abbé Beauregard, ascended the pulpit on a Sunday, to deliver the usual sermon to a large and select audience in the Cathedral of Notre Dame in Paris. He began the discourse, and for some time he proceeded in the ordinary calm style of preaching. But all of a sudden this venerable old priest appeared invested with a prophetic spirit. His usually pallid countenance became flushed with a preternatural fire. With a louder tone of voice, and burning words, he announced as certain impending calamities over France, and the city of Paris in particular, and he gave an anticipated history of their future horrors to the astonished multitude. With the voice and spirit of a prophet, he spoke of the dethronement of the king,

* Béjol's History of the Conquest.

of the intended profanation and spoliation of churches and altars, of the entire abolition of feasts and divine worship. "In this holy temple," he said, "bloody and lewd songs will be substituted for sacred psalms and holy hymns." Then, turning towards the sanctuary of Notre Dame, and with his right hand trembling with emotion, pointing to the grand, high altar, "*There*," the holy priest exclaimed, with a voice choked with anguish, — "*there upon that sacred tabernacle* the goddess of reason, the impure Venus, in the real person of a living infamous female, will receive incense and divine homage from impious and lustful men." It is more easy to imagine than to describe the surprise and commotion produced by these words in that large assembly. Very few in the audience were willing to believe these prophetic predictions. The venerable preacher was severely criticised and censured both by the laity and by the clergy. Those who had the greater cause for fear were the loudest and boldest in their condemnation of the supposed indiscretion of the old priest. The news of the occurrence spread through the city, and was soon brought to the Royal Palace. Everywhere the conduct of the preacher at Notre Dame was disapproved and condemned. The holy priest had to suffer. But in a few years the events verified the prophecy. Hundreds of witnesses saw with their own eyes in tears the realization of the predictions made to their incredulous ears. Some of the principal persons who were the least disposed to give credit to the prophetic words of the saintly Abbé Beauregard, were in less than fourteen years brought in disgrace to the fatal guillotine erected in the square De Grevé, in sight of that very cathedral now sacrilegiously profaned, where they heard the prophetic warning, — a warning they heeded not then, but which in their sad condition they remembered, to admire and implore the goodness and mercy of God. Therefore, "Extinguish not the spirit. Despise not prophecies. But prove all things, and hold that which is good." We may believe as certain that before any grave event transpires in any city, province, kingdom, God always gives beforehand warnings to mankind. Now, more directly to our point.

Everybody knows that during the last eighty years the most serious convulsions have agitated Europe. Had these *grave events been previously foretold?* Yes, by all means yes!—they were most clearly and repeatedly predicted. Again, a gigantic, most sanguinary and most destructive war is scarcely finished in France. The false prophets of this credulous generation, in *big words* and *capital letters*, announce peace. Material interests desire it. Christian charity more earnestly prays for it. But this world is not converted to God yet. Do not calculate too soon upon a permanent peace in France, Italy,—Europe. Who will give peace to France? The infidels Thiers, Fabre, & Co.? *Impossible!* France has not yet complied with the absolutely necessary conditions of peace demanded by a *Higher Power* than that of Germany. For a most Christian nation the conditions of a true, lasting peace is the faithful observance of God's holy laws, as the prophetess of La Salette lately declared. Much remains to be done in this respect. Hence, no wonder that rumors of wars sound through the air; thoughtful Christians look aghast at the dismal gathering storm in France, Italy,—Europe. More serious calamities are threatening the immediate future. Can we find, then, any authentic prophetical prediction foretelling these future events? Certainly we can, if we wish. Peruse, then, the present compilation of prophetical predictions, and you will be able to learn much important and useful information about the immediate future.

The style of this Introduction, as well as of the next chapter, and of the letter of Melanie to her mother, will be found somewhat different from the rest of this book. The reason is obvious. These articles were published in the "New York Freeman Journal" two years ago, when the writer had no fixed intention of compiling this present work. Hence, in respectful deference to the kind editor of the "Freeman," and of former readers, no essential alteration is made in them on the present occasion.

FIRST PART.
WARNING PROPHECIES.

CHAPTER I.

PROPHETICAL PREDICTIONS OF THE SOLITARY D'ORVAL RELATIVE TO THE PRESENT CONDITION AND FUTURE DESTINY OF FRANCE.

AS St. Paul desires Christians "to despise not prophecies, but to prove all things and to hold that which is good" (1 Thess. v. 19), before believing in any new prophetical prediction, we should be furnished with satisfactory proofs for the authenticity and veracity of the prophecy. By prophecy we understand the prediction of future events naturally unknown to man. This prediction, then, must exist before the fact foretold. Again, when the same prophet predicts various events for different periods of time, it is very clear that the realization of a considerable portion of his prophecies is a sufficient guaranty for the fulfilment of his future predictions. Now, these two proofs are found in a remarkable manner in support of the Prophecy D'Orval.

It is, beyond all doubt, established, that this long prophecy existed before the first French Revolution, and before anything was known about the very existence of Napoleon I., of whom it speaks so distinctly. Here I mention the principal periodicals wherein it was first published in France: *Journal des Villes et Campagnes* (City and

Country Journal), 20th June, 1839; thence it was copied in the *Propagateur de la Foi* (Propagator of the Faith), on two different occasions during the same year, Vols. IV. and V.; also in the *Tablettes du Chrétien* (The Christian Tablet); the Freiberg *Invariable* published the same, Tom. XIII., in 1839. In the following year, 1840, it was published in a more satisfactory manner in the Paris *Oracle* of Monsieur Dujardin. In that article the writer, Monsieur O'Mahony, gives a number of letters, which he obtained from different French priests and lay gentlemen, proving the existence and knowledge of this prophecy before the first French Revolution. I shall give the principal portions of these letters.

Remarks about the Predictions D'Orval.

"We feel bound to ask our readers to rely upon our word, when we assure them that they can place all confidence on the authority of the following attestations. They come from the most pure and respectable sources. They are the results of inquiry, and the literal expressions of venerable ecclesiastics, and lay persons of eminent piety. Were we allowed to mention their names, not the least doubt could remain upon this fact. Nobody can be surprised at the reserve imposed upon us, and why persons who live in France, or are engaged in the sacred ministry, do not wish to have their well-known names published. (During the reign of King Louis Philippe.)"

"This Prophecy D'Orval was well known in 1816, at Bar-le-Duc, by a very large number of persons, some of whom gave a copy of it to the Very Rev. Canon De ——, which he communicated to Monsieur De L——. Though this gentleman had no doubt of the exactness of such authority, he wished, however, to collect more proofs.

For this object he obtained new and confirmatory information from the inhabitants of Bar-le-Duc. He wrote upon this subject to the *curé* (parish priest) of Mande, a city near the ancient abbey D'Orval, who afterwards was made Canon and Vicar-General of O. After some considerable delay, this worthy ecclesiastic answered to the date 29th August, 1833 : —

"'I have in my parish a saintly person, who has full faith in these predictions. I do not censure her, but I leave her to her pious belief. However, I confess that I do not share in her convictions.'

"We like to give this first answer, because the disposition *not to believe* will add more authority to the subsequent change of opinion of this prudent ecclesiastic. This curé of Mande being pressed by the former gentleman, De L——, he, on the 4th of April, 1835, wrote a second letter to this effect : —

"'I have delayed some time answering the letter with which you have honored me. The cause of it has been the necessity I had of gathering better information which I could not procure without visiting the locality and exmining divers sources, in order to be able to offer you something certain about the subject of your letter. Now, behold here the result of my inquiry. It is a certain fact, which excludes every doubt, that the prophecies of the Solitary D'Orval, such as they are known to you, were written in the abbey D'Orval before the French Revolution, namely, before the year 1790. At that time they were known and read in that abbey. The Baron, Sir Manoville, a personage of sound sense and of religion, attests to having read them at that time, without attaching to them the importance which he felt obliged to give them afterwards.

"'French emigrated ladies knew these prophecies during their exile. Many ecclesiastics, among whom the curé of Sedan, had without doubt knowledge of them before the French Revolution in 1830. It is therefore a well-established fact that this prophecy, exactly as it is known at the present day, is proved to have had its origin at an epoch anterior to the events which are therein specified in a manner so precise and clear as to appear to have been written after their occurrence. In conclusion, every wise and prudent person can give to it his full and entire approbation.'

"So far the letter of the curé of Mande. But Monsieur De L—— went further in his inquiry. He wrote to the curé of Sedan, and received from him the following answer:—

"'During my emigration (exile from France on account of the Revolution of 1792), I often heard persons speaking of these prophecies. But I had not the opportunity then of reading the text. It is only since the Restoration (1815) that it has been communicated to me. It contains all that relates to Napoleon, the return of the Bourbons, their departure, and the rest, etc., etc., till the coming of Antichrist. Orval, through which I passed a few days before the Revolution in the year 1792, is no farther than six leagues (about eighteen miles) from here (Sedan). I had occasion to return thither and examine its ruins. I have been able to collect all the documents relative to this very interesting prediction. I am sure that the most respectable and trustworthy persons in these parts, and elsewhere, have in it, like myself, the greatest confidence.'

"Lastly, the curé of Mande, who, in 1833, did not believe this prophecy, yet, after examining its well-authenticated proofs, became more and more convinced of its reality. On the 23d September, 1839, he wrote to Monsieur De L——:—

"'The prophecies of the Solitary D'Orval have for some time attracted in a peculiar manner the attention of ecclesiastical persons in high positions. The fact that the Archbishop of Paris has requested some copies of it, shows that he fully and entirely believes in them. His conviction is common to many ecclesiastics distinguished for their learning, and to a great number of the faithful esteemed and commendable for their piety.'"

I shall close here with Monsieur O'Mahony's own words: —

"It is this kind of arguments that has to be answered by those who, with unmeaning words, and the worthless gossip of anonymous writers, sneer against this prophecy. After all these facts, the exactness of which we guarantee, and after all these testimonies, whose authority every wise and prudent person will admit, it remains for us to make known the last and final results of long researches made about this Prediction of Orval, — a result, certainly the most important, because through them we have succeeded in obtaining the real authentic version, which we now publish. This is no less than the original text of the Prediction, copied in the year 1823, from a book printed in Luxemburg in 1544."

This should be more than sufficient to demonstrate the pre-existence of this prophecy to the events foretold in it.

The hasty and unwise *brochure* against this prophecy of Orval by Monseigneur Rossat, bishop of Verdun, was triumphantly confuted by the Abbé Lacombe, canon of the Metropolitan church of Bordeaux, in a volume of 230 pages, printed in the same city in the year 1849, with the following title: "*The Authenticity of the Prophecy D'Orval since the Year* 1793 *demonstrated by material, logical, and mathematical Proofs; corroborated by numerous contemporaneous Testimonies, and deposed at the Public Library of Bordeaux by the Author of 'Diffidence and Confidence in Relation to Modern Prophecy.*'"

More authority could be given, but these will be considered sufficient to justify my motive in sending it for publication, and perusal by persons, like myself, interested in the present condition of France and Europe.

I have had opportunities to learn that the reading of these and other prophetical predictions has exerted considerable interest. In translating and arranging them to the best of my judgment for publication, I had no selfish motive. I desired in a plain and practical manner to show that a wise, divine, all-governing Providence directs, rules, and controls all the affairs and destinies of human society for the welfare of Christ's holy Church. With very few honorable exceptions, all human governments of the earth seem to have abdicated, or at least to overlook in practice, this fundamental maxim of Christian policy. No construction can stand long after its principal foundation has been undermined. The general uneasiness of the human mind is an ominous prognostic of impending calamities. These shall fall upon us much sooner than thoughtless and reckless men expect. The flaming sword of the avenging angel is ready to strike. It will cause frightful havoc in this self-conceited, infidel, mammon-worshipping generation.

The false prophets of the usurped pulpits palaver the blind passions and delusions of their Sabbath worshippers, proclaiming peace, peace, prosperity, security. The refrain is promptly answered by the giddy scribes of an infidel press. With them America is the model of Christian nations, the most perfect example of Christian morality. But boastful pride and presumption always go before a fall. With her large share of guilt, America cannot avoid her due share of punishment.

However, before Divine justice inflicts the deserved punishment, God's mercy warns both the guilty and the innocent, in order that the guilty may in time repent, and the just may not despond, but may be moved to prayer and hope. We have full faith in these timely warnings.

We Catholics firmly believe that the word of God has not been silenced by the Incarnation. For us the language of prophecy is no strange voice. On the contrary, our faith in our sacramental Emmanuel, continually abiding with his holy Church, makes us expect that in his loving goodness and compassionate mercy, he will, through his favorite servants, warn the faithful when his offended justice is forced to punish the prevailing wickedness of mankind.

Confining our glance to the last one hundred years, we shall easily find that God, *in divers ways and at sundry times, has spoken through prophetic predictions*, by miraculous apparitions, by prodigious signs given in sacred pictures and devout statues. These heavenly mysterious signs have been daily witnessed during many months by entire populations. These supernal apparitions, after the most irrefragable evidence, have been solemnly approved by competent ecclesiastical authority. Here, as a recent example, I mention the celebrated apparitions in the year 1858, to *Bernardette* at the rock of Massabielle, near Lourdes, in France. I should advise the readers of this to peruse the authentic account of the apparitions, and of numerous miraculous cures, given in a splendid work with the title "Our Lady of Lourdes." They will be satisfied that God speaks yet to the children of men.

Moreover, has not the present saintly Pope Pius IX., *at divers times and in various ways*, warned the faithful to prepare for impending calamities? Can we hear so many merciful calls, and remain indifferent? Can we suppose that in so many and such explicit heavenly voices there is no meaning? They are full of meaning, and also pregnant with danger for us, if we heed them not. We all desire peace, prosperity, and happiness.

When men shall practically recognize the sovereign dominion over them of the true living God; when we shall boldly proclaim our belief in the Divine authority of Jesus Christ, as exercised upon earth through his *infallible Vicar, the Bishop of Rome;* when every Christian government shall imitate the noble example of the Catholic Republic of Ecuador, in South America, and conform their conduct to the maxims of the gospel, —then, but then only, lasting peace, true prosperity, and real happiness shall be enjoyed by mankind.

My personal opinion in relation to these prophecies is founded upon the following considerations: First, the proofs of the authenticity of the Predictions D'Orval. Secondly, the agreement of these predictions, especially about the imminent future, with many other prophecies made by different canonized saints and eminent servants of God, very distant from each other in point of time and country: for instance, St. Bridget, of Sweden; St. Francis de Paula, already mentioned. To these I could have added St. Malachy, of Ireland; St. Thomas, of Canterbury; St. Francis, of Assissium; St. Margaret, of Cortona; St. Catherine, of Sienna, etc., etc. Also the venerable Abbot Werdin, of Otranto, who died in the year 1279, distinctly foretold the future appearance in France of the youthful prince mentioned by St. Francis de Paula, and in these prophetical Predictions D'Orval. A goodly number of similar predictions contemporary with, or subsequent to, this of D'Orval have likewise been made by persons of acknowledged sanctity in France and Italy. All this, and much more, is contained in the *sixth edition*, issued in 1864, in Turin, of a collection of these and other prophecies, gathered with great care by several learned priests. As soon as published, these predictions have been sought after with such avidity that each successive edition was soon exhausted. They have been perused by scores of thousands of Catholics, and by thousands of pious and learned ecclesiastics of every degree, from the most humble curé to the highest personages of Rome. Thirdly, if we except some few infidel sceptics in France, nobody has attempted to deny or contradict them. Now, could we not safely interpret this prudent and respectful silence of the Church in a matter of such importance as a kind of at least indirect sanction of these prophetical predictions? My remarks, of course, are not exclusively confined to D'Orval's predictions; for I have corroborated them with several others. Fourthly, for me, the events already transpired, the present condition of Europe, and the restless agitation of the human mind in every nation of the globe, very strongly incline my judgment to expect that the fulfilment of these predictions will in a few years be effected.

We remarked above that the second and perhaps best guaranty for a prophecy is the actual realization of a considerable portion of the events foretold. We are now going to give this proof. The predictions of the Solitary D'Orval, at the present time, form naturally two distinct parts, namely, past and future prophecies; the first part is the longest, the second the most important. In the original and copies the principal predictions are given in distinct paragraphs; but these are not marked by any numbers; on this occasion I have concluded to mark them with Roman numbers: first, to facilitate their intelligence; secondly, for the sake of reference; thirdly, to render more convenient some desirable comment. After this explanation, we pass to the prophecy, the title of which is this:—

Sure Prophecies revealed by the Lord to a Solitary for the Consolation of God's Children.

I. At a certain time a young man, coming from over the sea to the country of Celtic-Gaul (France), will make himself remarkable by his power and counsel (*sagacity ?*). [N. B. Napoleon Bonaparte I.; from the island of Corsica, went to France.] But the great ones, beginning to fear him, will send him to fight in the land of captivity. (Egypt, in the prophetic style of the Bible, is called the land of captivity.)

II. Victory shall bring him back to the first country (France). *The Sons of Brutus* will be very much stupefied at his return, for he will domineer over them, and assume the name of Emperor.

[N. B. In this, as well as several other modern prophecies, the *Red Republicans*, or rather *secret societies and conspirators*, are decorated with the ignoble title of *Sons of Brutus*. Pagan Roman history can supply the reason for this title. This word *Brutus* can also. Those who desire the best explanation, in the words of our divine Redeemer, may read it in the gospel. St. John viii. 44.]

III. Many high and powerful kings shall conceive much fear because of the Eagle, which shall seize many sceptres and crowns. Infantry and cavalry Eagles and blood shall with him fly like midges in the air. All Europe is greatly terrified at the shedding of blood, for he shall be so powerful as to induce the belief that God is fighting with him. [Napoleon, like Attila, was God's scourge in Europe; he took the Eagle for his war standard.]

IV. God's Church is *somewhat consoled* in beholding again her temples opened to her own sheep entirely dispersed; and God is praised. [During the first French Revolution by the *Red Republicans*, Christianity was officially and totally abolished in France. Bishops, priests, religious, pious lay Catholics, were martyred. Napoleon I. abolished this impious law, and restored our holy religion in France. But his motive was more political than religious. The good attempted by bad men is always imperfect, and of a short duration. We are going to witness this fact.]

V. But it is finished.; the moons are passed. The old man of Zion (Pope Pius VII.) cries to God from his heart very much oppressed by burning grief. [This holy Pope was confined in prison, and much harassed by order of Napoleon. Temporary success always makes bad men proud, arrogant, and tyrannical. But when they dare persecute the Church of Christ, and his holy Vicar upon earth, their punishment and humiliation is inevitable. Our Holy Father, Pius IX., is at the present kept prisoner in his own capital, and oppressed with burning grief by an apostate and impious government. He and the whole Catholic Church is crying to God. We are certain of final victory.]

VI. Behold the powerful man (Napoleon) blinded by sin and crimes. He leaves the grand city (Paris) with such a splendid army that the like nobody ever saw. But no military man is able to resist the face of the weather. Behold a third part of his army, and again a third part, perish (in Russia) through the cold of the Almighty Lord. [God is always at every time and in every country the Lord of hosts. "And now, O ye kings, understand : receive instruction, you that judge the earth. Serve ye the Lord with fear. Embrace discipline, lest at any time the Lord be angry, and you perish from the just way, when his wrath shall be kindled in a short time. Blessed are they that trust in him." Ps. ii.]

VII. But now ten years are passed after the era of desolation, as I have said in its place. (See No. V.) Widows and orphans have raised vehement lamentations. Lo! God is no longer inexorable. [Observe the efficacy of the fervent prayer of afflicted souls in moving God to mercy. He uses what instruments he likes for the welfare of his people. On this occasion, to restore peace to his Church, the Lord of hosts employed the power of *three schismatical and heretical nations*, — Russia, Prussia, and England.]

VIII. The depressed potentates recover their strength, and form an alliance for the overthrow of the man so much feared. Coming with them, behold the old blood of former ages (the Bourbons), which recovers its dignity and place in the great city (Paris), whilst the above-mentioned man, deeply humbled, goes to a place on the same sea whence he came. [The small island of Elba, to which Napoleon I. was exiled, in April, 1814, is not far from Corsica, his native island.]

IX. God alone is great. The eleventh moon is not yet risen, and the bloody scourge of the Lord chastises again the great city, and the old blood flies away from Paris. [Napoleon, after ten months of exile, broke his parole, returned again to France, where he remained during the one hundred famous days, was again defeated at the battle of Waterloo, sent to St. Helena, where he died in 1821.]

X. God alone is great. He loves his people, and abominates blood. The fifth moon shone upon many soldiers from the East. France is covered with military men and war machinery. It is all over with the man of the sea. Behold, the old Capetian blood returned once more.

XI. God wills peace. May his holy name be blessed.

Now a great and prosperous peace will flourish in France. The white flower is held in great honor. Many sacred canticles are sung in the house of God. . . . . In the mean while the *Sons of Brutus* look with rage at the white flower. They obtain an important decree.

[N. B. The white lily is the emblem of the old royal house of Bourbons. Their flag is also white. The lily is the emblem of purity; the white flag that of peace and honesty. No wonder, then, that the impious Sons of Brutus, or rather of Belial, like their father, hate the very sight of such emblems, as the Devil hates the sight of the cross. Look, if you can penetrate into their secret conventicles; they are busy at their old work; they are conspiring in the great Babylon; they obtain a decree against the Jesuits and other religious-teaching communities in France. This is always and everywhere the first attempt of that antichristian sect.]

. XII. For this cause God is again grievously offended, because he loves his elect (religious), and because the sacred days (Sundays and holy days) are profaned. God will try, during eighteen times twelve moons, their return to him. [Some explain that God will await the return of the French to faith and piety during the period from the first exile of Napoleon to 1830, which not being obtained, then the punishment follows.]

XIII. God alone is great. He purifies his people through various tribulations, but always to the detriment of the wicked; therefore, through the instrumentality of a numerous and accursed sect, which walks in the dark (secret societies), a terrible conspiracy is formed against the white flower, and the poor old blood of the Capet (Bourbons, Charles X.) has to fly from the great city (Paris), for which the Sons of Brutus are very much rejoiced.

[Who can be so wilfully blind as not to see in these prophetic words the spirit, character, and aim of secret European societies? During the last one hundred years they have been the forges of all revolutions and persecutions against the Catholic religion.]

XIV. Listen how the servants of the Lord very strongly cry to the Most High God, and he does not hear on account of the noise of his arrows, which he tempers in the fires of his wrath to transfix the heart of the impious. [Reflect, here, why sometimes the fervent prayers of the just are not immediately granted by God: it is for the greater punishment of their enemies; for, according to St. Augustine, God delays to hear our petitions, in order to grant them to our best advantage.]

XV. Woes to France! The Gaul [Gallican?] will erase the white flower, and a great one will be saluted King of the People. A strong commotion shall be experienced among nations, because the crown will be imposed by those artisans who fought in the vast city. [Louis Philippe was not, like the old Bourbon, King of France, but King of the French. He was crowned by the victorious mob of Paris: hence he was styled the citizen-king, — better, perhaps, the King of Democracy.]

XVI. God alone is great. The power of the impious shall sensibly increase; *but let them make haste!* [our divine Lord used a like expression with Judas,] for behold the opinions of the Gauls [Gallicans?] come in collision, and there is great dissension in their councils. The King of the People, who at first was considered very weak, yet will go against many of the wicked. But he was not well established [in faith and religion; he was a high Freemason]; lo! God casts him down.

[At the bloody revolution in Paris, July, 1830, when Charles X. was dethroned, Louis Philippe, Duke of

Orleans, his cousin, was elected King of the French. But history shows that only a truly Christian Catholic monarch can reign long and prosperously in France. Louis Philippe was not a good Catholic king, much less a *Most Christian King*, as all monarchs of France were styled; hence, in his turn, he was expelled in February, 1848, when a French Republic was again proclaimed. *But France can never be long a Republic!* For France, a Republic, is inevitable civil war. Only a solidly established kingdom or empire can procure peace and happiness to France; for such monarchy the foundation must be laid in *the heart of the French nation*, and *this must rest on St. Peter's Rock!* As only a true Pope can be the real Bishop and legitimate King of Rome, so only a monarch, *indeed most Christian*, can be able to govern France well. Such is the decree of Heaven. The second part of this prophecy, as well as several other prophetical predictions, have proclaimed it. Do you, reader, cry, Superstition? Is it superstition to believe that Jesus Christ, very God and man, *is the King of kings and Lord of lords?* "*Every creature in heaven and on the earth and in the sea, I heard all saying, To him who sitteth on the throne, and to the Lamb, benediction and honor and glory and power for ever and ever.*" (Apoc. v. 13.) This evidently embraces more than France and Europe. I believe it embraces the whole universe; therefore this earth, and every human government. But the history of at least fifteen hundred years sufficiently shows that *only a monarch indeed most Christian can govern France well.* In the year 505, the apostle of France, St. Remigius, wrote to his great spiritual son, Clovis, the first Christian king of Catholic France, offering, for his acceptance, the best charter for the successful government of the French people: "Choose wise councillors, who will be an honor to your reign. Respect the clergy. Be the father and protector of your people. If you do this, you will draw down upon yourself the divine blessings." Does not this also imply that these promised divine blessings will be withheld from every ruler in France who does not live and act as a most *Christian monarch?* The evidence of the past is the best guaranty for the future.]

XVII. Howl, ye *Sons of Brutus.* Call upon you the wild beasts, which are ready to devour you. God alone is great! What booming of arms! There is not yet a full number of moons, and, behold, many warriors are coming.

[We are arrived at the threshold of the future. No wonder, then, if this portion of the Predictions of D'Orval appears more mysterious and obscure than the former, which had for us relation to the past. Let the past, then, be our light and guide to the dark future. For the present, those who desire to understand the highly important meaning of the above prophetic words should never forget what is signified by *Sons of Brutus.* Let us hold this fact of *secret history* as certain, that, during the last one hundred years, the principal revolutions, at least in Catholic countries, and consequent persecutions of the best classes of Catholics and religious, have been precipitated upon society by the worthy *Sons of Brutus.* This has been the fact in France, Spain, Portugal, and in all their dependencies; in Italy, Hungary, Austria, Bavaria, and other parts of Germany. By the same class of men the attempt has lately been made in Ireland. It will soon be more successful in England. Simple-minded Christians may not believe this truth, secret accomplices in these intrigues may affect to deny this assertion, or pretend to sneer at this statement. But others, more sincere, have acknowledged the fact. Let American Catholics be upon their guard; the storm so long brewing in the East (Orient) is fast spreading to the far West. Is it very improbable that the secret wire-pullers may soon use it as a political machine? Watch, and you will discover more than one ominous sign! What is the object and intention of the so-called Grand Army of the Republic? It forebodes no good for Catholics. We may fear, but we shall not despond. Read again the prophecy No. XIII. Reflect on these words: "He (God) purifies his people through various tribulations, but always to the detriment of the wicked." Here again the prophet says: "Howl, ye *Sons of Brutus*" (to express their distress and rage). "Call upon you the wild beasts, which are ready to devour you." Men not guided by superior lights of faith and reason, but impelled by passion, always act with precipitation; this very precipitation forms the pit, which, under the wise and just, but mysterious design of Divine Providence, they dig for their own fall and destruction. "There is not yet a full number of moons." In his long-suffering patience, God would have allowed some years' longer tranquillity and peace to France and Europe; but the violent passions and impatient eagerness of the *Sons of Brutus* precipitate the calamity. But lo! they suffer a crushing defeat where they expected certain victory; they bring upon themselves the wild beasts, prepared and ready to devour them. . . . . What these wild beasts are, we may learn from the epithets used by the defeated *Sons of Brutus* against the German armies and their leaders in France. The *Sons of Brutus* fight against, but are defeated by, their brothers! God punishes his people through various tribulations; but always to the detriment of his wicked enemies.]

XVIII. It is finished. The mountain of God, desolated (the Church), has cried to God, the children of Juda have invoked God from a strange land, and, behold, God is no longer deaf. [N. B. By these children of Juda, in the prophetic style, we should understand the priests and faithful Catholics, who shall be soon exiled, or who will emigrate through the impending civil war, and religious persecution by the *Sons of Brutus* in France. We may also understand the old royal Bourbon family so long exiled from their country, and that will in a few years be restored to the throne of St. Louis.]

XIX. What fire goes together with his (God's) arrows! Ten times six moons, and again six times ten moons have nourished his wrath (about eleven years). Woes to thee, populous city (Paris)! Behold kings armed by the Lord! . . . . But fire hath already burned thee to the ground. . . . . Thy just ones, however, shall not perish; God has heard them; the place of wickedness is purged by fire; the ample river (Seine) has carried to the sea its waters all red with blood.

XX. France (continues the Prophecy D'Orval), France, that appeared dilacerated, is on the point of being reunited. God loves peace. Come, young Prince, leave the Island of Captivity. Join the lion to the white flower. Come. God wills what has been foreseen. The ancient blood of centuries will also put an end to long divisions. Then shall be seen in France one shepherd only.

[N. B. More than twenty different prophecies in this book distinctly predict the appearance in France of a young Prince, a lineal descendant of the old Capetian blood.

Who this young Prince can be it is difficult to tell. It is one of those mysteries with which the wisdom of God likes to baffle the calculations and designs of men. He is invited by the prophet D'Orval to leave the Island of Captivity. What is meant by this island we cannot explain. In relation to Napoleon I., by this expression the same prophet indicated Egypt. In this particular case it may be Egypt, or it may be England.]

XXI. The powerful man, assisted by God, will establish himself well. Many wise laws shall restore peace. This scion of Capet will be so prudent and wise that all men will believe God to be with him. Thanks to the Father of mercies, the Holy Sion (Holy Catholic Church) sings again in the temples, One only God. Many poor wandering sheep (Protestants) shall come to drink of the living spring of truth and grace. Three princes and kings shall throw off the garb of error, and will see clearly in the faith of God. At this time two thirds of a great nation of the sea (England) shall reassume the true faith. [Several other prophecies foretell these consoling future events even in more clear expressions. In fact, they announce the general conversion of mankind to Catholic Christianity before the end of twenty years from this date, through the zeal of the future Angelic Pope (Papa Angelicus), with the energetic co-operation of the future Monarch of France and the new religious Order so distinctly foretold by St. Francis de Paula, and by other saints and servants of God. I do not expect that all those who read these announcements will believe them. For my part, I like to say with holy Job: *I know that my Redeemer liveth.* . . . . *This my hope is laid up in my bosom.* (Job xix. 25.)]

XXII. God is again praised during fourteen times ten moons, and six times thirteen moons. God is the only Master of Mercies, and for this he will, moreover, for the sake of his elect, prolong the peace during ten other times twelve moons. [All this gives about forty years.

However, this last sentence indicates that, during the period of peace and prosperity, many Christians will begin to grow cold; hence the Lord of Mercy has to exercise this divine attribute for the sake of his elect.]

XXIII. God alone is great. Much good has been accomplished. The saints are about to suffer. The man of sin arrives. He (Antichrist) is born from two bloods. The white flower becomes obscured during ten times six moons, and six times twenty moons (during about one hundred and eighty months), and it disappears, nevermore to be seen. In that time much evil will be done; little good. Many flourishing cities shall perish through fire. Israel, with good heart, comes to Christ-God. The accursed sects and the faithful believers shall form two distinct parties.

XXIV. All is over. God alone shall be believed. A third part of the Gauls (France), and again a third part and half, shall have no more faith. The same shall be with other nations. And, behold, already six times three moons, and four times five moons, which are separated, and the age of the end is begun.

XXV. After a number of moons not full (those evil days shall be *shortened*, as promised by our Divine Saviour, *because of the elect.* Matt. xxiv. 22) God fights through his two just ones (Henoch and Elias), and the man of sin (Antichrist) will get the upper hand (he will kill them). But all is finished. [The apparent temporary success of the wicked is ever the most certain sign of their impending defeat; and this defeat is always more complete in proportion to their success.]

The high God sets a wall of fire that obscures my understanding. I can see no more. May he be forever praised.

(End of time, and beginning of eternity, in about one hundred years hence.)

CHAPTER II.

PROPHECY OF ST. REMIGIUS.

ST. REMIGIUS, Bishop of Rheims, in Celtic Gaul (France), baptized King Clovis, with three thousand of his principal nobles and officers of his court and army, on Christmas morning in the year 494. The famous Archbishop of Rheims, Hinemar, who lived in the ninth century, says that St. Remigius, on the eve of Christmas, made to Clovis the following prophecy. This prophecy is related by the great ecclesiastical historian Baronius in the years 494 and 512, in his ecclesiastical annals. Many other authors, in different ages and in different countries, mention the same. Among them, Vincent de Beauvais (*Speculum Historiale*, Tom. XX, c. 49); Gerson, in his panegyric of St. Louis, King of France; Godefrid, of Viterbo; Aimoin (Tom. V, c. 21); Hyppolitus, Bishop in Sicily, — add *that the great French monarch, who shall subject all the East, shall come about the end of the world.* Several Byzantine writers, among whom Agathias and Chalcondyle, have taken notice of this prophecy of St. Remigius, which is as follows : —

"Take notice, my child," St. Remigius said to King Clovis, "that the kingdom of France is predestined by God for the defence of the Roman Church, which is the only true Church of Christ. This kingdom shall one day be great among the kingdoms of the earth, and shall embrace all the limits of the Roman Empire, and shall submit all other kingdoms to its own sceptre.

"It shall last until the end of time.

"It shall be victorious and prosperous as long as it will

remain faithful to the Holy Roman See, and will not be guilty of any of those crimes which ruin nations; but it shall be rudely punished every time that it will become unfaithful to its vocation."

The uninterrupted tradition of all ages combine in asserting the authenticity of this prophecy.

All ecclesiastical writers of France, all the ancient chronicles, and all agiographers, from Venerable Beda, who lived in the seventh century, to Baronius, in the sixteenth century, and M. Ch. Barthelemy, in his history of the Saints of France, mention it, when they have occasion to speak about St. Remigius and King Clovis. But the realization of this prophecy is no less attested by the uniform testimony of every age. To be convinced of this fact, it is sufficient to open the history of France. Everybody will be forced to admit that this prophecy is the programme and compendium of French history. All great events in France continually revolve on this point. All that astonished humanity observed at the times of King Clovis, of the Emperor Charlemagne and St. Louis, men are ever surprised to see repeated in France.

The greatest writer of our age, M. the Count de Maistre, could pen these celebrated words:—

"It is sufficient to open history in order to see that the punishment, inflicted on France when she is culpable against God or his Church, goes out of all ordinary rules, and that the protection granted to her by God is also of an extraordinary character.

"These two prodigies combined are reciprocally multiplied, and present one of the most astonishing spectacles that the human mind has ever contemplated."

This prophecy of St. Remigius became famous both in the West and East.

The Saracens of Sicily relied on this prophecy when,

without fear, they resisted the attack of the great Emperor Nicephorus, saying that it was not he whom the oracles foretold as their future victor, but that it would have to be a great monarch of the French nation, which would have to attain the highest power before the end of the world, and then put an end to the Ottoman Empire.

The Venerable Bede, in the seventh century, supports this prophecy with the oracles of the ancient Sibyls (*Carmina Sibyl*, Tom. VIII). More than a thousand years ago, Rabanus Maurus, who was a Benedictine abbot in Fulda in the year 822, and afterwards Archbishop of Mayence, made the following statement: —

"Our principal doctors agree in announcing to us, that towards the end of time one of the descendants of the kings of France shall reign over all the Roman Empire; and that he shall be the greatest of the French monarchs, and the last of his race.

"After having most happily governed his kingdom, he will go to Jerusalem, and depose on Mount Olivet his sceptre and crown.

"This shall be the end and conclusion of the Roman and Christian Empire."

The monk Adson repeats this ancient tradition in the tenth century. He made use of this prophecy to prove that the end of the world should not, as some persons believed, take place at the end of that century; because, he said, the great French monarch is not yet come. This prophecy is found in the book of Antiquities in an appendix to the works of St. Augustine (Tom. VI., Benedictine edition). This work is attributed to the celebrated Alcuin, the friend and teacher of Charlemagne.

CHAPTER III.

PROPHECY OF ST. BRIDGET, OF SWEDEN.

ST. BRIDGET was the daughter of a royal prince of Sweden, called Birger, and of Ingeburgis, a lady descended from the kings of the Goths. Bridget was born in 1304. At ten years of age, listening to a sermon on the Passion of our Divine Saviour, she was so strongly affected that the impression lasted through her whole future life. In obedience to her father, Bridget, when only sixteen years of age, married Ulpho, a very pious and religious young prince of Nericia, in Sweden. They had eight children. Their house was like a most exemplary and fervent religious community. Ulpho died in the year 1343. Bridget made pilgrimages to Compostella in Spain, to Palestine, and to Rome, where she died on the 23d of July, 1373. St. Bridget wrote several pious works, one of which is about her revelations. These were printed in Lubec, 1492; at Nuremberg, 1522; in Rome, 1521, 1556, 1606, 1608; at Antwerp, 1611; at Cologne, 1628; at Munich, 1680.

A considerable number of these revelations were written from her relation by Peter, a Swedish Cistercian monk, who was her confessor, and companion in her many travels, and who died 1390. The eighth book was written by Alphonsus, surnamed the Spaniard, and the hermit, who resigned the bishopric of Jena, in Andalusia, and who was also her confessor. (See Butler's "Lives of Saints, 8th October.")

The following prophecy of St. Bridget was found in a

lead case in the vaults of the Benedictine Fathers in the city of Naples, which they preserved in their library. The copy, which we herein publish, was taken from the convent of St. Dominic, in the town of Mareno, where it was discovered by Francis Famesone Biondi, a notary-public of the same place, and which was published in a collection of prophecies with the title of Oracolo, in the year 1856. St. Bridget prophesied the fall of the Greek Empire in the following words: —

1. Let the Greeks know that their empire, their kingdoms, or dominions, shall never be secure or in settled peace, but will always be held in subjection by their enemies, from whom they shall have to suffer most grievous hardships and constant distresses; until, with true humility and good-will, they shall have devoutly submitted themselves to the Church of Rome and to her faith, conforming themselves entirely to the holy ordinances and rites of that Church.

II. When the Feast of St. Mark (the Apostle), April 25, shall fall on Easter Sunday, the Feast of St. Anthony of Padua, 13th of June, shall occur on the Feast of Pentecost, and that of St. John the Baptist, 24th, shall come on the Feast of Corpus Christi, the whole world shall cry, Woe!

[During this present century this has nearly happened already twice, namely, in the year 1848 and 1859, when the Pope and the Church were severely tried. It will happen once more, namely, in 1886. But we must particularly remark this last event, in which alone the Bridgitine warning will be literally verified; for then Easter shall exactly occur on the twenty-fifth day of April, Pentecost on the 13th, and Corpus Christi on the 24th of June. Whereas, in the years 1848 and 1859 it was very near, but not exactly on the same dates; it will be the same in the following century, namely, **1943**, but few of the present readers shall be able to witness this last calamity. In reciting on St. Mark's day the Litany of the Saints, as commanded by the Church, Catholic clergymen might think of this.]

III. For the Lily reigning in the superior part shall move the encampments against the seed of the Lions, and shall surround the children of men that will fight against the Lily. At that time the sign of impiety shall be raised. (The famous tree of liberty in the year 1792 in France, and in Rome, 1849.)

[Observe that in the year 1791, Easter, Pentecost, and Corpus Christi fell as above, 1848.]

IV. At that time will come out of the island (of Corsica) a terrible son of man (Napoleon Bonaparte), carrying war in his powerful arm, and with the French he will fight against the Italians, Germans, Sarmatians, Spaniards, and Turks. Everything shall be upset. During three consecutive years there shall be fighting among the faithful. The Lily, or Bourbon kings, shall lose the crown, which shall be taken up by the Eagle, and with which shall be crowned the son of an obscure man risen from the sea, who will carry the admirable sign in the promised land. Woe! woe!! woe!!! when the son of man shall seat himself on the throne of the Lilies (on the throne of the Bourbons in France), then great tribulations shall be in the Church.

V. During the six following years there shall be many and great wars among Christians, and in some country the war shall be so cruel that men never saw the equal. Ah! child, consider well whether thou will be on the side of good, or of evil! If thou art on the side of good, or right, why dost thou not raise up again the columns of the Church? Why dost thou not restore them to their proper place?

[Should not these words of our holy prophetess be considered as addressed to Napoleon the First, who pretended for a time to be a true Catholic, exhorting him to give a practical proof of his religion by restoring the true, legitimate French bishops to their vacant or usurped sees, by respecting the rights of the Church, and protecting the Pope?]

VI. Then shall rise the congress of iniquity (Freemasons and Jansenists), that will be able to excite the Gallicans against the Church of God. However, Gallicanism shall perish, of its own disease. But the son of man, the parvenu of the sea, shall be most invincible in war, and shall subdue all Germany. The great house (Austrian Empire) shall almost be pulled down. But at last the Eagle will come from the North to the West, and shall together with her children be surrounded by the towers of Spain, and they will raise Germany up again.

VII. The Eagle (of Napoleon) will also invade Mahometan countries (Egypt and Syria), and will carry the admirable sign in the land of promise. Peace and abundance shall return to the world.

But shortly after new wars shall break out. Woe to you, Venice! Woe to you, Lucca and Genoa, *Italian republics!* Woe, because after the year 1790 you shall all be pulled down by the hands of the French. Then in Europe there will be very many wicked men (wicked and impious men, then, are the real enemies and destroyers of true republican governments). New wars! wars carried on with much cruelty and fierceness, many cities shall be destroyed, an innumerable quantity of men shall be killed, the very head of the world shall be shaken. This most unhappy war shall end, when an emperor of Spanish origin will be elected (see "Letters of St. Francis de Paula"), who will in a wonderful manner be victorious through the sign of the Cross. He shall destroy the Jewish and the Mahometan sects; he will restore the church of Santa Sophia (in Constantinople), and all the earth shall enjoy peace and prosperity; and new cities will be erected in many places.

[It is well known that a grandson of Louis XIV., the great king of France, was made king of Spain, and the royal families of Spain and Naples, as well as the Duke of Parma, are its lineal descendants. In order, however, to understand better this prophecy, read the "Letters of St. Francis de Paula," chapter v., page 155.]

VIII. Sweden shall see again the true light of Faith, when it will be governed by a queen born with eleven fingers.

IX. Antichrist shall be born from an accursed woman, who will pretend to be well informed in spiritual things, and of an accursed man, from the flesh (semine) of whom the Devil shall form his work. The time of this Antichrist, well known to me, will come when iniquity and impiety shall above measure abound. Before, however, Antichrist arrives, the gate of Faith will be opened to *some nations*, and the Scripture shall be verified. *People without intelligence shall glorify me, and deserts shall be inhabited.* Hence, when many Christians will be lovers of heresies, and wicked men will persecute the clergy and will hate justice, this should be the sign that Antichrist shall come without delay. [Are we not at present in these bad times?]

X. Lastly, he shall arrive, the most wicked of men, and, helped by the Jews, he will fight against the whole world; he will reign during three years, and shall have dominion over the whole earth; he will make every effort to abolish from the earth the Christian name, and very many Christians shall be killed.

In the copy of the above prophecy transmitted to us, the following dates are connected with it, but we cannot vouch that they were made by St. Bridget:—

In the year 1740, great earthquakes.

1760. Africa shall be on fire.

1783. Most awful earthquakes in many places.

1791. The wrath of God shall be over the whole earth.

1800. God shall be acknowledged by few men.

1829. A portion of Spain shall fall; Italy shall experience fears.

1830. Very many shall fight.

1846. There shall be no pastor.

1847. New wars.

1848. People shall rise against people.

1849. Rome shall be defiled with blood.

1860. The most wicked of men (Garibaldi) shall come forth.

1886. The great monarch shall appear.

1890. Mankind shall acknowledge the Unity and Trinity of God, and there shall be one Shepherd and one Fold.

1900. There shall be a great sign in the heavens.

1980. The impious shall prevail.

1999. The luminaries shall cease to give light.

CHAPTER IV.

PROPHECY OF FATHER JEROME BOTIN, A HOLY BENEDICTINE MONK.

MR. BERGASSE had in his possession a copy of this prophecy in writing, since the year 1790. It was first published in a book, by Mr. Bricon, in the year 1830; republished by Mr. Demonville in the year 1832, and by Mr. Dujardin in 1840. In the monastic register of deaths in the Abbey of Saint Germain des Pres, in Paris, the following notice about Father Jerome Botin is found: "On the 10th of July, 1420, died Jerome Botin of Cahors, aged 62 years. He was a person remarkable for his learning, piety, and holiness. May he rest in peace."

Prophetical Predictions.

In the name of the Lord, the Creator of all things, behold the words which the Holy Spirit has dictated to Jerome, servant of God, and written in the Monastery of St. Germain des Pres, in Paris. In the year 1410, of the Incarnation, Pope John XXIII. governing the Church of God, Charles VI. reigning in France, behold what the Spirit hath said to him.

I. Woe to nations, woe to kings and princes, who govern people; for times of mourning and of bitterness shall come, the storm of tribulation shall divide and scatter men; the earth shall be soaked with the blood of ecclesiastics, of the nobility, and of the people. Woe to those who carry the sword, for it shall be stained in their own blood (of relatives). Nor far distant is the epoch when these men shall come, says the Spirit to me.

II. After one century (the fifteenth, says Bricon) the Lord's inheritance shall be divided (through Luther's schism), and, on account of it, princes shall fight against princes, nations against nations, and egotism, under the pretext of reformation, shall attempt to upset everything. But after another century (the sixteenth century) the Church of God will be found all safe, because the hand of the Almighty is more powerful than that of the strongest potentates of the earth. This is what the Holy Spirit says to me.

III. Woe to the sea, woe to the earth, and woe to those who live at present, and during a century. Woe to France, and woe to the people of the Island (England), because the inheritance of the Lord shall abandon them, and for the few remaining faithful in it there shall be much affliction, says the Spirit.

IV. In about another century (the seventeenth) the inheritance of the Lord shall no longer be divided, at least in France. In this country a king shall reign (Louis XIV.), of whom it is written, *Arm thyself with thy sword, and carry it at thy side.* Being a most powerful monarch, he will reunite kings, princes, and people; he will govern with wisdom and power. This is what the Spirit says. His reign shall be very long; it will be a reign of justice and strength; his memory shall be glorious, and held in great veneration.

V. After another century (the eighteenth) the princes of the earth and all the nations shall be in great agitation and fury (on account of the first French Revolution), and this shall be a time of iniquity and desperation; scarcely a man shall be found that will do good. It is this that the Lord inspires me to announce. Then shall reign in France a prince, the anointed of the Lord (Louis XVI.), a man endowed with virtue and mildness.

But the ministers of iniquity shall put a price upon his head; they will exhaust against him all their malice; they will put him in prison, and his end shall be more wretched than his beginning; so says the Spirit.

VI. After having cast him and his relatives into prison, the princes and great men shall be dragged to destruction; and then great mourning and lamentations shall be in the Church of God. A stone shall not be left upon a stone. The altars and churches shall be destroyed, the virgins consecrated to the Lord shall be outraged, these men of iniquity shall be drunk with folly, because they shall have signs over their heads, and houses (the cap of liberty), says the Spirit.

VII. Woe to princes and to great men, because their power shall be destroyed. Woe to the people, because their hands shall be imbrued in blood. Woe to those who govern them, because they shall walk in the way of iniquity, and they shall become drunk with the blood of an innocent king, of great men, and of the people, and their government shall be a dominion of perversity, and a reign of abominations, and in a short time they shall be expelled from power and shall perish. It is this that the Spirit says to me.

VIII. Woe to princes and great men! Woe to the people, because their king shall be sacrificed like a lamb; their neighbors shall be slain, and others shall be exiled, and those who have committed these crimes will cry, *Amen.* Before the end of the eighteenth century, the ministers of the altar shall weep and suffer persecution, the Shepherd shall be struck and the Flock dispersed.

IX. Woe! yes, thousand times woe, to the people who rebelled against all authority, and abolished the laws; they pulled up from the root the source of their prosperity; they tore to pieces the Lily, but the Eagle (Napoleon) shall seize upon them; it shall catch and destroy its prey, said the Spirit.

X. The earth shall be deluged with the blood of its inhabitants. Her children, armed with iron, shall perish by the sword. Her innumerable calamities, says the Lord, shall not appease my wrath. My right-hand shall be lifted up against the people; the power that will oppress them shall be my instrument of indignation against them, and against other nations. This is what the Spirit says.

XI. But some time after four centuries (*from* 1410, *namely, during the nineteenth century*) the altars of Beelzebub shall be destroyed. (See here to what excess of impiety men have arrived.) The workers of iniquity shall be punished and shall perish; the heavenly dew shall fall upon the desolated earth, and over the Church afflicted.

XII. A son of royal blood shall be born from the race of Artois. (Charles X. of France was Count of Artois.) He shall govern France with prudence and with honor; the spirit of God will be with him; the Spirit said so.

XIII. Before the end of the nineteenth century another Pastor (Papa Angelico) shall rise, who will lead the people in equity, and the kings in justice. He shall be honored by princes and by the people; but before his empire is established, let those who have not bowed down before Baal fly from Babylon (Paris), says the Spirit.

XIV. Let everybody think how to save his life; for behold the time wherein the Lord will have, with the severity of his punishments, to demonstrate the multitude and enormity of the crimes with which she (Paris) is defiled. The Lord will cause to revert upon that city all the evils with which she has tyrannized over others.

XV. This impious city, the ravager of nations, the executioner of her own priests, of her kings, and of her own children, has been used by the Lord as the hand for presenting the cup of his vengeance to all the nations of the earth. All nations have drunk the wine of her frenzy; they shall suffer the anguish of her captivity and of her barbarity. (They shall suffer on account of her atheistic doctrines, of her antichristian revolutionary conspiracies, of her impious and bloody secret socities, of her immoral and scandalous books, of her manifold instruments of depravity, of her Parisian modes and fashions, of her altars erected, and human victims immolated to demons.)

XVI. But on a sudden this Babylon (Paris) is fallen, and in her fall she is broken to pieces, said the Spirit.

XVII. *All this shall come to pass for the purification of the just, and for the destruction of the wicked; in order to make men honor the Church of God, and fear and serve the Lord.*

Such are the words which the Spirit revealed to his servant Jerome, who wrote these things by his orders, the truth of which shall, in due time, be acknowledged.

CHAPTER V.

PROPHECY OF FATHER NECKTOU, A JESUIT, ABOUT FRANCE.

THE Rev. P. Neckton was a Jesuit before the suppression of that illustrious Order, in the year 1773. He foretold very clearly this suppression. After the suppression, this holy religious lived, during many years, as a most exemplary secular priest, in the city of Poitiers, where he acquired such high esteem for his holiness, that a pious mother brought to him the dead body of her little babe, which he restored to life.

On another occasion the Abbé Necktou casually met in the street a young boy, by name Davion, to whom he foretold, that he should not only become a priest, but that he should be raised to the dignity of archbishop, and, under another name, greatly contribute to the reestablishment of the Jesuits. All this has been fully realized, as the same archbishop testified on different occasions. The Abbé Raux related to several trustworthy persons in Paris and in Lyons, that Rev. P. Necktou, before the suppression of the Jesuits, on two different occasions, called him into his room, and for several hours spoke to him about the approaching dissolution of his Order, and of the imminent French Revolution, in consequence of which both had to fly from France into Spain. They were kindly received in the hospitable house of a Spanish prince, to whose children the Abbé Necktou became tutor. During an apparent calm, both resolved to return to France. On leaving the house of their kind and noble benefactor, the Abbé Necktou turned to his younger companion in exile, and said to him: *You see, my dear friend, this house; look well at it; when you shall be again obliged to leave France, this is the place wherein you will find shelter.* The fact verified the prediction. "Shortly after our return to France, I was obliged," the Abbé Raux says, "once more to fly away from it into Spain, and to seek an asylum in the same princely mansion."

These private prophecies, so literally fulfilled, gave the Abbé Raux a strong confidence in the fulfilment of the other prophecies of a more general character. The Abbé

Raux states: "After having in the most minute and circumstantial manner foretold to me all the horrible events of the first French Revolution, the Abbé Necktou added:—

"'A reaction will follow which shall be taken for a counter-revolution; this shall last for some years; but this shall only be a patch sewed together. There will be no schism; but the Church shall not yet triumph in France; there will be more trouble.

"'A man disliked by France will be placed on the throne; a man of the house of Orleans shall be made king.

"'It is only after this event that the counter-revolution shall begin. It shall not be effected by foreign powers; but two parties will be formed in France which shall fight unto death. The party of evil will at first be stronger; the good side shall be weaker. At that time there shall be such a terrible crisis that people, frightened by events, shall believe that the end of the world is come.

"'Blood shall flow in several large cities. The very elements shall be convulsed. It will be like a *little general judgment*. A great multitude of persons shall perish in these calamitous times.

"'But the wicked shall never prevail. They indeed shall conspire for the destruction of the Church; but time shall not be allowed them, because this frightful crisis shall be but of a short duration. *When all will be considered lost, all shall be found safe.*

[This expression is found often repeated by other prophetical seers, and should give great confidence to the faithful, persecuted children of the Church. *Porte inferi non prevalebunt. The gates of hell shall not prevail.*]

"'During this revolution, which shall very likely be general, and not confined to France, Paris shall be destroyed so completely, that, twenty years afterwards, fathers walking over its ruins with their children, these will inquire what place that was. To whom they will answer: *My child, this was formerly a great city, which God has destroyed on account of her crimes.*

" 'After this most terrible event, everything shall return to order; justice shall reign in the world, and the counter-revolution shall be accomplished.

" 'The triumph of the Church will then be so complete that nothing like it shall ever be seen, for this will be the last victory of the Church upon earth.

" 'As, when the fig-tree begins to sprout and produce leaves, it is a certain sign that summer is near, so when England shall begin to wane in power, the destruction of Paris shall be near at hand.

" 'This shall be a sign. England shall, in her turn, experience a more frightful revolution than that of France. It shall continue so long as to give time to France to recover her strength, when she will help England to return to order and peace.'

"The Venerable Abbé Necktou did not assign any precise time for all these events, which he predicted to me," says the Abbé Raux, his friend. "He stated, however, that *those persons who shall behold this last revolution will thank God for having preserved them to witness this glorious triumph of the Church.*"

A lady, well known in Lyons for her great piety, on hearing the Abbé Raux relating this prophecy about the destruction of Paris, said to him: "Reverend sir, this seems too hard. What will become, then, of so many good souls living in that great capital of France?"

He answered: "Paris, madam, shall certainly be destroyed; but before this occurs, such signs and portents shall be observed, that all good people will be induced to fly away from it."

Finally, the Venerable P. Necktou foretold, that when the above-mentioned events shall be near at hand, everything upon earth shall be so upset and confused, as if God had entirely withheld his providence from mankind, and that, during the worst crisis, the best that can be done would be to remain where God has placed us, and persevere in fervent prayer. During more than fifty years this remarkable prophecy is perfectly known in France.

CHAPTER VI.

PROPHECY OF SISTER MARIANNE, AN URSULINE NUN.

SISTER MARIANNE, an Ursuline nun in the Convent of Blois, France, famous for her sanctity of life, during her last illness, in the month of August, 1804, made the following prophecies to Mademoiselle Leyette, living now in the same convent, under the religious name of Sister Providence:—

1. That her mother, in six months' time, should no longer be able to put any obstacle to her religious vocation.

In fact, her mother died before the end of six months.

2. That she should become a religious in that community.

Such was the case.

3. That she should be elected several times Superior. All this has been done.

4. That she should not die before the accomplishment of the great events which she had announced to her.

Sister Providence is at present ninety-three years old, and enjoys perfect health.

5. That the religious community, then very small and poor, should greatly flourish.

Such has been the sequel.

6. That they should later change the locality, and that some religious on that occasion would separate themselves from the community, which in reality took place.

7. That in the new locality they would build a wall for the enclosure by using for it a silver coffee-pot.

It is a remarkable fact, that a pious benefactress of that community, observing how indispensable the wall was, came to the Mother Superior and said to her: "Fear not, have courage; *Le bon Dieu,* the good God, has inspired me to spend for the erection of the needed wall the price of a silver coffee-pot, which I had intended to purchase."

8. That some time later a bishop would be elected for Blois, whom such and such sisters should see, but that such others should not see.

The event verified this prediction.

The Abbé Richaudeau, chaplain to the Convent of the Ursulines of Blois, where Sister Providence lives, has composed and published a conscientious and lucid dissertation upon these prophetical predictions, which ecclesiastical authority has approved as an historical document.

We give here a sketch of it.

1. *Times which precede actual Events.* — Monsieur Abbé Richaudeau says that, according to the older copies of previsions and predictions, and in conformity with the oral

traditions of that religious community, Sister Marianne predicted all the great events that have happened since the beginning of the present century; so likewise the fall of the first Emperor Napoleon; the restoration of the Bourbon dynasty; the hundred days of Napoleon's treacherous return to France; the assassination and death of the Duke de Berry, brother to Louis XVIII., and father to the Count de Chambord, whose unexpected birth was predicted by Sister Marianne. Also the revolution of 1830, and that of 1848.

In announcing all these events, this holy nun entered into little details which have all been literally verified.

2. *Actual Events.* — Monsieur Abbé Richaudeau is of opinion that the present occurrences, according to the authentic traditions of the community, are really the great events predicted by Sister Marianne. The present Mother Superior of the Ursulines of Blois has, on the 15th of October, 1870, written the following words to the Dominican Father Delatrie:—

"Although Sister Marianne did not state the precise epoch of the events which she revealed to Sister Providence, yet this latter has never confounded the events of 1848 with those which have relation to the present time.

"During these last years, when the political horizon began again to become clouded, to our interrogations Sister Providence answered, 'No! it is not yet the moment of the great event.' But at this day she believes that the time is arrived.

"Many details not published by the journals of France, but well known to us, leave no doubt in our minds in relation to these events.

"The present foreign war is mentioned, the invasion and its consequences are most clearly predicted, but the final conclusion, which Sister Providence constantly calls *le grand coup* (the grand event), makes us fear an *internal convulsion.*"

According to the Abbé Richaudeau, Sister Marianne gives seven indications so precise that they leave no doubt about the epoch in question.

1. Before these great calamities, a certain construction will be effected in the convent, the principal portion of which will be erected, but the projected building shall not be finished before these events predicted take place.

At present in the Ursuline Convent at Blois there is a building in such condition.

2. The great misfortunes shall begin before the vintage.

The French war with Germany was declared on the 19th of July, and actually begun in 1870.

However, the Abbé Richaudeau remarks, that from these predictions it cannot be gathered that these evils will end in the same year. The work of regeneration which God has commenced is very great and most important.

God is working for the reformation of Christian nations, especially that of France.

We cannot naturally expect that moderate and short calamities can effect the cure of great and inveterate diseases.

3. The Seminarians (in the Episcopal city of Blois) will have gone out of the seminary when the great misfortunes shall arrive. Before the end of it they could have returned, but they shall not do so.

So far this has taken place; the Seminarians are away.

4. During these calamities the great Fair of Blois shall occur.

Every year this Fair takes place on the 5th of September. During many years, people remember and speak of these prophetical predictions.

5. During the war, men will be obliged to go by small parties, until only the old men shall remain at home.

6. During these calamitous times nobody shall be able to learn the true news, except through some private letters; so much so, that people shall not know to what government they belong.

7. People shall hear the rumbling of heavy wagons drawn by bullocks, and loaded with the movable property of those who fly before the enemy.

This prophecy is very remarkable, because in Blois, wagons so drawn are very seldom seen; yet this has actually taken place during the late war.

Old Sister Providence, however, asserts that the occurrences of the late war are not the great calamities predicted by Sister Marianne. This holy nun used to say:—

"So long as public prayers will be made, nothing shall happen; but a time will come when public prayers shall cease. People will say, 'Things will remain as they are.' It is then that the great calamity shall occur. This great calamity shall consist: 1, in a great fight; 2, great tribulations in many large cities of France; 3, a horrible massacre in the capital, namely, Paris. During the battle, people shall hear the noise of the cannon nine leagues, or twenty-seven miles, distant.

"Before the great combat the wicked shall be masters. They will perpetrate all the evils in their power, but not as much as they desire, because they shall not have the time. Good and faithful Catholics, less in number, shall be on the point of being annihilated, but a stroke from

Heaven will save them. [Shall this be the three days and nights of complete darkness predicted by the Venerable Maria Taigi of Rome?]

"O power of God! O power of God! All the wicked shall perish, and also many good men. O, how frightful shall these calamities be! The churches shall be closed, but only for the space of twenty-four hours. Religious women, being terrified, shall be on the point of abandoning the convent, but, however, they shall remain. At this time such extraordinary events shall take place that the most incredulous will be forced to say, *The finger of God is there.* O power of God! *There shall be a terrible night,* during which no one shall be able to sleep. These trials shall not last long, because no person could endure them. *When all shall appear lost, all will be saved.* It is then that despatches shall arrive, announcing good news, when the *Te Deum* shall be sung, in a manner in which it has never been heard before. It is then that shall reign the Prince, whom people will seek, that before did not esteem him. At that time the triumph of religion will be so great that no one has ever seen the equal. All injustices will be repaired, civil laws will be formed in harmony with the laws of God and of the Church. The instruction given to children will be most Christian; pious guilds for workmen shall be re-established; the triumph of the Church and of France shall be most glorious."

Mademoiselle De Leyette, now Sister Providence, asked Sister Marianne how long should this happy time continue. To whom the holy nun answered: "O, neither you, nor any of the religious who shall then be with you, will see the end of it"; and then added: "I have many other things to tell you. O, what beautiful things I have to tell you! what beautiful things! Come again to see me."

But one hour later Sister Marianne rendered her beautiful soul to God.

CHAPTER VII.

PROPHECY OF A FRANCISCAN CAPUCHIN FRIAR.

THIS prophecy is preserved in the library of the Capuchin Fathers, in Genzano, between Albano and Veletri, near Rome, which has been transcribed from a copy dated 1776 :—

1. From the year 1780 to 1792 of our Redemption, the Emperor of Germany (Joseph II. of Austria) will in an incredible manner afflict the orthodox faith, the Holy Church of Jesus Christ.

2. A new empire shall rise up in France (the first French Revolution and the first Napoleon); then woe to you priests, because you shall be persecuted, dispersed, and exiled!

3. The German Emperor will form close alliance with Oriental and Northern powers (with Russia, Prussia, and England) against his enemies. In union with these powers he will wage a desolating war in France and in Italy.

4. Through this alliance the new empire shall be broken up, and the Church of Jesus Christ will enjoy her peace, but for a short time.

5. Between, however, these allied powers shall arise most bitter dissensions, and the Emperor (of Austria) shall be constrained to fight against his former allies.

[All this portion of the prophecy has relation to the past. It has been literally verified. The Emperor Joseph II. of Austria persecuted the Church. The first French Revolution and the Empire of Napoleon and its fall is well known. England, the former ally of Russia, fought against it in Crimea with France. France and Italy fought against Austria. Prussia has been at war both with Austria and more lately with France. Let us now proceed to the remaining portion of the prophecy, which has relation to the immediate future.]

6. All the ecclesiastics, both secular and regular, shall be stripped of all their possessions, and of every kind of property, and obliged to beg from lay persons their food and everything necessary for their support, and for the worship of God.

7. All religious orders will be abolished, except one having the rules of the most rigid and most severe institute of the ancient monks.

8. During these sad calamities the Pope shall die.

9. Through the death of the Supreme Pontiff the Church will be reduced to the most painful anarchy, because from three hostile powers (through their influence) three popes will be contemporaneously elected: one Italian, another German, the third Greek. This, by force of arms, shall be placed on the throne.

10. During this time much human blood shall be shed in Italy, and many cities, country towns, and castles shall be brought to ruin, with the deaths of many thousands of persons.

11. By the Catholic clergy and people the true and lawful Pope will be elected, who shall be a man of great holiness and goodness of life, selected from the surviving monastic Order mentioned above.

12. A scion of the Carlovingian race, by all consid-

ered extinct, will come to Rome to behold and admire the piety and clemency of this Pontiff, who will crown him, and declare him to be the legitimate Emperor of the Romans, and from the Chair of St. Peter the Pope will lift up the standard, the crucifix; and will give it to the new emperor. (See other similar prophecies in this book.)

13. This new emperor, with the robust Italian and French people, and with those of other nations, will form a most powerful host, called the Church Army, through which he shall destroy the Ottoman Empire, all heresies, and shall also totally defeat the Emperor of the North, who is called *Mystic Antichrist.*

14. The above-mentioned new emperor, with the assistance of God and of the Pope, will co-operate to the reformation of abuses; will assume (with the free consent of the Pope) the management of the temporal government; will assign a decent pension to the Supreme Pontiff, and also to the bishops and clergy; and they all, being detached from every earthly covetousness, will live in peace, which shall last till the end of time.

15. Finally, the Pope will select twelve subjects of his religion, whom he will send through the world to preach missions. They shall have the power of converting the nations to the faith of our Lord Jesus Christ, excepting the Hebrews, who are reserved for the end of the world.

CHAPTER VIII.

PROPHECY OF GEORGE MICHAEL WITTMAN.

GEORGE MICHAEL WITTMAN, the pious and devoted Bishop of Ratisbon, was born January 23, 1760. He was distinguished for extraordinary learning and erudition, vigorous orthodoxy, and great aptitude in teaching, an ardent zeal for souls, and for his charity towards the poor.

In 1788 he became Vice-President and in 1803 President of the Ecclesiastical Seminary of Ratisbon; in 1821, Canon of the Cathedral; in 1829, Suffragan Bishop Provost of the Cathedral, and Vicar-General. At the death of Bishop Tailor, in 1832, he became his worthy successor, and died March 8, 1833. The popular voice proclaimed him a saint, and all who knew him said, "He was a man of the first apostolic days of the Church, — a priest according to God's own heart."

The illuminated eye of Wittman foresaw the future when he spoke in the following manner: —

"Woe is me! Sad days are at hand for the Holy Church of Jesus Christ. The Passion of Jesus will be renewed in the most dolorous manner in the Church and in her Supreme Head. In all parts of the world there will be wars and revolutions, and much blood will be spilled. Distress, disasters, and poverty will everywhere be great, since pestilential maladies, scarcity, and other misfortunes will follow one another.

"Violent hands will be laid on the Supreme Head of the Catholic Church; bishops and priests will be persecuted, and schisms will be provoked, and confusion reign amid all classes. Times will come, so pre-eminently bad, that it will seem as if the enemies of Christ, and of his Holy Church, which he founded with his blood, were about to triumph over her. *But the priesthood will remain firm and resolute, and good people will adhere faithfully to that body.* A general separation will be made. The wheat shall be winnowed, and the floor swept. *Secret societies will work great ruin, and exercise a marvellous monetary power,** and through that many will be blinded, and infected with most horrible errors; however, all this shall avail naught. Christ says, *He who is not with me is against me, and he who gathereth not with me scattereth.* Scandals will be but too rife, and woe to those by whom they come! *Although the tempests will be terrible, and will turn away many in their passage, nevertheless they cannot shake the rock whereon Christ has founded his Church. Porte inferi non prevalebunt.*

"The faithful sheep will gather together, and in *Unions of Prayer* will offer potent resistance to the enemies of the Catholic Church. Yes, yes, the flock will become small. Many of you will see those sad times and days which will bring such evil in their train; but I shall not behold them. A marvellous thing will occur, (may this not apply to the proclamation of the dogma of the Pontifical Infallibility, and the overpassing by Pius IX. of the years of the Pontificate of St. Peter?) but then hell will rise in opposition against it, and terrible agitation will ensue. Great confusion will reign amid princes and nations. The incredulity of the present day is preparing those horrid evils."

* See page 195.

CHAPTER IX.

OUR LADY OF LA SALETTE. — REVELATIONS OF THE BLESSED VIRGIN MARY TO MELANIE AND MASSIMIN.

I. — *Preliminary Remarks.*

THE wonderful apparition of the Blessed Virgin Mary, on the now famous mountain of La Salette, to two young children, is well known to the Catholic world. La Salette is the western portion of the Alps, which divide France from Piedmont, in Italy. The nearest town to La Salette is Corps, which belongs to the large diocese of Grenoble. The great Chartreuse was in that neighborhood. This apparition, then, took place on the borders of France and Italy, and has, evidently, relation to both those unhappy countries, which have, by impious men, been made the forges of an antichristian revolution against the Church and legitimate governments. God, as usual, chooses the weak and humble to overcome the strong, and the poor and ignorant to confound the wise. A little shepherd boy, eleven years of age, and a poor, timid girl, fourteen years old, suddenly became famous in France, Italy, Europe, and over the whole Catholic world. The name of the boy is Peter Massimin Giraud, that of the girl, Frances Melanie Mathieu. Since the apparition, both are better known by their second names, namely, Massimin and Melanie. Both were natives of Corps. Melanie was hired to assist the young Massimin in tending his father's cattle on the mountain of La Salette. They were both at this humble employment on Saturday, September 19, 1846, being the eve of the Feast of the Seven Dolors of the Blessed Virgin

Mary, between two and three o'clock in the afternoon, when both beheld the apparition.

They saw a lady surrounded by a brilliant light, sitting on a stone near a dry fountain, in an attitude of profound grief. At this unexpected spectacle, the two children remained stupefied. Melanie allowed her shepherd's staff to fall to the ground; little Massimin, with more natural courage, kept his own, and told Melanie to take up her stick immediately, that they might defend themselves in case of need. At this moment the unknown lady stood up, and crossing her arms upon her chest, she spoke thus to them: *Come near, my children; have no fear; I am here to communicate to you some great news.* The two children, reassured by her attitude, kind looks, and gentle words, moved a few steps towards the lady, whilst she also came to meet them, and placing herself between them, spoke to them in the following manner, shedding many tears at the same time: "If my people will not obey (God's commandments), I am forced to let free my Son's arm. It is so strong and heavy that I can no longer retain it. It is a long time that I am suffering for you. If I wish to prevent my Son from abandoning you, I must pray incessantly. . . . . Yet you make no account of this. Whatever you may do, you shall never be able to compensate all my solicitude for you. I gave you six days for work, but reserved the seventh for myself; yet it is refused to me; this is what renders so heavy the arm of my Son. Drivers mix up the name of my Son with their oaths. If the harvest is spoiled, it is through your own fault. Last year I wished to make you understand this by the rottenness of the potatoes; but you paid no attention to this; on the contrary, when you found your potatoes spoiled, you swore, and mixed the name of my

Son with your oaths. Your potatoes shall rot so fast that for Christmas you shall have no more. Worms shall destroy your wheat; the little that shall grow shall be reduced to dust at the thrashing. A great famine shall come. Your chestnuts shall be spoiled, and your grapes shall rot." After these words, the Holy Virgin turned towards Massimin, and confided to him a secret. The same she afterwards did to Melanie. Whilst she was speaking to one, the other could see her lips moving, but could not hear her words; she commanded each separately to keep the secret inviolate. They both promised so to do. The Blessed Virgin added to both in common some other kind words, which, for brevity's sake, we omit, and then said twice : *Well, my children, make these things known to all my people.*

Here the Lady began to walk towards the place where their cattle were grazing, followed by the two children, who observed that her feet only softly touched, like a light zephyr, the top of the green grass. She began then to rise up slowly into the air, when she gave a look towards heaven, and down again towards the earth ; by degrees *and degrees* her head began to disappear, then her arms, finally her feet, leaving behind, for a short time, a bright halo.

According to the description of the two privileged children, the following was the appearance of this heavenly Lady : She had on her feet white shoes, adorned round with roses ; over a white dress, besprinkled with pearls, she wore a yellow apron ; on her shoulders and round her neck she had a white kerchief, or a small shawl ; and a high head-dress, surrounded by a crown of roses. Attached to a small chain, hanging from her neck, and resting upon her chest, was a cross and crucifix, having a pair of pincers at the right, and a hammer at the left ;

from the extremity of the cross hung a larger chain. In her hand she held an ordinary handkerchief, adorned with roses. Her countenance was oblong, very beautiful, and so resplendent that nobody could, for any length of time, fix his looks upon it. At this apparition the children observed that the Blessed Virgin spoke a much longer time to Melanie than to Massimin. As it might be expected on such extraordinary events, the two children were subjected to the most minute and searching examination. In their artless simplicity they were ever found consistent and inflexible in the statement of this fact. But nobody could, either by promises or by threats, induce them to reveal their respective secrets. Melanie especially attracted attention, on account of her longer colloquy with the great Queen of Heaven, and because she appeared more deeply impressed with the sacred solemnity of the apparition. From that time both children were placed under the care of pious and prudent religious teachers. In the month of July, 1851, Monseigneur de Bruillard, the venerable Bishop of Grenoble, succeeded in persuading Melanie and Massimin to write privately their respective secrets, and to send them in two distinct sealed letters to the Pope.

Reverends Rousselot and Gerin, two priests of the diocese, were commissioned by the bishop to convey these two mysterious messages to his Holiness, who received them with great amiability. The Pope read the two letters in the presence of the two ecclesiastics; he appeared particularly impressed with the longer account of Melanie. But he only uttered these words: *There are chastisements for France; but Germany, but Italy, but many other nations, are equally guilty.*

In a few years after, Melanie embraced the religious state of life in France; but by Napoleon she was exiled to England, where she made her religious profession among the discalced Carmelite nuns, under the name of Sister Mary of the Cross, Victim of Jesus, in the convent in Darlington, near Durham, in the diocese of Hexam, in the North of England. Some years ago she returned to France, and for some time lived in the Convent of Providence in Marseilles, but was forced to abandon it, when she went to Castellamare, near Naples, in Italy. From that place she wrote the following very important prophetic letter to her mother, which has been authenticated by the curé of Corps, near La Salette.

II. — *Letter of Melanie to her Mother.*

September 21, 1870.

MY VERY DEAR AND WELL-BELOVED MOTHER, — May Jesus be loved by all hearts. This letter is not only intended for you, but also for all the inhabitants of Corps, my very dear native town.

A father of family, full of affection for his children, seeing that these were forgetful of their duties, and after abandoning the law which he had given them had become ungrateful, resolved to punish them severely. His spouse, mother of the family, prayed for their forgiveness, and went immediately to visit the two youngest, namely, the two weakest and most ignorant of all her children. This lady, who cannot weep in the mansion of her spouse, which is heaven, found abundance of tears in the fields of these wretched children. She announced to them the complaints and threats of their lord and master, if they did not return to him and observe his commandments. But only a small, very small number of them embraced from their hearts a sincere reformation, and attached themselves to the observance of the holy law of the father of family. The majority continue in their crimes, and fall more deeply into vice.

In consequence of this their father inflicts upon them various punishments in order to bend their obstinacy. But these wretched children, instead of falling upon their knees to ask his pardon and mercy, and above all promising to him a change of conduct, seize and break the rod with which they are punished, imagining that in this manner they escape the chastisement. But their father, becoming more than ever irritated, takes hold of a stronger scourge and strikes them, and will continue to strike till they acknowledge their guilt, humble themselves, and implore the mercy of him who is the Lord and King of heaven and earth. (This is a very simple, modest, but touching allusion to the apparition of La Salette.)

You understand, dear mother, and dear fellow-citizens of Corps! this father of family is God! . . . . We all are his children. Neither you nor I have loved him as we ought. We have not observed his commandments as we should; in consequence of this God punishes us. A great number of our brothers die in war. Many families and entire cities are reduced to misery. But if people return not to God, the punishment is not finished. Paris is guilty, and very guilty, because it has rewarded an impious man (Renan) who has written a book against the Divinity of Jesus Christ. . . . . Men have only a limited period of time for committing sin, but God, being Master of Eternity, chooses what time he likes for punishing the wicked.

God is irritated by a multitude of sins, and because *he is almost unknown and forgotten by men*. Who will then be able to stop this war that causes in France so much desolation, and which will soon begin in Italy and elsewhere? Who shall be able to arrest this scourge of the war?

It is necessary, in the first place, that France recognize in this war the true hand of God. Secondly, that she humble herself, and beg from her heart and soul pardon for her sins. Thirdly, it is necessary for France to promise sincerely to serve the good God with her whole heart and soul, and to observe his commandments without any human respect.

There are persons who pray, and ask the good God for the success of our French armies. But this is not what God wills. (Was not this a clear, plain prophecy of the imminent defeat of the French armies by the Prussians?) God demands the conversion of the French. The most holy Virgin came to France (at La Salette), but France is not converted.

She is more guilty than other nations. If she do not humble herself before the good God she shall be greatly humbled. Who will save the city of Paris, that centre of vanity and arrogance, except fervent and continued prayers ascend to the heart of the good Master?

I remember with pleasure, my very dear mother, and well-beloved inhabitants of my dear native town, — I remember those devout processions that you made on the holy mountain of La Salette to keep the cholera away from your neighborhood, and the Holy Virgin was pleased with your fervent prayers, your penances, and with all your good works performed for God's sake. I believe and hope that you continue at present to make those beautiful processions for the salvation of France. May France at length return to the good God, because he awaits only for this conversion to withdraw the rod with which he chastises his rebellious people. Let us then pray much; yes, let us pray. Make your processions as you did in 1846 and 1847. Believe that God will hear you, because he always hear the prayers of humble hearts. Let us pray together; let us pray continually.

I never liked Napoleon, because I have in my memory his whole history. May the Divine Saviour of the world forgive him the evil that he has done, and which he is actually doing.

Let us remember that we are created for the love and service of God, without which there cannot be any true happiness. Let mothers bring up their children in a Christian-like manner, because the time of tribulations is not yet finished. If I divulged to you the number and qualities of these trials, you should be terrified! But I do not wish to frighten you. Have confidence in God, who loves us. Let us pray! let us pray! and the sweet, the good, the tender Virgin Mary will always be with you. Prayer disarms the anger of God. Prayer is the key of heaven. Let us pray for our poor soldiers. Let us pray for so many mothers desolated at the loss of their sons. Let us consecrate ourselves to our good Mother of heaven. Let us pray. Let us pray for those blind, deluded people, who do not see that it is the hand of God that punishes France in this moment. Let us pray much, and let us do penance.

Be all most strongly attached to holy Church, and to the holy Father, who is the head of the Church, and the visible Vicar upon earth of our Lord Jesus Christ. In your processions, in your penances, pray much for the Pope.

Lastly, be ye all in peace. Love one another like brothers. Promise God to keep his holy commandments, and do this in practice, and thus through the Divine Mercy you will be happy, you will have a good and holy death, which I ardently desire for you all, whilst I place you under the protection of the august Virgin Mary.

My salvation is in the Cross.

MARY OF THE CROSS, *Victim of Jesus.*

The heart of Jesus watches over me.

So far Melanie's letter. I add a few sentiments, which the perusal of this letter has suggested to my mind.

The style and sentiments of this remarkable letter stamp it with the gift of inspiration. The simplicity of a country shepherdess utters the most sublime ideas. Her mind is horrified at the manifold crimes committed by men against her good God. She sees the justice of an eternal God provoked to anger against them. Her tender, loving heart is moved to pity. From the seclusion of the cloister Melanie sends forth the cry of alarm and warning, inviting sinners to repentance and to prayer. In the name of God she promises mercy and pardon if they repent, but threatens more severe chastisement if they remain obstinate.

The spirit of prophecy pervades this letter. Dreadful calamities are clearly foretold as impending upon France and Italy, because *men have forsaken and forgotten God.* But, in the words of the Pope, *many other countries are equally guilty.* The arch-demon of infidelity has perverted the minds and corrupted the hearts of millions of men in every Christian nation. Principles of religion and maxims of morality have been undermined and shaken to the foundation. Might has supplanted right. Jove has been substituted for Jesus. Gold is the god of the present age, and Venus its goddess. Barabbas has been preferred to Jesus Christ. His Vicar upon earth has been rejected by an impious crowd for the sake of an excommunicated monarch. European and other earthly governments sanction the usurpation and sacrilege either by their expressed words or by their silent apathy. When the majority of the human race is impious and wicked, then a general punishment becomes inevitable. Because God is obliged to give a practical proof not only of his divine justice, but of his very existence. Moreover, the spirit of impiety, of which Voltaire was the apostle in France, galvanized at present into life by such reckless men as Gambetta, Garibaldi, Cremieux, and *their red craft*, conjured into action by their high-priest Mazzini, — this impious spirit, I say, is now fully determined to make the most desperate effort for the total overthrow of Catholic Christianity. These are not idle imaginations. Those who know the real character of this impious class of men expect all this as imminent. Those who have perused "The Jew of Verona" and "Lionello" of the late learned Father Bresciani are prepared for these events. We can judge the tree from its fruits. See what they have already attempted in France, in Spain, and especially in Italy and Rome. Moreover, their organs of the press publicly announce the intended attack and their final intentions; weekly correspondence from Rome confirms my assertions.

Again, the black storm of revolution and religious persecution, so long conceived in iniquity, deeply brooding and violently pent up within the dark recesses and impious *Vendite* or lodges of antichristian secret societies of the *Carbonari*, is ready to burst with diabolical fury upon unhappy Italy. They feel that this is their hour, and the power of darkness. Their long-sought opportunity is arrived. In Spain and Portugal, but more especially in France and in Italy, these bad men have political power and military weapons in their strong grasp. They will not let their *tight grip* loosen, nor surrender them without a fearful and bloody struggle. They have made up their mind. They are impatient for the assault. Secret orders have already been issued. Co-operation has been secured and promised in different parts of the world. We shall soon hear that the attack against our holy religion has begun in France and Italy, and very likely also in Spain.* This fight of the power of darkness against Catholicity will and must last for some years. First, because the contending parties are numerous and strong. Secondly, because time and opportunity will be given to this impious revolution fully to manifest her real character and aim in horrible deeds of blood and sacrilege, in order to undeceive those short-sighted Christians and Catholics who sympathize with it.

It is hard, it is painful, it is a scandal to the weak, to be obliged to hear and see, not only lay Catholics, but also ecclesiastical persons, publicly fraternizing with the antichristian revolution, and, in spite of most grave censures of their Church, sanction and encourage by their words and personal conduct the sacrilegious usurpation of the Papal States, and by their silence and apathy approve the outrages against the sacred person of Christ's Vicar. But the time is not far distant when not only true Catholics, but every honest man with natural principles of justice and feeling of humanity, will be forced to detest with horror the cruel excesses of the impending revolution, the worst that has ever afflicted Christianity and human society. Its authors, leaders, and followers

* This was written two years ago.

will be condemned to universal and everlasting infamy.
I have strong motives for writing all this. The third
reason why this infamous revolution will be suffered by
God to last for some considerable time—very likely a
decade—is in order to render the wisdom and power of
Divine Providence, in the protection of his holy Church,
so strongly and universally evident that no man of
sound reason will be able to deny it; *for the gates of hell
can never prevail against our holy Church.*

This public divine manifestation seems necessary in
this unhappy age of practical atheism, wherein a ruling
Divine Providence is excluded from the government of
human society. In this boasted nineteenth century of
civilization and progress, human society has fallen into
material Paganism. Melanie has forcibly expressed this
melancholy fact in these words: *God has been forsaken
and forgotten by men.*

A cruel persecution of the Church and of her venerable
Head *will*—contrary to all calculations of blind infidelity—*and must* stir up and rouse the dormant faith
and fervor of all true Catholics. Spain and Portugal,
France and Italy, have foolishly allowed their civil power
as Christian nations to fall into the hands of the secret
enemies of their faith and religion. They have had already to suffer much for it. Like true Christians, they
have suffered with exemplary patience. But as soon as
the attempt is made to deprive those Catholic people of
their faith and religion, then we shall see the unity, the
power and strength, of Catholicity. Spain and Portugal
are in mind and heart Catholic nations. France is by
no means without faith; that truly Christian nation has
a large number of true and devout Catholics, who will,
if necessary, bravely fight for their holy religion, which
is at present the only hope and effective means for their
salvation and preservation of their afflicted country from

dismal anarchy and utter ruin. Fighting for their religion, they are certain of achieving a most complete and most glorious victory.

In Italy we have every hope of a complete triumph of the Catholic faith in the prudent and firm attitude of the Pope, and with him all the Italian Episcopal and ecclesiastical hierarchy; in the manly tone of the Catholic press, in the renewed faith and fervor of the Italian Catholic youth, in the general manifestation of devotion to the Holy Father by the people, and in their silent, patient abhorrence of the Freemason government by which they are oppressed in soul and body. The two columns of Catholic Italy are patience and hope. Rome has by Jesus Christ been chosen as the capital seat of his kingdom upon earth. The Pope, his Vicar, is and shall be the Bishop of Rome to the end of time. No earthly king shall ever reign long in Rome. Two hundred and fifty millions of Catholics cannot permit this sacrilege. God is pledged to protect both his Church and his Vicar upon earth. He will infallibly do it even in Rome.

III.—*On the 23d of June, 1871, Melanie, in Answer to a Letter of a Religious Sister of Providence in Corenc Dauphiné, wrote as follows:—*

"CASTELLAMARE, KINGDOM OF NAPLES.

"Our poor France, you say, is greatly humbled. Ah! my dear sister, she had done much better to humble herself without awaiting for the blows of the Most High; and she would do well now to strike her breast, to revive her faith, if she does not wish to be entirely annihilated. Ah! my good sister, in beholding the state into which society is plunged, one should shed tears night and day. O, the worst of all evils is that some men hate God! they are determined to fight against him. I never have said that the Dauphiné (Province of France) shall be protected. Ah! if people haste not to return sincerely to God, what is already arrived is as nothing! nothing!! nothing!!! I do not wish to dishearten anybody; you, my dear sister, you know God a thousand times better than I do; therefore, if we pray to him, he is full of mercy, and he ever desires to pardon all those who sincerely return to him. In the opinion of some persons, I am nothing but a deluded visionary; in consequence of this I abstain from speaking, lest the words of truth, of which I am only a feeble and very unworthy channel, should be despised. Poor France! she has a veil over her eyes; she is, as it were, paralyzed regarding the truth. Poor France! unhappy France! Ah! my dear sister, how my heart is filled with bitter grief in witnessing the fall of a nation formerly so full of religion. When will God, in his mercy, give us a handful of brave souls, that do not fear men, and who, stripped of everything, shall announce holy truths, and will sacrifice themselves for the glory of Jesus Christ? If the good God makes me return to France, I will thank him with my whole heart. I do not ask to re-enter a convent; I would only wish to live in a small village and teach a small school. [Here there are some mysterious words.] If the persom whom I would petition for such favor were in France, and were what he shall be, I would have already written to him for it. The statue of Voltaire is still erected in Paris; it seems to me that the first act of Monsieur Thiers should have been the destruction of that monstrous statue. But I understand. Voltaire is the idol of France. I have written to Monsieur Thiers. Worse for him, and worse for France, if he does not act as a Christian. I do my duty. When there is question of the glory of God, I fear neither death nor prison. France has been ruined because the clergy fear man more than God. Ah, if I am correct upon this point, poor clergy! poor clergy! But no! I am wrong; in the opinion of the clergy, I am deluded. The clergy are good, the clergy are disinterested, the clergy are full of zeal, full of charity towards the poor. It is the flock that is bad." (These words are ironical. Melanie is deeply grieved because the apparition of La Salette, the threatened punishments, and herself have been treated as a delusion. We should remember that these private letters were not intended for publication by Melanie.)

IV. — *Portion of a Letter of Melanie to a certain Monsieur Gerard, dated August 15, 1871.*

"It is very near twenty-five years since the good, the sweet Virgin Mary, Mother of God, came to shed tears over our mountain. She cried, and for whom ? and for what ? It is because her people have deviated from the path of virtue, and, with rapid strides, hasten to precipitate themselves into the abyss of perdition. Poor people! poor France! Thou knowest not that thou mightest be grounded like grain under the mill-stone of God's anger and justice! At the present time it is useless to speak to men; their blindness is supreme. It is necessary that God should speak; and he will speak; but they cannot form an idea how. The earth must be punished, purified. You desire, sir, some information about the letter which I wrote to Monsieur Thiers. As I always write only one copy, so then I could not tell you what I wrote in my letter. I only remember to have said to him to remove from Paris the statue of Voltaire and all that is not of God and for God. It seems to me that I likewise told him that if the government return not to God, and does not procure the observance of God's commandments, the chastisements already inflicted are as nothing. I did not give him my address, and my letter, directed to him, was mailed in Marscilles. When the time for writing to . . . . shall have arrived, I will do so gladly. In this moment France is not worthy of him."

V. — *Letter of Melanie to Victor C—— de Stenay, Author of " The Future Unveiled," and of " Last Prophetical Warnings."*

CASTELLAMARE, May 2, 1872.

J. M. J. SIR, — May Jesus be loved by all hearts.

I thank you very much for your charity in sending me your book, *Le Grandeurs et Malheurs de la France*. I have read it in haste. I shall peruse it over some of these days. This is the first time that I read prophecies. I believe that, to understand them, we should not look at things in a human way, or with human eyes. Before seeing Mr. Brandt, I never heard anybody speak of the future hero, David Lazzaretti; neither am I aware of any pamphlet or writing concerning him. But if I ever come to the knowledge of anything of this kind, I shall send it to you with pleasure. I am nothing but most vile dust. I am guilty in many ways, but I hope not in having disobeyed the most Holy Virgin. In proof of this I may mention the persecutions which I have had to endure, and which I suffer at present. When I asked some one the cause of my expulsion from the Convent of Providence, and of my exile to England, I received no answer, especially in the presence of other persons. *Eh bien!* Well, I shall not answer for so many persons. Charity forbids it. I will give an answer to only one person that spoke to me as follows: "Melanie, if you continue to speak against our Emperor (Napoleon), you shall not be allowed to remain in this place. You are deluded; it is the Devil that makes you speak. Napoleon is a saint, and all that he does is for the good of religion. Therefore, do not venture to speak any more so ill of Napoleon, and to exaggerate the holiness of the Pope, who is a man like ourselves. The Pope ought to celebrate mass, and that is all." To these words I answered: "I ought to obey God. As long as I live I shall speak the truth. If the Pope, whom I do not look upon as a man like you, forbid me to speak, I shall be silent, because I ought to obey the Vicar of Jesus Christ, and him alone, about what relates to my secret. If a bishop is not subject to the Vicar of Jesus Christ, I am neither bound to believe nor to obey the word of such bishop, who is without the Church." Therefore, sir, I have spoken, and, as I am going to tell you, I have also written, but as a religious person I cannot do much.

In the year 1860, I delivered this portion of my secret into the hands of a person dear to the heart of God, namely, to the Assistant of the Superior-General of the Sisters of the Compassion of Marseilles. I was then in that convent, and was associated to it. That writing was sent to a Vicar-General of the bishop of that city; it was returned with the following words: *France is at peace; these are things relating to the end of the world; too much attention should not be paid to them. Beware of illusion!* The same paper was afterwards put into the hands of a reverend Jesuit father, who returned it, saying that *there were some things about the end of time, and some others taken from the Apocalypse.* I wished to write, and did write to Napoleon. But I have got the letter in my possession, because I was not allowed to forward it, and it was the same Jesuit who did not judge it prudent. I have lately learned that this good Jesuit father could find it prudent to disguise himself in order to avoid the prison, and if, like many others, he had been killed, he should without doubt have believed that, if it were not the end of the world, it was at any rate the end for himself. Behold, sir, how this writing has remained in obscurity. No person knows whether I may manifest all the entire secret, or if at a fixed epoch the remaining portion shall be known. I believe it is better for us to be converted, to expiate, to atone, to serve the good God with our whole heart; to imitate your example, by having no fear of displeasing men in serving God and in making truth known. The good God will reward you, sir, for your zeal in promoting the glory of God and of the most Holy Virgin. Persevere. You shall have God for your defence and support. My poor France is very ill. However, if she would shake off the yoke of her slavery, she should become free with the freedom of God's children. France is the slave of the Devil, because she is the slave of the enemies of the Most High. Hence, alas! poor France. . . . . . She is about being crushed.

Please, I beseech you, to pray for me, for I am in great need of it; and I, though very unworthy, — I will pray for you. Pray also, I beg of you, for my companion, who is the person of whom I spoke to you above, namely, the Assistant of the Superior-General; she, through devotion and love of the most Holy Virgin, has followed me into exile; pray, then, for her and for those who belong to her.

I have known Monsieur Frochon on the mountain of La Salette, where I left him when I started for England, whither I was accompanied by a prelate (Monseigneur Newsham, the late venerable President of Ushaw College, near Durham), and a canon, both English. I have never travelled with Monseigneur Bishop of Birmingham. I have never gone to his diocese.

My extraordinary confessor being in Naples, and not coming here except once a month, I must await in order to acquaint him of your desire in relation to the declaration of the entire secret. But I do not think he will permit any change in the portion which I transmitted to the Abbé Bliard, because he might say that one would not know what part he should believe. Poor Mr. G—— has much to suffer. . . . . O my God! . . . . Darkness is where light should be! Let us be attached to the infallible Pontiff. Let us love the Church!

Please to accept the homage with which I am, monsieur,
Your most humble and most grateful servant,
MARIE DE LA CROIX, *Victime de Jesu.*
(MARY OF THE CROSS, *Victim of Jesus.*)

The eye of God over me watches; my salvation is the cross. *Vive Notre Dame de la Salette.*

VI.—*A Second Letter of Melanie to the same Gentleman.*

CASTELLAMARE, May 15, 1872.

J. M. J. May Jesus be loved by all hearts.

SIR,—I thank you for your charity in sending me the three books. I have received them with great pleasure. May the sweet and merciful Virgin Mary reward you for them. I have read almost entirely *Le Avenir Dévoilé*, "The Future Unveiled." I have arrived at page 172, where an important remark is made in the following words: "One is prompted by a spirit of religion to ask himself why Mother Mary of the Cross is made to play a semi-political *rôle* or character incompatible with her vocation, howsoever profitable it may be to souls. Melanie is a Carmelite; she should be dead to the world. Instead of giving here and there pieces of her secret enveloped in pious exhortations, she should reveal them fully *in extenso.*"

Since in another passage of the same book it is well said, that I have been persecuted, and still I am, people should know that I have not entered into any convent. I keep, indeed, my vows as a Carmelite; for which I am more than happy. When I wrote to my poor old mother, I was far from thinking that my letters to her would be printed. I had not, therefore, any intention to play a semi-political character. In beholding our poor France marching with rapid strides towards her ruin, one should indeed be without blood in his veins not to be moved, and not to cry, *Do penance, observe the law of God.* Is it because I am a Carmelite religious that I ought to be insensible to the evils of my mother, the Church, and to the perdition of all my brothers in Jesus Christ? Is it because I see some bishops and many priests who, if not all in word, yet in their actions, abandon the Holy Church and our Holy Father,— is it for this that I should have to hide myself, that I should have fear of Napoleon, of the government, and of the persecutors of the holy Church? Alas! it is just because some had fear that the evil is come thither. Well, I, the most unworthy, the most ignorant, the most weak and vile of creatures, I have no fear of any person. I am firmly attached to the infallible Pope, and to the holy Church, and I shall combat evil with all my power. I dread nothing, and I am not afraid of men, because they are as nothing in the hands of the Most High. Thiers, *all little and great as he is,* — Thiers is nothing else but the anger of God on my poor France. But let him wait a little longer, and we will see what shall happen.

People wish to know all my secret. But what does our Divine Master desire from us? It seems to me that he wills our conversion. What profit have we drawn from that small portion of the secret which we know? None. The more shall we have received, the stricter will be our account with God. I will not render our poor France more culpable. She wishes to see with her own eyes; she shall be obliged to see such things that she will have to close her eyes. Yes, she shall see to her great misery, she shall be surfeited. Let us pray, let us pray, let us pray without ceasing; let us atone. If the chastisements have to come, at least they could be mitigated by many prayers and much penance. Let us pray, let us pray. No person can form any idea of the nature of the punishments. . . . . Let us pray much. God is good. He wills not our perdition. . . . . Please to accept the humble homage with which I am, monsieur,

Your most grateful and most humble servant,
MARY OF THE CROSS, *Victim of Jesus*.

The eye of God watches over me; my salvation is in the cross. *Vive Notre Dame de la Salette.*

CHAPTER X.

MANIFESTATION OF THE SECRET OF LA SALETTE MADE BY MELANIE TO THE ABBÉ FELICIAN BLIARD.

MY REV. FATHER, — I deliver into your hands that portion of the secret that I received from the Holy Virgin on the 19th of September, 1846, and which, however, should now no longer be kept secret. You may do with it what you judge best before God and before men.

MELANIE MATHIEN,
Shepherdess of La Salette.

Given at CASTELLAMARE this day, January 30, 1870.

I. — *Words of the Most Holy Virgin to Melanie.*

What I am going now to tell you shall not always be kept secret. You may publish it in the year 1858.

The priests, ministers of my Son, through their 5· 9 7· 4 9 6· 6 3· 4 6· 3·, through their irreverences, and their

6· 5· 4· 6· 3· 2· 3·, whilst celebrating the holy mysteries; through their love of 1· 9 9· 2 3· 1 2·, love of honors and of 4· 1· 9 6· 6 6· 9· 6·, — yes, priests cry for vengeance, and vengeance is suspended over their heads. Woe to the priests, and to persons consecrated to God! who through their infidelity and their 5 9· 7· 4 9 6· 6 3· 4 6· 4· crucify again my Son. The sins, 5 3· 6 4 3· 9· 6 3 1 1 3· 6· + 3 1 6 9· + 9· 3· 3· 6· 9 5 6· 3· 7·, cry to heaven, and call for vengeance, and behold vengeance is at their doors. For no person is any more found to implore the mercy and pardon of God in behalf of the people; there are no more generous souls, no more any person worthy of offering the Immaculate Victim to the Eternal Father in behalf of the world. God is going to punish in a manner without example. Woe to the inhabitants of the earth! God is going to exhaust his wrath, and nobody shall be able to evade so many combined evils. At the first stroke of his fulminating sword the mountains and the whole nature shall shake with terror, because the disorders and crimes of men pierce the very vaults of the heavens. The earth shall be stricken with every kind of plagues. (Besides the pestilence and famine, which shall be general. Glossa of Melanie.) There shall be wars until the last war, which shall be waged by the ten kings of Antichrist. All these kings shall have a common design, and they only shall govern the world. Before this comes to pass the, etc. . . . . . Society is on the eve of the most terrible and the grandest events. People must expect to be governed with a rod of iron, and to drink the chalice of God's indignation. After the year 1859, the Vicar of my Son, the Sovereign Pontiff, Pius IX., should not go any more out of Rome. Let him be firm and courageous. Let him fight with the arms of Faith and of Love. I shall be with him. He should distrust Napoleon, whose heart is double; and when this will aim at being both emperor and Pope, God shall then abandon him. This eagle, determined ever to lift itself higher, shall fall on the very weapon which he uses to oblige the people to raise him up (universal suffrage). Italy shall be punished on account of its ambition of wishing to shake off the yoke of the Lord of lords. Hence she shall be given up to war; blood shall flow from every side; the churches shall be shut up or profaned. Priests and religious shall be hunted; they shall be butchered in a cruel manner. Many shall abandon the faith, and great shall be the number of priests and religious who shall separate themselves from the true religion; among these there will be found likewise several bishops. Let the Pope be upon his guard against miracle-workers, for the time is arrived when the most astounding prodigies will take place on the earth and in the air. (Is it Spiritualism?)

[The schism which, according to the Carthusian prophecy, shall take place at the death of Pius IX., is herein most clearly indicated.]

In the year 1864, Lucifer, with a very great number of demons, will be unchained from hell. By degrees they shall abolish the faith, even among persons consecrated to God. They shall blind them in such a manner that, without very special graces, these persons shall imbibe the spirit of those wicked angels. Many religious houses will entirely lose the faith, and shall be the cause of the loss of many persons.

Bad books will abound upon the earth; and the spirit of darkness shall spread over the earth a universal relaxation about everything relating to the service of God. Satan shall have very great power over nature

(God's punishment for the crimes of men)*; temples will be erected for the worship of these demons. Some persons shall be transported from one place to another by these wicked spirits, even some priests, because these will not be animated by the holy spirit of the gospel, which is a spirit of humility, charity, and zeal for the glory of God.

Some will make the dead rise and appear as holy persons. The souls of the damned shall also be summoned, and shall appear as united to their bodies. (*Such persons, resurrected through the agency of demons, shall assume the figure of holy persons, who are known to have been upon earth, in order more easily to deceive men. These self-styled resuscitated persons shall be nothing but demons under their forms. In this way they shall preach a gospel contrary to that of Jesus Christ, denying the existence of heaven.* Glossa of Melanie.)

In every place there shall be seen extraordinary prodigies, because the true faith has been extinguished, and a pale light shines in the world.

My Son's Vicar shall have much to suffer, because for a time the Church shall be exposed to very great persecutions. *This shall be the time of darkness.* The Church shall have to pass through an awful crisis. France, Italy, Spain, and England shall have civil war. Blood shall flow through the streets. French shall fight against French. Italians against Italians. After this there will be a frightful general war. For a time God shall not remember France, nor Italy, (for two years or for one?) * because the gospel of Jesus Christ is no more understood. The Holy Father will suffer much. *I will be with him to the end to receive his sacrifice. The wicked shall many times attempt his life.* A precursor of Anti-

* Words of Melanie.

christ (Garibaldi), with his troops, composed of persons from several nations, will fight against the true Christ, the only Saviour of the world. He shall shed much blood, and will strive to destroy the worship and religion of God, in order to make himself honored like God. Nature demands vengeance against men, and she trembles with fright in expectation of what will befall the earth sullied with crimes. Tremble, O earth! And tremble you also who make profession of serving Jesus Christ, but inwardly worship yourselves, because God has delivered you to his enemies, because corruption is in holy places. (Many convents are no longer houses of God.)*

In the year 1865, the abomination shall be seen in holy places, in convents, and then the demon shall make himself as the king of hearts. Let Superiors at the head of religious communities be very circumspect about the candidates they receive . . . . because of the disorders and love for carnal pleasures. . . . . It will be about that time that Antichrist shall be born from. . . . . At his birth he shall vomit blasphemies. He shall have teeth; in a word, he shall be like an incarnate demon; he shall utter frightful screams; he shall work prodigies; and he shall feed on impure things. He shall have brothers, who, though not incarnate demons like him, shall nevertheless be children of iniquity. At the age of twelve years they shall have become remarkable for valiant victories, which they shall achieve; very soon each of them will be at the head of armies. *Paris shall be burned,* and *Marseilles shall be submerged;* many great cities shall be shattered and swallowed up by earthquakes.

I address a pressing appeal to the earth. I call upon the true disciples of the living God, who reigns in the heavens; I call upon the true imitators of Christ

* Glossa of Melanie.

made man, the only true Saviour of mankind; I call upon my children, those who are truly devoted to me, those who have offered themselves to me that I may lead them to my Son, those whom I carry as it were in my arms, those who have been animated by my spirit. Finally, I call on the apostles of these last days, these faithful disciples of Jesus Christ, who have lived despising the world and themselves, in poverty and humility, in contempt and in silence, in prayer and mortification, in chastity and union with God, in suffering and unknown to the world. It is time for them to come out and enlighten the earth. Go ye forth and manifest yourselves as my darling children; I am with you and within you, so that your faith may be the light which illumines you in these unhappy days, and that your zeal may make you hankering for the glory and honor of the Most High. Fight, ye children of light; combat, ye small band that can see, for this is the time of times, the end of ends.

Behold the reign of the ten kings! Woe to the inhabitants of the earth; there shall be sanguinary wars, and famine, and plagues, and contagious maladies; there shall be showers of a frightful hail of animals; thunder shall shake entire cities; earthquakes which shall swallow up some countries; voices shall be heard in the air; men (in despair) shall knock their heads against the walls; they shall call on death, and death shall be their torment; blood shall flow from every side. Who shall be able to overcome (all these evils)? Fire shall rain from heaven, and shall destroy three cities. The whole world shall be struck with terror, and many will allow themselves to be seduced, because they have not believed the true Christ living among them. *The sun becomes dark.* Faith only shall survive. So the time! the abyss opens. Behold the king of the kings of darkness! Behold the beast with his subjects! . . . .

[It is necessary to remember that Melanie has not yet divulged all her entire secret.]

To A. M. l'Abbé Cloquet.

This portion of my secret is truly a copy of that which I gave to M. F. Bliard.

SISTER MARY OF THE CROSS,
Shepherdess of La Salette.

September 22, 1871.

II.—*Words of Melanie, and Portion of Some of her Letters.*

Since her vision on the mountain of La Salette, Melanie has often been heard saying: "The great chastisements will come, because men will not be converted; yet it is only their conversion that can hinder these scourges. God will begin to strike men by inflicting lighter punishments in order to open their eyes; then he will stop, or may repeat his former warnings to give place for repentance. But sinners will not avail themselves of these opportunities; he will, in consequence, send more severe castigations, anxious to move sinners to penance, but all in vain. Finally, the obduracy of sinners shall draw upon their heads the greatest and most terrible calamities."

From a letter written by Sister Mary of the Cross (Melanie), dated June 16, 1872, we extract the following considerable portion:—

"We are all guilty! Penance is not done, and sin increases daily. Those who should come forward to do good are retained by fear. Evil is great. A moderate punishment serves only to irritate the spirits, because they view all things with human eyes. God could work a miracle to convert and change the aspect of the earth without chastisement. God will work a miracle; it will be a stroke of his mercy; but after the wicked shall have inebriated themselves with blood, the scourge shall arrive.

"What countries shall be preserved from such calamities? Where shall we go for refuge? I, in my turn, shall ask, What is the country that observes the commandments of God? What country is not influenced by human fear where the interest of the Church and the glory of God are at stake? (Ah, indeed! what country, what nation upon earth?) In behalf of my Superior and myself, I have often asked myself where could we go for refuge, had we the means for the journey and for our subsistence, on condition that no person were to know it? But I renounce these useless thoughts. We are very guilty! In consequence of this, it is necessary that a very great and terrible scourge should come to revive our faith, and to restore to us our very reason, which we have almost entirely lost. Wicked men are devoured by a thirst for exercising their cruelty; but when they shall have reached the uttermost point of their barbarity, God himself shall extend his hand to stop them, and very soon after, a complete change shall be effected in all surviving persons. Then they will sing the *Te Deum Laudamus* with the most lively gratitude and love. The Virgin Mary, our mother, shall be our liberatrix. Peace shall reign, and the charity of Jesus Christ shall unite all hearts. . . . . Alsace shall return to France. . . . . Let us pray; let us pray. God does not wish to chastise us severely. He speaks to us in so many, so many ways to make us return to him. How long shall we remain stubborn? Let us pray, let us pray; let us never cease praying and doing penance. Let us pray for our Holy Father the Pope, the only light for the faithful in these times of darkness. O yes, let us by all means pray much. Let us pray to the good, sweet, merciful Virgin Mary; for we stand in great need of her powerful hands over our heads."

Lastly, Melanie has written to her brother, who lived in Paris, and to her married sister in Marseilles, to go away immediately from these two large and populous cities, because the catastrophe is imminent.

III. — *Present Mode of Life of Melanie.*

Melanie wears the religious habit, so does likewise her faithful companion. She teaches five or six girls. She is under the immediate obedience of the Rt. Rev. Bishop of Castellamare di Stabia, a city about eighteen miles distant from Naples. She has very frequent visions, and often she is in spiritual intercourse with Palma Maria d'Oria (whom she has never seen in an ordinary way). Through bilocation or other supernatural way, they speak together almost every day, though living at a great distance one from the other. Palma Maria has been, during many years, confined to her poor room by extraordinary sufferings. This holy woman spoke, last year, a great deal about Melanie to a French priest, the Abbé Brandt, and Melanie did the same to him about Palma Maria, of Oria. These are, indeed, marks of holiness.

IV. — *Secret of Massimin Girand.*

On the 19th of September, 1846, I saw a lady brilliant like the sun, whom I believed to be the Holy Virgin. However, I have never said it was the Holy Virgin. I have always said that I saw a lady, but never ventured to affirm that it was the Holy Virgin.

From what I am going to state here, it appertains to the Church to judge whether it was truly the Holy Virgin or some other person. She gave me my secret about the middle of her conversation with me, after these words: *The grapes shall rot, and the chestnuts shall be bad.* The Lady began by saying to me: —

1. Three fourths of France shall lose the faith, and the other fourth, that will preserve it, will practise it with tepidity.

2. Peace shall not be given to the world until men will be converted.

3. A Protestant nation in the North shall be converted to the faith, and, through the means of that nation, the others shall return to the holy Catholic Church.

4. The next Pope shall not be a Roman.

5. When men shall be converted, God will give peace to the world.

6. Afterwards this peace shall be disturbed by the monster (Antichrist).

7. The monster shall arrive at the end of this nineteenth century, or, at latest, at the commencement of the twentieth.

CHAPTER XI.

PROPHECY OF THE VENERABLE ABBÉ VIANNAY, CURÉ D'ARS, FRANCE.

A SHORT time before his death, which happened August 4, 1859, this holy priest prophesied the sad and happy events that the justice and mercy of the Lord reserves for France. He communicated these prophecies to a pious countryman of the neighborhood of Rhodes, who went to consult him about his vocation, and by whom he was advised to join the Lazzarists as a lay brother. His Superiors have judged proper to make him declare the following revelations in the presence of, and authenticated by, a notary-public. Here we give the last portion, which has relation to the future, which we have extracted from the books of the Rev. Father Maria Anthony and of the Abbé Curcque: —

"After this victory their enemy (the Prussians) shall not quit entirely the occupied country." Here the Curé d'Ars spoke to the young man of the negotiations between France and the German Empire for the liberation or evacuation of France; then he added: "They (the Prussians) shall come back (for a second invasion of France); but this time our army shall fight well everywhere. For during the first war our men would not combat well, but in the second war they will fight. O, how they will fight!

"The enemy (the Prussians) will allow the burning of Paris, and they will rejoice at it, but they shall be beaten; they shall be driven entirely from France.

"Our enemies shall return, and will destroy everything in their march. They shall arrive near Poitiers without meeting with any (serious) resistance, but *there* they shall be crushed by the defenders of the West, who shall pursue them. (Here the Papal soldiers of Cathelineau and of Charette will cover themselves with immortal glory. This shall be the beginning of the successive triumphs of virtue and justice.) From other directions their provisions shall be cut off, and they shall suffer very serious losses. They will attempt to retire towards their country, but very few of them shall ever reach it. *All they took from us shall be returned, and a great deal more.*

The Communists of Paris, after their defeat, shall spread themselves through all France, and will be greatly multiplied. They shall seize arms; they shall oppress people of order. Lastly, a civil war shall break out everywhere. These wicked people shall become masters in the north, east, and southwest (of France). They will imprison very many persons, and will be guilty of more massacres. They will attempt to kill all the priests and all the religious. But this shall not last long. (This persecution shall not last a long time.) People will imagine that all is lost; but the good God shall save all. It will be like a sign of the last judgment. Paris shall be changed, also two or three other cities (Lyons and Marseilles are mentioned above in several places); God shall come to help; the good shall triumph when the return of the king shall be announced (Henry V.). This shall re-establish a peace and prosperity without example. Religion shall flourish again better than ever before.

"I know not why I tell you all this," said Monsieur Viannay to his confidant; "but, the time being come, you will remember this; and you will be very tranquil, as well as those who will believe you." This good Lazzarist Brother says, "The great calamity is not yet passed. Paris shall be demolished and burnt in earnest, but not entirely. Events shall transpire more terrible than what we have seen. However, there shall be a limit beyond which the destruction shall not go." When asked which will be the limit, he answered: "I do not know; but I shall not leave our house of St. Lazzarre."

CHAPTER XII.

PROPHECY OF THE VENERABLE ANNA MARIA TAIGI.

WE extract a few interesting particulars from the life of this venerable servant of God, published in Philadelphia, by Eugene Cummiskey, 1872.* Anna

* A most interesting life of this venerable servant of God, has been published by Messrs. Richardson and Sons, 26, Paternoster Row, London, and Derby.

Maria was the privileged daughter of Louis and Santa Gionetti. She was born to them on the 29th of May, 1769, in the beautiful city of Sienna, in Tuscany. At her baptism she received the names of Anna Maria Antonia Gesualda. In the year 1775, she, with her pious, but poor parents, went to live in Rome. Here her good and virtuous mother assisted in laying out the body of Blessed Joseph Labré. In due time Anna Maria was married to Domenico Taigi, or rather Taegi, a pious and virtuous young man, but of uncouth and rough manners, which contributed much to her sanctification. She was a perfect model of a Christian wife and mother. She had seven children. Though profoundly humble and retiring, yet the perfume of her extraordinary sanctity spread far and wide. Anna Maria enjoyed a very singular and most wonderful gift from God. During forty-seven years, a mysterious supernatural light, a species of sun, was ever before her eyes. In it she could read and tell the state of consciences, the revolutions, the wars, the designs of governments, the aims of secret societies, superstitions, and crimes, the reward of the saints, and the punishments, both temporal and eternal, prepared by God for all human transgressions. During her life and after her death she wrought many prodigies. She died in Rome, in great odor of sanctity, on the 9th of June, 1837. The process of her beatification is advancing very rapidly in Rome. Hence her title of Venerable. The prophetical previsions of this admirable seer reach till the day of universal judgment. The greatest portion of her prophecies are in the secret archives of the Congregation of Rites in Rome. But many of these prophecies were by her made known to a considerable number of persons eminent in virtue, and several also in high dignities. The Venerable Vincent

Maria Strambi, Bishop of Macerata, was one of these; so also Monseigneur Natali, who, during twenty-five years, enjoyed her entire confidence. He died only three years ago. By them and by others several fragments of Anna Maria's prophecies have been made known. The following important extracts have been published in Paris, in the first volume of the *Avenir Dévoilé*, "The Future Unveiled," p. 53. But further details can be read in the above-mentioned Life, published in London, and edited by Edward Healy Thompson.

1. *A very thick darkness shall envelop the earth during three days.* This awful darkness shall be impregnated with such pestilential vapors, and filled with such frightful apparitions, that they will cause, in a more special manner, the death of the hypocritical or avowed enemies of the Holy Church.

Anna Maria announced that on this terrible occasion so many of these wicked men, enemies of his Church and of their God, shall be killed by this divine scourge, that their corpses round Rome will be as numerous as the fish which a (then) recent inundation of the Tiber had carried into the city. All the enemies of the Church, secret as well as known, will perish over the whole earth during that universal darkness, with the exception of some few, whom God will soon after convert. The air shall be infected by demons, who will appear under all sorts of hideous forms.

On this subject, Anna Maria has given several directions to the faithful. One of these was, to procure blessed candles, which alone shall give light during the darkness; also, to remain in prayer, to recite the holy rosary, not to attempt to *look out for idle and vain curiosity*.

2. A heavenly apparition shall come to reassure the

faithful. St. Peter and St. Paul will appear on the clouds, and all men shall see them; and, in a supernatural manner, faith shall return to their hearts. Innumerable conversions of heretics shall cause universal edification.

From the process of the beatification of Venerable Anna Maria Taigi, which was published in the *Analecta juris Pontificii*, we learn the following circumstance, deposed upon oath by Cardinal Pedicini (who was personally known by the compiler of this):—

"One day," says the Cardinal, "Anna Maria, while shedding a torrent of tears, prayed and offered her actions and sufferings for the conversion of sinners, for the destruction of sin, and that God might be known and loved by all men. Then God manifested to her the horrible sins of persons of every condition, and how grievously he was offended. At this sight the servant of God experienced a profound sorrow, and sighing, she exclaimed: 'Dearly beloved! what is the remedy for this disaster?' Jesus Christ answered: 'My child, the Church, my spouse, my Father, and myself shall remedy everything. For after a punishment . . . . those who shall survive shall have to conduct themselves well.' At this point she saw innumerable conversions of heretics, who will return to the bosom of the Church; she saw, also, the edifying conduct of their lives, as well as that of all other Catholics." So far Cardinal Pedicini.

We may here remark, that the gap after punishment, left by the editor of the *Analecta*, might have been that of the three days' darkness. But we shall not insist upon this interpretation. We have more conclusive proofs. The Very Rev. Father Calixtus, Superior in the Monastery of the Trinitarian Fathers in Cerfroid, Asine, France, wrote a volume with the title, "The Venerable Anna Maria Taigi." Our extracts are made from its second edition. This book, written with the approbation of the Superior-General of the Trinitarians, postulator of the cause of the venerable servant of God, has been carefully examined at Rome, and, in every point, found comformable to the authentic documents of the Apostolic process for the beatification of the Venerable Anna Maria Taigi. The following are the particular details : —

3. *During several successive days, Anna Maria beheld a most excessive darkness spreading itself over the whole world.* She likewise saw falling ruins of walls, accompanied by much dust, as if a great edifice had tumbled down. This scourge was shown to her on divers occasions. This may indicate the ruins caused by frightful earthquakes, or the destruction effected by the wicked Communists. We presume, and assume as pretty certain, that this darkness will be sensible, similar to that of Egypt, mentioned in Exodus, tenth chapter, and that it shall continue during three days. Though the venerable servant of God has not mentioned this duration, yet Monseigneur Natali, having been questioned on this particular point by a large number of persons, has invariably assured them *that the darkness shall last during three days.*

In spite of all these proofs, the generality of the people refuse to believe it. Some attempt to contradict them, and others pretend to laugh at the threatened punishment. The same was done immediately before the universal deluge; but the unbelievers perished; the eight believers in the ark only were saved. Our best answer will be given in the following words of Monsieur Amedeus Nicolas: "For my part, I shall not affirm that *physical darkness* shall come; but it seems to me that the subject is too grave to laugh at. Scriptural prophecies, history, and the state of the human mind at the present epoch, may well justify the apprehensions of many persons upon this subject. Since a physical darkness of three days' duration took place in Egypt, it follows that we may have again the same phenomenon at the present time; for, from the fact that an event in nature has taken place, we may conclude that a similar thing may happen again."

The Apocalypse, at the opening of the sixth seal, seems to foretell a sensible darkness when it says that after a great earthquake the sun became as black as *sackcloth of hair*. (Apoc. vi. 12.) If we are arrived at the epoch of the world mentioned here by St. John, how shall we be able to see light if the sun is in darkness? It is universally admitted that God chastised the Egyptians with material darkness, in punishment of their wilful internal blindness, corruption, and obstinacy. But a little knowledge and experience of the present state of human society is more than sufficient to prove that the aberrations, the corruption and stubbornness of men, are much worse than at the time of King Pharaoh. It is only a striking event, bearing an evident mark of the Divine hand, that shall be able to bring back human society to the belief of the very existence of God, and to that of the spiritual world. Now, this dreaded darkness would be this irrefragable and unanswerable proof; it is therefore more opportune and more necessary at the present time than it was three thousand three hundred and sixty years ago in Egypt. St. John, in this chapter, repeats more in detail a similar prophecy, which we read in the second chapter of Isaias. These are the words of the Apocalypse: *I saw when the Lamb had opened the sixth seal, and behold there was a great earthquake, and the sun became black as sackcloth of hair, and the whole moon became as blood; and the stars fell from heaven as the fig-tree (apple-tree) casteth its green figs (or apples) when it is shaken by a mighty wind; and the heaven withdrew as a book (long parchment) rolled up together; and every mountain and the islands were moved out of their places. And the kings of the earth, and the princes, and the tribunes, and the rich men, and the strong men, and every bondman, and every freeman hid themselves in the dens and in the rocks of the mountains; and they say to the mountains and to the rocks, Fall upon us and hide us from the face of him that sitteth upon the throne, and from the wrath of the Lamb. For the great day of their wrath is come, and who shall be able to stand?* (Apoc. vi. 12–17.)

It is necessary to remark here that this horrible scene does not represent the commotion at the end of the world, because it is followed by a grand religious revival, as may be observed at the sixth epoch of the Church, at the opening of the sixth seal, and at the sound of the sixth trumpet. This scene does not represent the last judgment of the dead, but a kind of ante-judgment of the living, which is well expressed in these words of the Psalmist. *The Lord has sworn, and he will not repent. Thou, Jesus, art a priest forever according to the Order of Melchisedek. The Lord at thy right hand hath broken kings in the day of his wrath. He shall judge among nations. He shall fill ruins. He shall crush the heads* (modern civil governments) *in the land of many."* (Ps. cix.) (*In the land of many* might be the same as in *many lands* or nations; or, more likely, *in the land of many* signifies the sham and corrupt governments of infidel democracy, wherein many wish to command, and nobody likes to obey.)

But, to return, what more than this universal darkness of seventy-two hours' duration is calculated to strike this general terror into the hearts of degenerate humanity? There is no doubt that this darkness, dreaded by the humble minority, and ridiculed by the arrogant majority, would produce wonderful beneficial effects. Now, if the result of this awful punishment were to be the general conversion of mankind to the true religion of Jesus Christ, as so many prophecies announce, why would any true and good Catholic dread its arrival? We, on the contrary, in our charity and zeal for souls, for the welfare of religion, and the honor and glory of Jesus Christ, — we should pray fervently and without ceasing that God's kingdom and universal dominion may soon come, and that his adorable will may be done on earth as it is in heaven.

So far this learned and truly pious author. We now come to the other prophecies of Venerable Anna Maria Taigi.

4. The Pope shall convoke a (general) council (that of the Vatican). A new constitution of the Church shall be proclaimed in it. (The one *Dei Filius* and that on the Pope's infallibility defined in solemn session July 18, 1870.)

5. The venerable servant of God, about forty years before the event, pointed out distinctly one after the other all the Episcopal Sees in the Catholic Church, the respective bishops of which were to oppose the definition at the late council at the Vatican.

6. Anna Maria foretold that a *very short time* after the promulgation of the new Constitution of the Church by the general council, the Emperor of the French would declare war against Prussia, by which he would be defeated and made prisoner; that France should be hum-

bled, because she would not know how to profit by her advantages as first daughter of the Church, and the protectress of the Holy See.

(Remember that the venerable servant of God died in Rome, June 9, 1837.)

7. France, she said, shall fall into frightful anarchy. The French people shall have a desperate civil war, in which old men themselves shall take up arms. The political parties having exhausted their blood and their rage without being able to arrive at any satisfactory understanding, they shall at the last extremity agree by common consent to have recourse to the Holy See. Then the Pope shall send to France a special legate, in order that he may examine the state of affairs and the dispositions of the people. In consequence of the information received, his Holiness himself shall nominate a most Christian king for the government of France. (From this it appears that the Holy See shall be settled before France.)

8. During this time there shall be a great universal revolution.

9. The priests shall almost everywhere be massacred to such an extent that, in order to find one of them alive, it shall be necessary to travel several days. The churches shall be closed, but only for a short time. (In another copy more recently received from Rome this passage varies somewhat. It is in the following words: "Religious shall be persecuted, priests shall be massacred, the churches shall be closed, but only for a short time; the Holy Father shall be obliged to abandon Rome.")

This announcement of the massacre of priests and religious mentioned in this and several other prophetical predictions, especially by Melanie, may not be exe-

cuted to all the extent indicated by the prophetical
warnings, because prophetical menaces are always conditional. Adequate penance and much prayer may suspend the execution, or at least moderate its severity.
But this penance should be performed, and fervent and
continued prayers should be offered to God. This is
one of the principal objects of this compilation. We
desire to invite in all the charity of a Christian heart
all poor sinners of any class or condition of life to a
timely repentance and penance. We entreat all good
souls, who may chance to peruse these lines, to pray to
God for the Church, for the clergy and religious persons,
and for the conversion of all poor sinners, and for those
who are in error. God does not wish the death of the
sinner, but that he may be converted and live. If God
demands the immolation of a certain number of consecrated victims, let us beseech him to give strength and
grace to these victims, that they may be acceptable in
his sight, and their blood, united with that of Jesus
Christ on the cross, may satisfy his divine justice, and
obtain mercy, pardon, and salvation to a sinful world.

The priest, observes a pious and learned author, — the
priest is called by God to be in a state of perpetual victim and immolation in behalf of mankind. The priest
is charged with the sins of the world; he is bound to
grieve always, and atone for them daily. St. Alphonsus
Ligouri adds, "When God desires to chastise the people,
the punishment generally begins with the clergy, because they are the primary cause, or, at least, occasion
of the sins of the people, either through their bad example or through their negligence about the souls
intrusted to their charge." Hence, St. Peter said,
Tempus est ut incipiat judicium a Domo Dei. (1 Peter
iv. 17.)

In the massacre described by the holy Prophet Ezekiel, God commanded that the priests should be the first victims. *A sanctuario meo incipite.* (Ezek. ix. 6.) God may require the sacrifice of his ministers in order to avoid larger massacres of the common people. The worthier the victim, the more valuable is the sacrifice. Few holy victims can satisfy the justice of God more than thousands of others of an inferior condition.

Moreover, through their stronger virtues the sufferings and the death of God's priests and religious may give more edification and greater courage to secular persons who may have to undergo similar trials.

God then comes once more to ask his priests to offer their blood (especially in Italy, France, and Spain), in order to assuage his just indignation, to compensate for the voluntary immolation of penance, which too many may have neglected to offer to him through want of generosity. Those victims who may not be entirely free from some stains shall, like Monseigneur Darboy and a few others, have the grand opportunity of washing them in their own blood, and also of obtaining the glorious crown of martyrdom. Who knows whether at the head of this glorious band of approaching martyrs may not be found the most worthy victim upon earth, the heroic Pius IX.; thus realizing to the letter, as some prophecies announce, the terrible title, *Crux de cruce*, — A cross from the cross ! ! ! . . . .

It is, then, at the price of blood, but of the blood of innocent, holy, and heroic victims, blood which flows in the consecrated veins of holy priests and religious, blood worthy of being commingled with the divine blood of the Lamb, that God has decreed to grant the great triumph of the Church, and then the general conversion of mankind to the faith and religion of Jesus Christ.

May all the victims be found worthy of such honor; may the blood of new martyrs become the fruitful seed of Christianity for all mankind. Amen!

CHAPTER XIII.

PREDICTIONS OF SISTER ROSE COLOMBA, A DOMINICAN NUN.

SISTER ROSE COLOMBA was a religious of eminent sanctity and of the most profound humility. During the long course of her religious life she knew so well how to conceal her solid virtues under the veil of a holy and childish simplicity, that nothing extraordinary was by her allowed to transpire before the eyes of her religious community. All knew her exactitude in the fulfilment of all her religious duties, her spirit of prayer, her tears, her mortifications. But as she purposely accompanied many of these pious actions with some oddities, not much account was taken of them, and she was often the subject of innocent amusement to the community. The unexpected literal realization of many of her prophetical predictions attracted at last the more serious attention of her religious sisters, and her fame for sanctity spread far outside of her monastery. She died June 6, 1847.

By order of the Bishop of the diocese of Ventimiglia, near Nice, Monseigneur Dealbertis, a collection of the prophetical predictions of Sister Rose Colomba was made, both during the last years of her life and after her death, by duly sworn witnesses, which were, and are at present, carefully kept in the episcopal archives, from which the following extracts have been faithfully copied, in the month of February, 1850.

The translator and compiler of these pages having, in 1856, heard some of these predictions, wrote for further information to the Very Reverend Provost of Taggia, Don Stefano Semeria, the learned, pious, and prudent parish priest, well known to the translator, and received from him a copy of these prophecies, which agree in substance with those published by the Italian author, and mentioned in the previous paragraph. From the same worthy ecclesiastic the translator received a printed copy of a most interesting description of the prodigious motion of the head and eyes of a new devout statue of the Blessed Virgin Mary, sent as a present from Rome by a pious artist, a native of Taggia, which was placed in a side chapel of the principal parish church. The miraculous motion of the eyes, head, and neck was first observed on the 12th of March, 1855, at the close of a solemn celebration, which lasted eight days, in honor of the Immaculate Conception, defined as an article of faith the year before by the great and holy Pope Pius IX. The prodigious movements were still observed on the 29th of September of the same year, being the date of the letter from the above-mentioned parish priest. The expression in the eyes and face and the motions of the neck and head were similar to those of a living person under various strong interior emotions, sentiments of grief, dread, and supplication to God prevailing. Hundreds of thousands of persons of every class and condition, some from Turin and some from Genoa, had, during the six months, witnessed these public prodigies, which were duly sworn to by one hundred and twenty of the most intelligent and trustworthy witnesses, when, by order of the Bishop, the canonical process was instituted. As we shall soon learn from Sister Rose Colomba's prophecies that the town of Taggia shall have a large share in the coming trials, so it appears to the compiler that this statement will not be found entirely out of place. We may proceed, then, to the prophecies of the venerable servant of God : —

1. During the lifetime of Monseigneur Maggioli, Bishop of Albenga, Sister Rose Colomba foretold to Father Angelo Danea, a most pious and learned Dominican friar, that he was to be made bishop of the same diocese, and that he should find out the innocence of a certain Canon Cairashi, who had been unjustly calumniated. All this was fully realized in the year 1836. After his election and consecration, the Right Rev. Bishop Danea stated these facts, in presence of all the religious community of the Dominican nuns in Taggia.

2. Sister Rose Colomba foretold that Pope Gregory XVI. would give a solemn admonition to the Russian Emperor for persecuting the Catholics in Poland, and that in consequence of this the persecution would be much mitigated. The event verified the prediction.

3. She foretold that to Gregory XVI. should succeed a Pope, *pious of name and of pious natural dispositions and habits*, who was to lose his throne ; but should bo restored to his temporal dominions through Napoleon. This prediction has been attested upon oath by many persons that heard it from the mouth of Sister Rose Colomba, and in a special manner by the advocate Philip Ghue, of Taggia, the Monastery Procurator, who, in a pleasant way, often said to Sister Rose : *Well, Sister, we shall soon behold Napoleon risen from death.* She used to reply : *You, sir, do not understand these things, but you shall see the Pope restored to his throne by Napoleon.* During some beautiful evening recreations, Sister Rose

would point out with her forefinger to the brilliant vesper planet, and say to her religious sisters: "Do you see that star? That represents to my mind the splendid cross which the Pope will give to Napoleon, as a token of gratitude for having restored him to his dominions." Soon after the flight of Pius IX. from Rome to Gaeta, Monseigneur Dealbertis, then Bishop of Ventimiglia, wrote to the nuns in the Convent of Taggia, that he should believe in Sister Rose's prophetical predictions if he saw the Holy Father restored to his earthly throne by Napoleon. All the world knows that the French troops sent by Napoleon brought Pius IX. back to Rome with great triumph.

4. Poor Louis Philippe! Sister Rose would often repeat;—poor Louis Philippe! he shall fly from France, and shall go to die in England.

5. Many three-colored flags, together with that of the Pope, shall be raised in Italy, and the people shall constrain the priests to bless them. This shall be the signal of the war which shall soon after break out.

6. Charles Albert, King of Piedmont, will be the first to hasten to the combat; but he shall be defeated and forced to fly into exile, and shall die on the borders of Spain. To him shall succeed his first-born young son, by whom a weak government shall be formed, through the means of which the monarch shall be led to the loss of . . . . (his life and crown).

7. The Pope shall be deprived of his temporal dominions, and shall be styled only Bishop of Rome.

8. Sister Rose Colomba often said that after Napoleon's death a cruel and bloody persecution shall rage against religion in Italy, through the malice of wicked children of the Church. The persecution shall commence with the suppression of the Jesuits. Many Catholics in Italy shall die martyrs for their faith and religion.

9. A persecutor, whom she used to qualify as Antichrist, shall come forth; he is already born; he will call himself the redeemer. Many sectaries will be united with him, who will persecute the Church with false doctrines and with violence, and their malice shall be so superfine that they shall succeed with their craftiness and hypocrisy to deceive many well-disposed Catholics.

(Here Sister Rose evidently describes the wretched Joseph Garibaldi, who, in many cities of Italy as well as elsewhere, was saluted by his partisans and blind admirers with the blasphemous title of Redeemer of Italy, Messiah, Christ, and God. In their impiety these wicked men went so far as to apply to him the four sacred initials of Jesus crucified, *I. N. R. I.*, interpreting them in this abominable manner, *Joseph of Nice, Redeemer of Italy*. Yet this antichristian monster has many admirers in America.)

10. Not only religious communities, but also good lay Catholics, shall have their property confiscated. Many of the nobility shall be cast into prison. A lawless democratic spirit of disorder shall reign supreme throughout all Europe. There will be a general overthrow. Sister Rose spoke of this general war in very energetic expressions. She used to say that there shall be great confusion of people against people, and nations against nations, with clashing of arms and beating of drums.

11. The Russians and Prussians shall come to make war in Italy. They shall profane many churches, and turn them into stables for their horses.

12. Some bishops, Sister Rose said, shall fall from the faith, but many more will remain steadfast, and shall suffer much for the Church.

13. England shall return to the Catholic faith.

14. Speaking of her native town of Taggia, she said that during the persecution not all the religious shall

persevere, and that those who will remain faithful shall be crucified on a certain mound in the grounds of the Monastery called Mount Olivet, together with other persons who will take refuge in that place. During these terrible trials the faithful will be greatly encouraged by pious and learned priests, especially of the Order of St. Dominic.

15. She also foretold that the new chapel attached to the Monastery should be profaned and turned into a stable for horses. This church was just then being built; but Sister Rose Colomba always tried to prevent it; she refused to give her vote for the building of it. She assured the nuns that she should never hear mass in it. In fact, she died a few days before the new chapel was blessed.

16. In speaking of her decease, Sister Rose used to say that, before her death, her body should be reduced to the last stage of consumption, and become almost transparent and like a skeleton, and that she should die on a Friday within the octave of Corpus Christi, whilst the Dominican Fathers were engaged in making the procession of the Most Holy Sacrament. All this has been literally verified.

17. Whilst shedding many tears, she often repeated that many sins were overflooding the earth, and many terrible calamities were impending over Italy; that for this cause she could not be cheerful and pleasant, and that if her religious sisters could penetrate all that she knew, they also should feel very sad.

18. Several persons, worthy of confidence and well informed with the predictions of this venerable servant of God, affirm that they heard her often repeating, with evident anguish of mind, that *priests and religious persons, during the often-mentioned religious persecution, were to be butchered like cattle in the shambles, and that the*

earth, especially in Italy, was to be watered with their blood. These were, positively, her own words.

19. As it has been mentioned above, this servant of God foretold that the persecution in Italy was to begin by the suppression of the Jesuits; but, she added, they shall be called back again; then a third time they were to be suppressed and never more be revived.

20. During a frightful storm against the Church, all religious orders were to be abolished except two, namely, the Capuchins and the Dominicans, together with the Hospitaliers, who shall receive the pious pilgrims, who, in great numbers, shall go to visit and venerate the many martyrs in Italy, killed during the impending persecution.

21. Lastly, Sister Rose Colomba foretold that Austria, Russia, and Prussia were to be allied together in order to fight and subdue the rebels (Red Republicans, Communists, Garibaldians, Carbonari, Freemasons), and that Prussia (more likely Russia) shall be converted to the Catholic faith. . . . .

We have, upon the subject of these predictions, interrogated in person a venerable old religious of the Order of St. Dominic, who, during many years, had occasion to converse with Sister Rose Colomba, and he solemnly assured us to have numberless times heard from the mouth of this holy sister all the predictions mentioned in this chapter, though not in the same order; because she expressed them according to circumstances, without any intention or attempt on her side to arrange them in any particular order. Though this prudent religious paid much attention inwardly to what Sister Rose Colomba said, yet he pretended to have no confidence in them, and generally expressed himself in this manner to her, when she used to reply: *Well, Father, you shall witness the accomplishment of a portion of them.*

CHAPTER XIV.

PREDICTIONS OF PALMA MARIA ADDOLORATA MATARELLI.

PALMA MARIA was born 31st March, 1825, in the episcopal city of Oria, province of Lecce, in Apulia, Kingdom of Naples. She was baptized in the Cathedral church by the bishop on the 2d day of April, which in that year was Holy Saturday. At her baptism she received the name of Palma Maria. The name of Palma is rather singular among Catholics, because it cannot be found in the Roman Martyrology. But it was evidently given to this privileged child in a providential manner, for it signifies victory and triumph. It seems very certain that God has chosen Palma Maria as an extraordinary living instrument for obtaining great victories over Satan, and for contributing to and co-operating in the universal approaching triumph of his Holy Church.

It is also a remarkable coincidence that the Rev. Vincent de Angelis, now a worthy canon of the Cathedral, who was by God destined to be her future spiritual director, assisted at her baptism as secretary to the bishop.

In her youth Palma Maria, through devotion to our Blessed Lady, was inspired to take the holy habit of our Lady of Dolors, when she added to her two baptismal names that of *Addolorata*.

Her father's name was Antonio Antony Matarelli, that of her mother, Catalda d'Ippolito. Both were simple and poor, but very good Christians. They gave no education to their daughter. God alone wished to be her teacher.

Conforming with docility to the wishes of her beloved parents, Palma Maria married Domenico Lito, a pious young shepherd, from whom she subsequently had three daughters, who died in their infancy, and she was left a widow when only twenty-eight years of age. Her father also being dead, Palma Maria with her aged mother has for some years being living in the hospitable house of her pious and kind benefactor, *il Signor Federico Marzella*, whose only child Antonietta is day and night entirely devoted to her father's guest, Palma Maria Addolorata Matarelli, who, though once married, continues to be known under her maiden name.

This admirable woman is considered to be the greatest living saint of our present age. From her earliest years this privileged soul has been enriched by God with extraordinary graces and supernatural gifts. She is favored with the gift of bilocation, or with the faculty of being in two different places at the same time. From details gathered during her ordinary conversation it has been found out that she has been transported in spirit to France, Belgium, China, and other distant countries. She acknowledges to be often present in the humble cottage of Louise Lateau during her ecstasies and sufferings at Bois d'Haine, near Tournay, in Belgium.

Palma Maria, through a special divine light, is made acquainted with all great servants of God at present living upon earth. She assured the pious French physician, A. Imbert Gourbeyre, Professor of Medicine at the College de Clermont-Ferrand, France, that she knew him three years before he went to visit her in the month of October, 1871. She told him also that she knew the famous, truly Catholic, and zealous French journalist, Louis Veuillot, editor of the Paris *Univers*, though she never heard his name mentioned by any human being. *He comes*, she said, *often to my mind whilst I am in prayer. He is a powerful man. Tell him to persevere.* . . . .

She announces that in Paris there is a child at present seven years old, who is destined to become a great saint, and who lives near the great convent of the Sisters of Charity. She gives to this little girl the name of *Rita*.

Palma Maria received the stigmas in her hands, feet, and side, on the 3d of May, Feast of the Invention of the Holy Cross, in the year 1865. These, however, for some years bleed only during the Fridays in Lent. She has also the miraculous crown of thorns on her forehead from which blood flows frequently. When this blood falls upon, or is wiped off with, any cloth, it makes upon the same the impression of crosses, or of the various instruments of our Saviour's passion. The same and more wonderful impressions have been and are occasionally produced upon the portion of her ordinary clothes which come immediately in contact with her left side about the heart. Upon these clothes, or upon other articles, for instance, white handkerchiefs, which have been applied to her chest, impressions have been produced representing *hosts* and *monstrances* like those used in our Catholic churches for benediction with the most Holy Sacrament. Whilst we write these lines these marvellous impressions are before our eyes.

Many other wonderful prodigies are related about this admirable living servant of God, which for his greater honor and glory we hope to see soon published in the English language.

During the last eight years she has lived without taking any material food. Every morning she receives the Holy Communion from the hands of the priest appointed by the bishop to celebrate the Holy Sacrifice in the room where she is confined by her preternatural sufferings. Three times daily our Divine Lord and Saviour appears to her in the visible form of an ordinary host, and she receives from him Holy Communion. Persons of much merit, and worthy of all confidence, testify as having, to their great edification, been present at these extraordinary communions of the servant of God, which she receives with seraphic transports of love. The pious Imbert de Clermont Ferrand, a celebrated doctor of medicine, has visited Palma Maria several times, with the desire of obtaining all possible information and of writing a book about her. He declares her to be the most wonderful living saint of the present century. Since this was written, an edifying sketch of her life has been published in the Brooklyn "Catholic Review." Palma Maria speaks of future events with the same certitude as if she were to state actual facts.

In the year 1863 Palma Maria stated that she had to suffer much in order to appease the anger of God against the city of Oria, which he wished to destroy through an earthquake. God, in fact, assured her that he had been moved to compassion in behalf of her fellow-citizens by her great grief, sufferings, and prayers; that the earthquake would take place, but no person was to be injured. The event soon confirmed the prediction of the holy servant of God.

Let us learn from this that menacing prophecies are made by God's inspirations in mercy for sinners, in order to excite them to a timely repentance, if they wish to avoid both the threatened temporal and eternal punishments. Will this blind, deaf, and sinful world take notice of these divine warnings?

Palma Maria's predictions are, with great exactitude, forwarded to the Holy Father in Rome; the following portions have been divulged:—

1. The attempt of the sectaries to establish a republican government in France, Spain, and Italy.

2. The civil war, which will, in consequence, break out in these countries, accompanied by other dreadful punishments, as pestilence and famine.

3. The massacre of priests, as also of some dignitaries of the Church.

4. Rome shall have to endure severe trials from the malice of wicked men. But at the critical moment, when the *rebellious Republicans* shall attempt to take possession of the Holy City (*evidently after the fall of the robber king, Victor Emmanuel*), they shall be suddenly arrested at the gates and forced to fly away in terror, crushed under the deadly blows of the exterminating angel, who, in behalf of the Israelites, destroyed 185,000 men of Sennacherib's army.

5. The destruction of Paris.

6. Three days' darkness, during which the atmosphere will be infected by innumerable devils, who shall cause the death of large multitudes of incredulous and wicked men. For this awful occasion, which, sooner or later, will certainly arrive, Palma Maria recommends the use of blessed candles, which alone shall be able to give light and preserve the faithful Catholics from this impending dreadful scourge. (The same has been announced by Anna Maria Taigi. See page 90.)

7. Supernatural prodigies which shall appear in the heavens.

8. A short but furious war, during which the enemies of religion and of mankind shall be universally destroyed.

9. A general pacification of the world, and the universal triumph of the Church.

During the month of March, 1872, an important prediction, reported in Rome as having been made by Palma Maria, attracted much attention. Eminent persons read it with the most lively interest. *L'Echo di Roma* and the *Univers* of Paris published a sketch of it, which seems to agree in many points with the prophecies of the Curé d'Ars, and with other predictions given in this book. According to the statement made by the reporters of these Catholic papers, Palma Maria saw in a vision a large cross in the sky, from which proceeded eight rays darting down towards different parts of the earth; four of these mysterious rays indicated mercy, the other four announced justice. The beams of mercy illumined Turkey in the east, and America in the west, and England, with Poland and Russia, in the centre. The rays of justice struck France, Germany, Spain, and Italy.

Coming more to particulars, it was said that Palma Maria announced that Spain, France, and Italy were, during the month of July, 1872, to enter a phase of terrible convulsions; that the two kingdoms of Spain and Italy were to be upset, under the pretext of re-establishing social order and of restoring these monarchies, more especially that of Italy, which has the stronger sympathies of the Prussians. The German armies should once more invade France, punish and retake Paris.

At this time a general bloody war shall break out; Russia, America, England, and, later, Austria, will unite to the support of France. The fields of battle in Italy shall be strewed with the dead bodies of German, Russian, French, and Italian soldiers. After fearful alternatives, the Prussians shall be defeated, and everywhere so entirely crushed, that scarcely any of them shall return to their families.

Henry of France shall be proclaimed king, and Pius IX. shall re-enter Rome to enjoy the beginning of the great triumph of the Church.

N. B. — In relation to this last portion of the prophecy about the present Pope *re-entering Rome*, th re are some apparent contradictions between the different and various prophetical predictions mentioned in this book. As it may have been remarked by the reader, some affirm that Pope Pius IX. will not leave Rome, and this statement agrees with the words of his Holiness; others state that he will re-enter Rome. Now, the two apparent contradictory statements may be entirely reconciled, if we reflect that the Pope is at present an exile and a prisoner in the Vatican, which, in a certain sense, is out of the real city of Rome, where the true metropolitan seat of the Pope, as Patriarch of the West, is found, namely, in the Lateran Basilica, which is situated in the eastern, whilst the Vatican is in the western extremity of the city. Besides, the Vatican is surrounded by special walls, which constitute the Leonine city. Let us consider the Leonine city different from the older city of Rome, — for, in reality, it is as much as Brooklyn is different from New York, — and the apparent contradictions are perfectly reconciled.

Let us return now to the prophetical predictions of Palma Maria. These will be explained and confirmed by the following extracts from a letter written to Victor C—— de Stenay, author of the "Future Unveiled" and "The Last Prophetical Warnings," from which these and some other extracts have been compiled: —

"June 20, 1872.

"MY DEAR FRIEND, — You know the reputation of Monsieur Abbé de Brandt. He is just arrived from Frohsdorf, where he saw Henry V. during three hours; from Oria, where he conversed twice, for more than an hour each time, with the holy Widow Palma; from Naples and Castellamare, where he was with Melanie during half a day; from Rome, where he was admitted to a private audience with the Holy Father during at least two hours; lastly, he has received a letter from the Curé de Maleton, and has learned the precautions

' taken by persons in high positions who live in Paris. I intend to inform you of the result of this pilgrimage."

(For brevity's sake, we confine ourselves to his conversation with Palma.)

"From Frohsdorf, Monsieur Abbé de Brandt went directly to Oria. Having procured letters of introduction from a Cardinal, he was allowed to see Palma. This extraordinary servant of God wears the stigmas, and during the last seven years she has not taken any material food. Thrice daily our Lord presents himself to her in a visible manner, under the form of an ordinary consecrated host, and the Abbé Brandt has, with his own eyes, beheld one of these marvellous communions. Moreover, Palma Maria receives every morning the Holy Communion from the hands of a priest. The interpreter of Monsieur Abbé Brandt was an ecclesiastic whom you know.

"Behold here some particulars of the conversation of this extraordinary woman, which is most authentic, because communicated to me by the venerable and worthy Abbé Brandt, who is incapable of deceiving.

"Immediately after his introduction to Palma Maria, she told him that she knew of his having had some difficulties with his bishop, on account of his direction of souls, but that he, the abbé, had always kept in the right way, and that he should continue in it. Soon after, she added, 'There shall be frightful massacres of priests and religious in Spain, France, Italy, and, above all, in Calabria (Kingdom of Naples). This shall be very soon; we are near it.' At this point the holy servant of God suddenly became radiant with light, and, with ineffable accents, she spoke of the happiness of martyrdom.

"Though Monsieur Abbé Brandt had been advised not to ask any questions of the venerable servant of God from mere curiosity, yet he thought that he could venture to question her whether these massacres were to take place on the 15th of July, as she had been reported in the *Univers* to have foretold. At these words, Palma Maria calmly asked: '*Have I said this? I am not aware of it.* I do not recollect what I say while in an ecstasy. I know very well the epoch, but I cannot voluntarily or knowingly reveal it. *There shall be three days' dark-*

ness. Not one demon shall be left in hell. They shall all come out, either to excite the wicked murderers, or to dishearten the just. This shall be frightful! frightful!! but a grand cross shall appear, and the triumphs of the Church will make people quickly forget all evils.'

"Being arrived in Rome, Monsieur Abbé Brandt had to render a most detailed account of what he had seen and heard at Oria to the prelate, secretary of the Pope. Then he had a long conference with the Holy Father. His Holiness enjoys more than flourishing health; it is miraculous. The Pope believes the prophecies of the Ecstatic of Oria. He seems to be full of confidence in the future. He is fairly disgusted with all present governments."

As a proof of the extraordinary sanctity of Palma Maria, we may add that she is in frequent communication in spirit with Melanie, whom she has never known in a natural way, and who lives at a considerable distance from Oria. Palma spoke a great deal to Rev. Monsieur Brandt about Melanie, and Melanie has also spoken to him of Palma Maria. This great servant of God is occasionally also supernaturally conversing with Louisa Lateau, the stigmatized of Bois d'Haine, in Belgium. We must also remark, that in speaking with the Abbé Brandt, Palma Maria not only did not contradict the reported prophecies, but indirectly confirmed them in substance. She admitted that, whilst in ecstasy and naturally unconscious about what she might utter, she may have mentioned those things. She affirmed that, by divine revelation, she knew the time when at least some of these events were to happen, but that she would not voluntarily manifest them. But she did not contradict them. Moreover, it is evident to every intelligent and unprejudiced observer of events, that Spain, France, and Italy have actually entered a phase of terrible convulsions.

CHAPTER XV.

PROPHECY OF JANE LE ROYER, IN RELIGION SISTER OF THE NATIVITY.

JANE LE ROYER was born on the twenty-fourth day of January, 1731, in the village of Beaulot, diocese of Rennes, in Brittany, France. She entered into the Monastery of St. Clare of Fougeres, called Urbanists. Her religious name was Sister of the Nativity. She died on the 15th of August, 1798.

This holy sister was entirely illiterate. Many years before the event she foretold the great French Revolution, and the horrible injuries caused to religion, more particularly in France.

In the year 1790, Sister of the Nativity, by command of God, manifested all her visions and previsions to the Spiritual Director of the monastery, the Abbé Genet, in fifty conferences, who wrote them down. She used to say, "The knowledge of these things shall contribute to the salvation of many souls, and form a treasure for the faithful for the last age of the world." Through the care and exertions of the Abbé Genet, the collection of the revelations and predictions of that venerable sister were published several times in France, and translated into the Italian and German languages. We could give long extracts, but prefer brevity and precision; hence we select the following important passages, which have more immediate relation to the present time : —

"My father, God has manifested to me the malice of Lucifer, and the perverse and diabolical intentions of his emissaries (secret societies) against the Holy Church of Jesus Christ. At the command of their master these wicked men have traversed the earth like furies, with the intention of preparing the way and the place for Antichrist, whose reign is approaching. Through the corrupted breath of this proud spirit they have poisoned the minds of men. Like persons infected with pestilence, they have reciprocally communicated the evil to each other, and the contagion has become general. [Is not here well described the pestilential influence of the International sect?]

"What convulsions! what scandals!

"The thick vapors which I have seen rising from the earth, and *obscuring the light of the sun*, are the false maxims of irreligion and of license (falsely called liberty), which in part originated in France, and in part came to us from abroad. These have succeeded in confounding all sound principles, and in spreading everywhere such darkness as to obscure the light both of faith and of reason. The storm began in France, which shall be the first theatre of its ravages, after having been its forge.

"But the Church in council assembled (prophecy of the Ecumenical Vatican Council) shall one day strike with anathemas, pull down and destroy the evil principles of that criminal constitution. (The impious revolutionary constitutions of modern times founded on the pretended rights of man, which make him independent of God.)

"I saw in God's essence a numerous assembly of ministers of the Church, who, like an army in battle array, and like a firm and unflinching column, shall sustain the rights of the Church, and of their Head, and shall re-establish its ancient discipline. . . . .

"What consolation, what joy, for all the truly faithful! . . . .

"I saw in the Divinity a great power, guided by the Holy Spirit, which shall restore right and order. (France through its great monarch.)

"All false religions shall be abolished. All the abuses of the Revolution shall be destroyed; the altars shall be re-established, and religion shall more than ever flourish." Amen!

CHAPTER XVI.

POETICAL PREDICTION, WHICH EXISTS IN THE PUBLIC BIBLIOTECA OF PIACENZA, IN ITALY, WITH SOME REMARKS ABOUT REPUBLICAN GOVERNMENTS.

"BELLA, fames, pestis, fraudes Saturnia regna
Sternent, et veteres pellentur ubique tyranni.
Pastor erit claves, non regna gubernans.
 Monstra loquor! Tum cum pariet bos rubeus hydram,
Nec Deus extinguet flammas, nec deseret jram,
 Nisi prius Ausoniæ feriant mala singula gentes.
Tempus erit prope lustrum. Mox aliger ingens
 Surget ut e somno, rostro metuendus et ungue.
Colla bovis cædet, sitibundus iniqui draconis
 Viscera depascet. Gallorum trina colorum
Sternet humi; statuet in propria reges.
 Galatia genitus terra Vir justus et æquus
Pastor erit: toto surget Concordia Mundo.
Una fides, unus regnabit in omnia Princeps."

Translation.

Famine, pestilence, war, and frauds shall prostrate the Italian kingdoms, and the ancient kings shall everywhere be expelled. The Supreme Pastor will hold the keys of Heaven, but shall be deprived of earthly kingdoms.

Horrible spectacle! When the red ox shall give birth to the hydra, God will not extinguish the flames nor calm his anger until all these calamities shall have stricken the people of Ausonia (Italy). This state of affairs shall last about five years.

Then an enormous bird shall awake, as from a sleep, and with its terrible bill and claws shall sever the ox's neck, and shall eagerly devour the intestines of the wicked dragon. He shall drag to the mud the tricolor flag of the French, and restore to their dominions the legitimate kings. A just and pious man born in Gallicia shall be the Supreme Pontiff; then the whole world shall be united and prosperous. One faith only and one emperor shall reign over the whole earth.

This prediction is remarkably clear in its brevity. It embraces the whole world; but, like almost all other prophecies, it bears a special reference to Italy and France. Under the unnatural allegory of a *red ox* generating a hydra, it vividly expresses the unnatural and impiously absurd efforts of radical sectaries, or red republicans, in attempting to establish, without the principles of Christian faith and morality, a universal so-called republic, or brotherhood of humanity, which must necessarily be followed soon by lawless communism, the *red ox* monster giving birth to the hydra of reckless anarchy. For anarchy is the inevitable consequence of the abolition of the dogmas of religion, justice, and authority. This detestable work was first begun three hundred and fifty years ago by the apostles of Protestantism who practised and preached rebellion against all legitimate authority both human and divine, and which its progeny of modern sectaries madly hasten to accomplish to their own ruin and perdition. Satan can indeed be the great Architect of Babel, but God alone can be the real founder, builder, and protector of Sion. Satan can produce only confusion, ruin, and despair; God alone can be the author of order, harmony, stability, and of true, real happiness, temporal and eternal.

Let us be permitted in all charity to entreat all the Catholic readers of these lines to pray very fervently for the speedy enlightenment and sincere conversion of all the members of secret societies condemned by the Church. Among them there are men well disposed in mind and heart. In Christian charity we should love them as individual persons; but as sectarians, no confidence can be placed in them. They are under a dangerous delusion; sooner or later they will be used as tools in the hands of unknown and impious leaders for much evil against religion, and consequently against the real welfare of society, under the flimsy pretext of promoting the good of humanity. For a sincere Catholic it should be more than sufficient to know that secret societies are condemned by his Church, — the infallible organ of God's eternal truth. Being under the ban of excommunication, no Catholic can live and die a member of such societies without the risk of eternal damnation. These are plain and strong words, but they are words of evangelical truth and Christian charity. These sectarians have already been the principal agents of much injury to the Christian religion. They are very active at the present moment, and they will soon cause serious evils to society by their attempts against the Catholic Church. But they shall find her firmly established upon an impregnable rock, and defended by the infallible promises, and by the omnipotent hand of her divine founder, Jesus Christ, the King of kings and Lord of lords; as we are going to show in the next part of this book.

Few Words about Republics.

The attention of the readers of this compilation will surely be arrested, and some of them may be startled, by the fact, that in the above-quoted poetical prediction, as well as in several others translated for this work, the abolition of European republics is often foretold. In order to prevent misconception, we consider it our duty to make here a few remarks upon this subject, so interesting to our American readers.

The Christian religion, founded by the incarnate wisdom of God for the general and lasting happiness of mankind, is and should be adapted to all the exigencies of human nature, and consequently to every legitimate form of civil government. Every intelligent and honest mind must at once perceive and admit the truth of this first principle. It could not be otherwise. Jesus Christ, the divine founder of Christianity, emphatically commanded his Apostles, and in them and through them all their legitimate successors, to preach the gospel to all creatures, and to teach all nations, tribes, and tongues the saving dogmas and doctrines of his holy religion. To animate them in the difficult achievement of this great work, — the grandest ever intrusted to human agency, — he solemnly promised to be always with them, together with the divine Paraclete. Here it is evident to every intelligent Christian mind that the Apostles, and in them and through them the Church of Jesus Christ, received from him a solemn promise, and infallible, because divine guaranty of his perpetual presence, light, inspiration, and assistance in their work of instruction and conversion of mankind to Christianity in every age and in every corner of the habitable globe.

In his divine wisdom, Jesus Christ knew perfectly well that his Apostles were to preach the Gospel, and thus establish his Holy Church among Jews and Gentiles, among barbarous as well as civilized nations. He was well aware that the dispositions of the human mind, the changing inclinations of the human heart, as well as the various circumstances of time, places, and climates, would occasionally require the adaptation of civil constitutions, laws, and human governments to the existing wants of society. Empires, kingdoms, republics, and every legitimate form of human government, were present before the mind of the divine founder of Christianity. He sent his Apostles, commissioned and commanded them to proclaim his saving faith and establish his religion among all nations. It was therefore his own interest and that of his Church to adapt his religion and worship to every form of civil government, whenever this was conducted in conformity with the first principles of natural justice and equity. The guaranty of his perpetual presence in his Church secured this boon to every honest civil government of the earth. The existence of his Church in any nation or government brings to them in a special manner the presence, sanction, blessing, and protection of God, because Jesus Christ is wherever his Church is. For she is his inseparable spouse; whosoever receives her receives him, whosoever favors her pleases him; and he is pledged to bless, protect, and cherish all those men, and, above all, those governments favorably disposed towards his Holy Spouse, the Church of the Living God. These are not euphonic expressions and barren theories. The history of two thousand years of Christianity is our best guaranty. No true, no real objection can possibly be adduced against this fact. All that is alleged against the Church of Jesus Christ will, upon impartial examination, be found to be the effects, not of Christian doctrines or Christian practices, but of man's resistance to her, and of God's just anger against those nations and civil governments which opposed her introduction within their limits, or attempted to persecute and oppress her virtuous and faithful members, living in peace and charity with their fellow-men. For those who persecute his Church persecute Jesus Christ, and those who persecute him in her shall ever be punished by God.

We have more to say in behalf of true Catholic Christianity. This holy and divine religion not only brings with her presence special blessings wherever she is received, but she confers an essential perfection necessarily wanting to any and every civil government.

Man has been created by God for happiness. But man is composed of body and soul; therefore, to be happy, both the manifold wants of his body and the higher and more extensive aspirations of his immortal soul must be provided for and satisfied. In his divine wisdom and goodness, God has fully provided for all the wants of fallen humanity. He has instituted the civil government for what more immediately concerns the material wants of the body. To guide, direct, and satisfy the higher and more noble aspirations of the human soul, God has revealed and established upon earth a divine religion. These two governments are originally from him. Both reason and revelation assert this truth; divine and human history confirms this fact. These governments, then, are the two beneficent arms of Divine Providence, employed by God in the general welfare of mankind, for the guidance, help, protection, and perfection of human nature. Religion is God's right arm; the civil government is his left hand. So long as these two powers are inspired, moved, and directed by the holy spirit of God, they, like the two hands of a perfect musician, produce the most agreeable harmony in the concert of humanity. Both, combined, effectively succeed in promoting the material and spiritual, moral and intellectual, civil and religious, welfare of mankind.

God, however, uses, in the ecclesiastical as well as civil governments, human instruments, which, in spite of the ability of the performer, may become out of tune. For these living instruments are persons endowed with a free will and judgment, which they, as mere individuals, may abuse by opposing the supreme will of the Divine Legislator, just as the officials of the best government upon earth can violate human laws. But a most essential exception must be made in favor of the Christian Church. God has most wisely provided against this danger on her side, by constituting her the living organ of his Divine Spirit, of his holy grace, and of his eternal truth; and consequently, by permanently endowing her with the gifts of his wisdom, power, and strength, whereby she is most infallibly preserved from failure in her sublime and divinely imposed mission.

This prerogative has not only never been granted by God, but, on the contrary, it has always been denied by him, to secular governments, whom he has commanded to have, in respectful docility, recourse to his Church, in order to learn from her his saving truth, and to receive, through her, the authoritative sanction to their moral laws for the safe guidance of their respective subjects. The Church of the living God is to human society what the soul is to the human body. They were originally both made by God; they are united by him, not to be foes, but to be friends. Let no man attempt to separate what God has united.

Let civil governments act upon these first principles, which enlightened reason can understand, and divine revelation has proclaimed, and they will ever find themselves in harmony with the Church of the living God. But if, abusing their material power, they attempt to pervert the eternal order, established by God in the government of this world, and pretend to subject the spiritual to the carnal, the divine to the human will, they cannot blame the Church, the living representative and witness of God upon earth, if she courageously says to them: *If it be just in the sight of God to hear you rather than God, judge ye; for we cannot but speak the things that we have seen and heard.* (Acts iv. 19.)

Modern earthly governments, however, disdainfully affect to despise these sacred and solemn maxims. They not only refuse to acknowledge the superiority of the ecclesiastical to the civil order, of the spirit over matter, of the soul over the body, of God over man; but they seem to have conspired to subvert entirely the plan of divine economy.

Their conduct manifests their determination to subject the spiritual to the secular power, and to make the Church of Jesus Christ the slave and tool of the state.

The present attitude of the Russian and German Empires, of the Italian usurping government, of the Swiss and Spanish republics, of French radicals, Austrian infidels, and English Protestant officials, towards the Pope of Rome, and towards the Catholic Episcopate, evidently betrays their common conspiracy. These governments have, at different times and in various ways, been warned by the authoritative voice of the Church and of the infallible supreme Pontiff, that by their acts they are inevitably undermining the very foundation of their own authority, and, through their conduct and example, they teach their subjects baneful lessons of general insubordination. These charitable and most opportune admonitions have been disregarded. Intended to effect a reconciliation, they have, through the distemper of the body politic, produced irritation. Like the frantic patient, they raise their arms against the wise and kind physician. Doomed soon to perish by political suicide, God strikes them with judicial blindness. As they refuse, not only subjection, but even ordinary respect, to sacred persons invested with divine authority, what wonder if their scandalized and demoralized subjects refuse to recognize and obey godless men claiming superiority and dominion over them! All tyrants and all the persecutors of the Church of God have ever met with the same fate. The Old and New Testaments and the history of the world witness to this fact.

Intelligent Christians and true statesmen must see that this conduct of modern European governments is the principal cause and the real secret of modern aspirations after the so-called republican institutions.

Proud man refuses to acknowledge a fellow-man as his superior. Every notion of a divinely appointed or sanctioned authority having been blotted out of the mind and heart of men, these have learned to scout the very existence of any superior being, human or divine. With their tongues and with their pens first, then with their swords and battle-axes, finally with gunpowder and petroleum, they are impiously determined to level both heaven and earth. After long consultations, they have agreed to the unanimous adoption of the following fundamental maxims, which will soon prove in practice the five most dreadful scourges of humanity:—

I. The absolute denial of a personal God, and consequently the existence of any divine religion. Hence the worse than pagan practice of divorcing religion from the state, which means separating man from God, the earth from heaven, time from eternity.

II. The substitution of the human for the divine will and law. Hence the spiritual tyranny of modern governments over the conscience of mankind.

III. The supreme and absolute dominion of the brutal force of a vicious and bold minority over an upright but timid majority.

IV. The utter immolation of the spirit to matter. Hence the never-ending praises and perpetual worship of material progress in commercial enterprises and extravagant speculations.

V. The substitution of unbridled license, favoring all bad human passions, to the sacred liberty of the gospel, and to the essential salutary restraints imposed by Christianity for the preservation of human society. Hence their hankering after the barbarism of socialism and communism.

This is the programme of modern sectarians, stripped of all the hypocritical sound of euphonious words. This is their avowed object, announced in their books, published in their daily and weekly press, embellished in their magazines, discussed in their secret conclaves, made a subject of daily conversation, proclaimed in their public assemblies and in all the organs of their manifold sects, or, rather, the same sect under manifold names.

This horrible subversion of every divine and human right, constitution, and law will most certainly be soon attempted, at least in Europe, by the threatened and imminent bloody revolution, which, humanly speaking, is inevitable in the present demoralized condition of society. The *red ox*, or, rather, the bull of *red republicanism*, must give birth to the coming hydra of bloody socialism and communism of the Parisian fashion, which, being goaded and infuriated by former checks and past repulses, will madly rush to the indiscriminate slaughter of all whom he finds in the way, and suspects to be opposed to his impious and cruel designs.

But, in such detestable condition of human affairs, opposition shall become a necessity of self-preservation, which natural and positive, human and divine, law demands and justifies. It shall be found morally impossible to induce the soundest and best majority of mankind to adopt the maxims and follow the practices of lawless communism. All conservative men, of sound principles, in any form of civil government, shall find themselves forced to oppose this monster with all their might. All men of conscience and of faith, all persons of morality and of law, will then, at least, be convinced of the absolute and paramount necessity of union and organization, in order to combat, with system and with success, the common foe of God and man.

God Almighty, the Lord of Hosts, provoked to a just indignation by the impieties and crimes of his enemies, persecutors of his Church, will most surely come to the protection and defence of his faithful servants and followers, and thus enable them, even through miraculous interposition, to crush the infernal monster of anarchy, and obtain over him the most complete victory.

The gigantic bird of heaven shall awake as from a sleep, and, with its terrible bill and claws, will sever the ox's neck, and eagerly devour the very intestines of the impious and wicked dragon of Antichristian socialism and anti-social communism.

Here we are at the turning-point for America. We should not be at all surprised if the onslaught against Catholics were to be made simultaneously over the whole earth. We have strong grounds to suspect this to be the intention and plan of the revolutionary Archons. In this case the storm will soon burst over our unsuspecting heads.

We are, however, inclined to opine that the trial will come later. This will be soon after the general defeat of communism in Europe. To understand our position and danger, we should reflect that socialism or communism in Europe will assume the fair name of republic, a it did two years ago in Paris, and as it does at the present moment in Spain. Now in America the majority of the people are, or affect to be, attached to republican institutions. Moreover, the Catholic religion, and Christianity in general, has in this country many more enemies than some simple people wish to suspect. Besides, there are too many ambitious persons anxious to ride at any moment on the swell of popular agitation to political eminence and coveted salaries. The mind of the people, agitated by European events, shall be found in fermentation and ready for explosion. In the mean time the dragon of Communism, to escape total destruction, will from Europe swim over the Atlantic Ocean to the more safe American shores, where it will be promptly met in friendly embrace by many thousands of congenial persons. We can conclusively argue this from their past conduct in relation to the late Paris Commune, and from their present friendly attitude towards the so-called Spanish Republic and persecuting Switzerland and Germany. It will be then, if not before, that the insane cry will be raised, and re-echoed from the anti-Catholic pulpit and infidel press, *The republic is in danger! down with the Papists!! death to the priests!!!*

Roman Catholics will be represented as inimical to all republican institutions, because, forsooth, they, in self-preservation, and in union with all the truly conservative men of Europe, were forced to combat the bloody dragon of Socialism, wearing on his gory head the republican cap of liberty.

The strong but dormant prejudices of the non-Catholic population will by demagogues be lashed into fury, and the inevitable consequence will be the massacre of Catholics, but especially of priests and religious; the burning of Catholic churches and schools, of Catholic colleges and seminaries, of monasteries and convents. Such is our prevision and prediction, though by no means do we desire in this case to be a prophet.

We can, however, foresee that, after this perhaps required baptism of fire and blood, the Catholic Church, purified by persecution, and fertilized by the sacred gore and holy ashes of many thousands of glorious martyrs, will more than ever flourish, and bear abundant fruit of sanctity in America as well as in every nation of the earth.

Then, though rather late, it will be found out, and humbly acknowledged, that Catholic Christianity is not and cannot be opposed to any legitimate form of civil government. Her divine origin, the very nature of her constitution, the heavenly object of her mission, forbid and prevent this opposition. The Catholic Church has never attacked any government legitimately established on account of its chosen civil livery or form. During more than eight centuries the Catholic Church has lived in peace and harmony with the Italian republics of Genoa, Venice, Pisa, Lucca, and Florence. During fourteen centuries she has cherished and nourished in the very bosom of her temporal States the small and weak Republic of San Marino. All these republics have lasted so long, not because opposed, but because guarded and protected by the keys of St. Peter and the sword of St. Paul; whilst the great American Republic has to prepare yet for the celebration of her first centenary. We shall conclude by affirming that the external government of the Roman Catholic Church is both in theory and in practice more truly liberal, and in this sense republican, than any other government upon earth. All the offices and dignities of this Church are open to the humblest as well as to the highest of her members, provided they qualify themselves for them by learning and holiness of life. We have daily instances of this fact, which no sane man can venture to deny.

The senseless clamor, then, raised by impious and designing men against the Catholic Church, that she is opposed to any form of civil government, is entirely groundless and calumnious. But when truth and facts fail an inveterate enemy, he is by his hatred forced to invent calumny, in order to palliate his persecution. God, however, knows how to justify, and he is powerful enough to protect, his divinely established Church, which he has built upon an impregnable rock.

CLEF CHIROGRAPHIQUE.

a	b	c	d	e	f	g	h	i	j	k	l	m
9	8·	+	5	3·	0·	2	7	6·	0	k	1·	5·

n	o	p	q	r	s	t	u	v	x	z	y
1	3	4·	8	9·	6	2·	7·	4	x	z	y or 6· 6·

N. B. This chirographic key was originally intended for the writing and reading French words. Hence, those only who can understand the French language can use it. For obvious reasons we leave it as it is. *Qui potest capere capiat.*

Every letter of the French alphabet is here represented by a cipher, except *c*, for which a cross is substituted. *K* and *x* are preserved. *Y* is either used as usual or two 6· 6· Attention should be paid to the points, to avoid confusion.

When time, the phrases should be formed and punctuation added.

In case of some typographic error, be indulgent.

SECOND PART.

TRIUMPH OF THE CATHOLIC CHURCH.

CHAPTER I.

JESUS CHRIST EVER TRIUMPHS IN AND THROUGH HIS CHURCH.

"HE shall have dominion from sea to sea, and from the river unto the end of the earth." (Ps. lxii. 8.) The eternal and consubstantial Son of God became man for the redemption and salvation of mankind. *For God so loved the world as to give his only begotten Son, that whosoever believeth in him may not perish, but may have life everlasting.* (St. John iii. 16.)

Faith, then, in Jesus Christ became an essential condition for man to obtain eternal salvation. Hence our Lord Jesus Christ said: *Father, the hour is come: glorify thy son, that thy son may glorify thee. As thou hast given him power over all flesh, that he may give life everlasting to all whom thou hast given him. And this is life everlasting, that they may know thee, the only true God, and Jesus Christ, whom thou hast sent.* (John xvii. 3.)

In conformity with these divine dogmas, Jesus Christ, *the author and finisher of our faith*, went forth among men; and through the brilliant example of his holiness, by his wonderful and frequent miracles, by the sublimity of his heavenly doctrines, he attracted to his saving faith a large number of proselytes.

But the maxims of the gospel being opposed to the perverse spirit and corrupt practices of the world, this world has been ever obstinately hostile to the doctrines and to the practices of genuine Christianity. *Hence the chief priests and the Pharisees gathered a council, and said: What do we, for this man, Jesus, doeth many miracles? If we let him alone so, all men will believe in him.* (St. John ii. 47.) These wily and powerful men of the world, having in their secret conventicle taken council together, come to the determination to condemn Jesus to death, and thus with the same blow put an end to his new doctrine and religion. The sentence of death was soon pronounced in an official form, and immediately executed upon this innocent and Divine victim with extreme barbarity. *The wicked man,* we read in the Book of Proverbs, — *the wicked man impudently hardeneth his face. . . . . But there is no wisdom, there is no prudence, there is no counsel against the Lord.* (Prov. xxi. 29.) The death of Jesus Christ proved to be his most complete victory over sin and hell; and his resurrection soon became his most glorious triumph over all his present and future enemies in the world. *He humbled himself, becoming obedient unto death, even the death of the cross; therefore God hath exalted him, and given to him a name which is above every name, that in the name of Jesus every knee should bow, of those that are in heaven, on earth, and under the earth; and that every tongue should confess that the Lord Jesus Christ is in the glory of God the Father.* (Phil. ii. 8.)

The Jewish priests and hypocritical Pharisees condemned our Divine Saviour to death in order to deprive him of some few thousand followers; and behold! he receives from the Godhead the empire of the universe, and the most absolute power and dominion over all creatures. *He shall have dominion from sea to sea, and from the river* (the Roman Tiber) *unto the ends of the earth.* (Ps. clxxi. 8.) Hence, immediately after his resurrection our Divine Master could say to his Apostles: *All power is given to me in heaven and upon earth. Go ye, therefore, and teach all nations, baptizing them in the name of the Father, and of the Son, and of the Holy Ghost. Teaching them to observe all things whatsoever I have commanded you.* (Matt. xxviii. 18.) *He that believeth and is baptized shall be saved; but he that believeth not shall be condemned.* (Mark xvi. 16.) *In the world you shall have distress, but have confidence; I have overcome the world.* (John xvi. 33.) *Behold I am with you all days, even to the consummation of the world.* (Matt. xviii. 18.) *And they going forth preached everywhere, the Lord co-operating with them, and confirming the word with signs that followed.* (Mark xvi.)

In obedience to the directions received from their Divine Lord and Master, the Apostles began to preach and to teach in Palestine; but they were persecuted and dispersed by the Jewish magistrates. This very persecution, however, accelerated the propagation of the gospel among all other nations of the earth with such prompt and rapid success that, a few years after, St. Paul, the apostle of the Gentiles, writing to the converted Colossians, could say: *The word of the truth of the gospel, which is come to you, as also it is in the whole world, bringeth forth fruit and groweth, even as it doth in you.* (Col. i. 6.)

In less than a hundred years from the resurrection of our Lord, Christian churches were formed and bishoprics were established in almost all the principal cities of the earth, but more especially in those of the vast Roman Empire. St. Peter, the infallible Vicar of Jesus

Christ and Prince of the Apostles, went to fix permanently the throne of spiritual power and of supreme ecclesiastical jurisdiction in the very city of Rome, the proud capital of the pagan world. The rapid increase and spread of Christianity alarmed the Roman emperors. They resolved to extirpate this new religion from every part of their dominions. *That was their hour*, and all the power of darkness was in their mighty hands. During three long centuries every engine of oppression and instrument of cruelty was used to torment and put to death every known professor of the Christian religion. Christians were forced by the violence of persecution to fly into remote deserts or to bury themselves alive under the earth in the catacombs. This made the pagan world believe and proclaim that Christianity was dead and buried. They boasted of having at last succeeded in their work of utter extermination. Some of the bloody emperors claimed as one of their greatest titles to human glory, praise, and gratitude their having blotted out from the annals of the world the hated name of Christian. But, in the words of the wise man, we shall repeat: *The wicked man impudently hardeneth his face. . . . . But there is no wisdom, there is no prudence, there is no counsel, against the Lord.*

The frost of winter may succeed in keeping down vegetation for a short time; it comes forth, however, with new vigor, as soon as it is enlivened by the genial warmth of spring and summer. The sacred blood of Christian martyrs is the prolific seed of Christianity, and the caves of the desert and of the catacombs were the living granaries preserved by Divine Providence for spreading over the face of the earth the sound wheat of Christian faith and holiness, which soon produced rich harvests of fervent souls. The more warm blood had been shed, the earlier and more abundant was the crop of faith and virtue in the widening field of the Christian religion.

At the end of the third century, the bloody persecutor, Diocletian, was succeeded in the government of the Roman Empire by the brave, youthful Constantine, who obtained the imperial throne of his persecuting predecessors by his faith in Jesus Christ, and by his open profession of Christianity. He promptly abolished every obnoxious law from the Roman code. With his whole noble soul he thoroughly discarded the absurd impieties and idolatry of paganism, and in a few years he rejoiced to see the formerly proscribed religion of Christ established and flourishing in every part of his vast and now prosperous dominions in Europe, Asia, and Africa.

The following century was the most glorious in the history of the Christian Church. Such is ever the effect of persecution.

Before, however, we go out from Rome, we will assist at the grand solemnity of St. Peter's public instalment on his Roman see of universal spiritual dominion, which was the most glorious triumph of Christianity at the close of three hundred years of bitter persecution. The highest honors and the most profound homages were, by the Roman Senate and people, paid to their triumphant military conquerors, and to the Roman Emperor in the Capitol of the Empire. At the time of Constantine, this famous Capitol was a magnificent palace, erected upon a high, rocky eminence, as it were a brilliant diadem on the proud head of imperial Rome. To make the contrast between the highest honors and the lowest infamy, the most complete human happiness and the extremity of human wretchedness, more striking and more keenly felt, a most horrible dungeon was constructed, partly hewed in the rock and partly built with solid masonry, at the base of the Capitoline Hill, and was called the Mamertine Prison. This filthy and frightful living sepulchre was intended for the worst criminals condemned to capital punishment.

By command of the tyrant Emperor Nero, St. Peter had been thrust, chained, and locked up in this dungeon. It was from this prison that he was dragged to a high hill, called the Janiculum, about two miles distant, where he was crucified. After his death, the Christians of Rome buried his sacred body at the base of the same hill, called the Vatican Field. This is what human hatred and pagan persecution did against the first Vicar of Jesus Christ.

But let us witness now a contrast between the Emperor Nero, his murderer, and St. Peter, his innocent victim. Whilst nobody can point out the burial-place of this persecuting Emperor, Christian faith, devotion, and gratitude have raised the most splendid sacred monuments in memory and honor of St. Peter, marking the great triumphs of Christianity.

A beautiful church was soon built on the hallowed spot of St. Peter's crucifixion. Over his grave at the Vatican was, by the imperial hands and generosity of Constantine, commenced the foundation of the grandest temple that human genius ever conceived and human efforts have ever attempted to build, which has been consecrated to the memory and honor of St. Peter, and to the perpetual worship of Jesus crucified. St. Peter's Mamertine Prison became a venerated sanctuary, whence the cross, hated and abhorred by paganism, has been carried in triumph by Christian faith and devotion, and permanently planted on the highest pinnacle of the Roman Capitol, whereon it has since stood, during seventeen centuries, as the victorious standard of Jesus

Christ, and the symbol and pledge of Christian hope and life.

O, when will the enemies of Christianity and the mad persecutors of Christ's holy Church learn, at least from history, if they refuse to believe divine revelation, that this Church is the masterpiece upon earth of Eternal Wisdom and of Divine Omnipotence, built by the hand of an incarnate God, and founded upon a solid rock, against which the gates of hell, combined with all the malice and power of bad men, cannot, and never shall, prevail? The infallible and effective promise of God protects her with an impenetrable shield, and his omnipotent arm defends her from all hostile attacks. When will the pretended sages and all the great men of the earth begin to understand that *no weapon that is formed against this Church can prosper, and that every tongue that resisteth her she shall condemn?* (Isa. liv.) The Catholic Church always outlives what she condemns. The long experience of centuries should warn them that, if they attempt to butt against this rock, they shall all break their heads, and some of them shall forfeit their crowns; and if this rock fall upon them, they shall be crushed to the earth and be ground to atoms, which the wind of heaven will scatter away, and consign their memory to everlasting infamy, like that of all persecutors of Jesus Christ.

We Catholics feel no dread and show no fear for our Holy Church and religion. This fact should not be overlooked in the present crisis of the world. We firmly believe that *this Church of the living God is the groundwork and the pillar of truth.* (1 Tim. iii. 15.)

1. *She is the groundwork of truth*, because originally founded by the God-Man Jesus Christ, *who is the way, the truth, and the life.* (St. John xiv. 6.)

2. *She is the groundwork of truth,* because owned and possessed by truth, by God, hence called *the Church of the living God,* who lives in her and for her; owned and possessed by Jesus Christ, who is her wedded and inseparable spouse.

3. *She is the pillar of truth,* because supported, protected, defended, and preserved by truth, by Jesus Christ, who is eternal truth; by the Holy Ghost, *who is the spirit of truth, and who is pledged to abide with her forever.* (St. John xiv. 16.)

4. *She is the pillar of truth,* because this Holy Catholic Church is constituted by Jesus Christ the only authoritative and infallible teacher of truth to mankind upon earth. She alone can and does teach, without the least danger of error, the existence of the Godhead in three real divine persons, Father, Son, and Holy Ghost, and of Jesus Christ the incarnate Son of God, *the Word made flesh, whom the Father has sent to us.* She is the unerring witness and the only sure voucher of his divinity and true humanity; of his dogmas and of his doctrines, of divine revelation in its integrity, and of genuine Christianity. Through this Holy Catholic Church alone Jesus Christ, the Saviour of mankind, can be known with infallible certainty, loved fully, and perfectly served by men.

As columns are erected in order that the statues of great men, benefactors of humanity, may be seen, remembered, and honored by present and future generations, so this Holy Church is the living column through which Jesus Christ is made known to the world, and duly worshipped by all true Christian believers. Hence it follows that, like persecuting Saul, all the enemies of this divine Church are necessarily the personal enemies of Jesus Christ, because it is impossible to attempt to pull down a column without at the same time and by the same wanton act upsetting the statue which stands upon it.

Remember, then, and reflect that *the Church of the living God is the groundwork and the pillar of truth.* But truth is unchangeable; what is unchangeable is eternal, and what is eternal cannot be destroyed or perish. *Magna est veritas, et prevalebit.* Fear not, Holy Church of the living God, *for thy maker is thine husband, the Lord of Hosts is his name; and thy Redeemer, the Holy One of Israel, shall be called the Lord of the earth, and thou shalt be founded in justice. . . . . No weapon that is formed against thee shall prosper, and every tongue that resisteth thee, thou shalt condemn.* (Isa. liv.)

From the first three centuries we shall now pass to the last three. Since the sixteenth century, and during more than than three hundred years, many and various weapons were forged by persecuting men of every class of society in different parts of the world against the body of Jesus Christ, the Church of the living God. Beginning with that of the apostate Luther, many tongues were whetted to fight against Catholicity with bitter words of calumny, with damnable heretical doctrines, and with maxims of impiety. In hatred of their divine faith and holy religion, faithful Catholics were persecuted, betrayed, and put to death in the largest portion of Europe (including persecuting Russia), in Eastern Asia, and also in North America. To this very moment we have been most stubbornly denied our full and equal civil and political rights in many European countries, and, at least in practice, in some other younger nations that boast of their liberality. During the last hundred and fifty years secret societies of professed infidelity and hatred against Catholicity have been organized with the sworn promise and determination to root out from the earth, and to crush down into the mud, what, to the horror of Christianity, the blasphemous tongue of Voltaire called the *infamous, ecraser l'infame,* namely, Jesus Christ and his Holy Church. Their malice is equal to their impiety. They know that, so long as the Catholic Church exists upon earth, Jesus Christ will be worshipped by men; hence their fiendish hatred against this Holy Church; hence their secret plots and extensive conspiracies against the infallible Pope and King of Rome; hence their determined and general efforts to deprive our children of Catholic schools; hence their general oppression of Catholics in every department of religious, civil, political, and military life. Since their impious leader, Voltaire, exhorted them to this work, they have been, and are more every day, determined to crush the infamous, *ecraser l'infame.* As their predecessors, the pagan persecutors in the first three centuries of Christianity, became furious with impotent rage, when the individual life of Christian confessors was preserved by the miraculous interposition of God, and in their malice invented new and more cruel instruments of torture for the destruction of their innocent victims, so the same practice is adopted at the present age by the modern persecutors of the Roman Catholic faith and religion.

They see that the last three hundred years of persecution, instead, as they expected, of crushing the Catholic Church, have, on the contrary, vastly contributed to her increase in numbers, in extent, in compact union, in strength, power, and influence. They should logically conclude from this, that this Church is a divine institution protected by the power of the Almighty.

But impiety is the derangement of human reason. Like the bat, these men are rendered more blind by the very light that should convert them to eternal truth. They are irritated by disappointment and maddened by failure. In imitation of the Jewish high-priests, chief magistrates, and hypocritical Pharisees, they have gathered their clandestine councils, and in their secret conventicles they have said, *What are we doing? This man, Jesus, doeth many miracles in favor and for the protection of his Church, and of his Vicar, the Pope of Rome; if we let him alone so, all men will believe in him.* (St. John xi. 47.) Their unanimous resolution has been to put him and his Church to a speedy and violent death. The death-warrant has been signed and issued; the executioners have been selected and appointed; the inexorable word of command has been given. Behold, then, the Prussian infidel, the Bavarian Doellingerite, and the Italian apostate governments in union with, and assisted by, the effete Turkish Empire, and helped by the red republicans of Spain and Switzerland, busy in forging weapons and in sharpening their malignant tongues against the infallible Vicar of Jesus Christ and against his Holy Church.

It is not unlikely, but, on the contrary, a well-founded rumor warns us, that an attempt will be made at the first opportunity to thrust upon St. Peter's throne an anti-pope, in order to create a schism in the Church Catholic. They have adopted the maxim: *Division is weakness. Divide et impera.* Divide to crush.

From the august prisoner of the Vatican we Catholics have been often warned that a bitter persecution is impending; but we have also been assured with even more positive and infallible certainty that the Catholic Church shall and must be victorious, and that the Holy

See of Rome will in a few years celebrate the universal triumph of Catholic truth over the whole world converted to the faith and worship of Jesus Christ crucified.

Persecutions are moral storms. They swell the angry billows of human passions that dash with mad fury against the rock of Peter, upon which the Church of Christ is divinely established; but they cannot do any serious or permanent injury to her. On the contrary, these boisterous waves break themselves against this solid rock of ages into a foaming spray, which only serves to wash off and carry away from the external ramparts and walls of the Church the accumulated filth and dirt of centuries; then, exhausted by their own violence, these stormy billows are forced by the command of Jesus to sink down in defeat and dishonor into a long and smooth calm. Meanwhile the triumphant bark of St. Peter, emerging from her secure haven with renewed sails and more powerful steam than ever, swiftly glides through every sea and ocean, carrying the victorious flag of faith and truth, of peace and happiness, to every nation and tribe of the inhabited globe.

Our invincible hope is founded upon the nature of the Church of Jesus Christ, and upon his infallible divine promises. *In the world you shall have distress*, he says, *but have confidence. I have overcome the world* (St. John xvi. 33.) *Behold I am with you all days, even to the consummation of the world.* (St. Matt. xxviii. 18.) We Catholics most fully and most firmly believe that *Jesus Christ is the Head of the Church. He is the Saviour of the body. Christ cherisheth the Church, for we are members of his body, of his flesh, and of his bones, that we may in all things grow up in him.* (Eph. iv. 15.)

In short, we believe that the Church of Jesus Christ,

the Roman Catholic Church, is nothing else and nothing less than the expansion, the extension, and the perfection of his divine incarnation. Hence we believe that, *of the increase of his government and peace there shall be no end upon the throne of David, and upon his kingdom, to establish it with justice and with judgment from henceforth even forever. The zeal of the Lord of Hosts will perform this.* (Isa. ix. 6.)

This throne and kingdom of David is the spiritual kingdom of Jesus, namely, his Holy Catholic Church. We have learned this truth from the words of the Archangel Gabriel, who said to the Virgin Mary: *Fear not, Mary, for thou hast found grace with God. Behold thou shalt conceive in thy womb, and shalt bring forth a son, and thou shalt call his name Jesus. He shall be great, and shall be called the Son of the Most High; and the Lord God shall give unto him the throne of David his father, and he shall reign in the house of Jacob forever, and of his kingdom there shall be no end.* (Luke i. 30.)

To this spiritual kingdom of Jesus Christ there shall be no end in duration, no limit to its extent, no check to its progress in the mind and heart of nations.

Lately, on a solemn occasion, a high personage, in reading his inaugural address to his civil and military officers, in the presence of the diplomatic representatives of earthly governments, and before a large multitude of his republican fellow-citizens, declared that in a short time he hoped to see all men united under one form of government, under one flag, and all speaking the same language. His words may perhaps have been inspired by the spirit of prophecy, because he is the high magistrate, *not for one*, but for four years, over many millions of people, representing almost every nation under the sun. We most firmly hope to see this anticipation verified *in about two decades of years* in the Catholic Church, under the spiritual government of the infallible Pope of Rome, having the *Labarum* of Constantine for its standard, and using in every temple of true divine worship the Latin language in the sacred liturgy of our holy religion.

Both good and bad men have for centuries been working hard to prepare the way for this long-desired and glorious event. Since the epoch of the sixteenth century, heresy, impiety, and consequently moral corruption, have radically subverted every human, civil, political, military, and religious institution. Human society is in a fever of excitement. A terrible confusion of ideas and practices predominates in every earthly, political, and religious system. The so-called ministers of the modern gospel are made and unmade, according to the passing whims of those who condescend to sit under their pulpits, and whom these licensed preachers study to please and flatter in order to secure a longer lease of their place and salary. This fact proves the actual realization of St. Paul's prophecy, who wrote: *There shall be a time when they* (false Christians) *will not bear sound doctrine, but according to their own desires they will heap to themselves teachers having itching ears, and will turn away indeed their hearing from the truth, and will be turned to fables.* (2 Tim. iv. 3.)

The antichristian maxims, adopted by modern sectaries and forced upon civil governments, have shorn them of their dignity and strength, and crippled their power and energy for good. The *sovereign people* refuse to be governed, but aspire to dominion, and those who should obey, pretend to command. Dignities are prostituted to personal ambition, the common good is sacrificed to official rapacity, immorality and crime are rather stimulated than checked and punished by many in high stations and official power. Humanity groans in a dismal and appalling chaos of disorder and misery. The human heart longs for order, stability, security, justice, and peace.

It is only the supernatural power of a religion with the sanction of divine authority that is able to draw order out of human chaos, and restore hope and happiness to the desponding heart of society. It is only an infallible Church that can promptly detect and authoritatively condemn all religious and moral errors, and teach all truths to humanity. The Roman Catholic Apostolic Church alone can appeal to the present and past generations of two thousand years, to witness that she possesses these divine prerogatives, because she alone has constantly exercised them for the general welfare of mankind.

Hence all true and good men ardently desire and fervently pray for her speedy universal triumph. Hence Catholic unions for supplications, and for the exercise of zeal and virtue and charity. Hence the universal revival of faith in the Catholic world. Hence the solemn declaration by the Ecumenical Council of the Vatican of the Pope's infallibility, which secures to Catholicity a safe, trusty, unerring, and victorious leader in the approaching spiritual conquest of the world. Unity is strength, and strength united is victory and triumph. *Magna est veritas et prevalebit.*

The proximity of this final victory and glorious triumph of the Catholic Church is announced by the actual accomplishment of the great prophecy made two thousand and six hundred years ago by the holy Prophet Isaias, and confirmed about two thousand years hence by the greatest of all prophets. (Luke iii. 5.) The following are their words:—

Be comforted, be comforted, my people, saith your God. Speak to the heart of Jerusalem, and call to her; for her evil is come to an end. The voice of one crying in the desert: Prepare ye the way of the Lord; make straight in the wilderness the paths of our God. Every valley shall be exalted, and every mountain and hill shall be made low, and the crooked shall become straight, and the rough ways plain. And the glory of the Lord shall be revealed, and all flesh together shall see the salvation of God. . . . . Behold, the Lord God shall come with strength, and his arm shall rule. Behold, his reward is with him, and his work is before him. He shall feed his flock like a shepherd. He shall gather together the lambs with his arm, and shall take them up in his bosom. (Isa. xl. 3.)

We discover the literal realization of this remarkable prophecy in the construction of railroads in almost every direction on the surface of the earth; in the long tunnels bored through previously impassable mountains; in the deep, wide, and extensive canals dug across isthmuses to unite the Mediterranean Sea with the East Indian Ocean, and in the contemplated one between the Atlantic and Pacific. We behold the accomplishment of this prophecy in the numerous and stately steamboats gliding over the waters. We read it in the public press and in the telegraph, claimed as the most ready and powerful auxiliaries to a universal dominion.

We most cordially believe that all the principal practical inventions of this present century are by a most wise and merciful Providence intended to facilitate the approaching general triumph of the faith and religion of Jesus Christ upon earth for the conversion, sanctification, temporal and eternal happiness of mankind. The pagan Romans also planned and constructed commodious roads in different countries of Europe, Asia, and

Africa, and spanned deep and rapid rivers with their solid bridges to enlarge their military conquests, to facilitate the effective administration of their government, and to stimulate and encourage trade and commerce. But without their knowing it, and in opposition to their designs, they served as instruments in the hand of God to prepare an easy way to the spiritual conquest of the Christian religion. The large Roman roads and convenient bridges were traversed by many Christian missionaries bringing the good tidings of the gospel to the benighted idolatrous nations of the earth, and in their constant intercourse with the infallible head of Christianity in Rome.

With more effective means at our disposal in our own days, we expect soon to witness more perfect results; and under this well-founded and cherished expectation, we pass to the perusal of the predictions which clearly and distinctly announce them to the world.

CHAPTER II.

PROPHECY OF ST. CESARIUS.

THIS prophecy is found in the first volume of the *Liber Mirabilis* (wonderful book), printed in the year 1524, in the Royal Library in Paris, letter Z, No. 2537. The older copies of this book bear the title of "Prophecies of St. Cesarius." The following is the passage which has relation to present events:—

"When the entire world, and in a special manner France, and in France more particularly the provinces of the north, of the east, and above all that of Lorraine and Champagne, shall have been a prey to the greatest miseries and trials, then the provinces shall be succored by a prince who had been exiled in his youth, and who shall recover the crown of the lilies. *Juvenis captivatus qui recuperabit coronam lilii.*

"This prince shall extend his dominion over the entire universe. *Dominabitur per universum orbem.* At the same time there will be a great Pope, who will be most eminent in sanctity and most perfect in every quality. *Per voluntatem Dei assumetur unus Papa, vir sanctissimus, et in omni perfectione perfectus.* This Pope shall have with him the great monarch, a most virtuous man, who shall be a scion of the holy race of the French kings. *Habebit suum virum sanctissimum qui erit de reliquis sanctissimi Francorum sanguinis Regum.* This great monarch will assist the Pope in the reformation of the whole earth. Many princes and nations that are living in error and impiety shall be converted, and an admirable peace shall reign among men during many years, because the wrath of God shall be appeased through their repentance, penance, and good works. There will be one common law, one only faith, one baptism, one religion. All nations shall recognize the Holy See of Rome, and shall pay homage to the Pope. But after some considerable time fervor shall cool, iniquity will abound, and moral corruption shall become worse than ever, which shall bring upon mankind the last and worse persecution of Antichrist, and the end of the world."

CHAPTER III.

PROPHECY OF ST. EDWARD, KING OF ENGLAND, AND OF ST. MALACHY, ARCHBISHOP OF ARMAGH.

ON the occasion of the re-establishment of the Catholic hierarchy in England, by the present great and holy Pope, Pius IX., with a bull dated 29th of September, 1850, an unexpected paroxysm of Protestant bigotry was roused into fury, with a threat of renewed persecution against inoffensive Catholics. In order to calm the public mind, and to encourage his fellow English Catholics, Mr. Ambrose Lisle Philipps, a fervent convert from the Church of England, published an eloquent epistle, addressed to his noble coreligionist, the Earl of Shrewsbury, dated October 28, 1850, from which the following extracts are taken: —

"Let the *no-popery* cry resound from the centre to the extremities of England; let the smoking ashes of Protestant bigotry be stirred up again; we Catholics shall calmly proceed in our career, from which we never have deviated, irreproachable models of loyalty to our sovereign and to the constitution, faithful to all our Christian duties, and aspiring to all those divine virtues inculcated to us by the Catholic religion. Our Christian revenge for the insults heaped upon our heads by our enemies will be to pray to God for them, and to beseech our Lord to open their eyes, in order that they may perceive the dangerous state to which they are reduced, and may at last be brought, by his divine mercy and grace, to acknowledge the authority of the Holy Catholic Apostolic Church, the only Church empowered and commanded by Jesus Christ to teach all nations, and to which alone he intrusted the keys of the kingdom of heaven."

Mr. Philipps, in giving a sketch of English Catholic history, relates the following vision and revelation made to St. Edward: —

"During the month of January, 1066, the holy king of England, St. Edward the Confessor, was confined to his bed by his last illness, in his royal Westminster Palace. St. Aelred, Abbot of Recvaux, in Yorkshire, relates that a short time before his happy death, this holy king was rapt in an ecstasy, when two pious Benedictine monks of Normandy, whom he had known in his youth, during his exile in that country, appeared to him, and revealed to him what was to happen in England in future centuries, and the cause of the terrible punishment. They said: 'The extreme corruption and wickedness of the English nation has provoked the just anger of God. When malice shall have reached the fulness of its measure, God will, in his wrath, send to the English people wicked spirits, who will punish and afflict them with great severity, by separating the green tree from its parent stem the length of three furlongs. But at last this same tree, through the compassionate mercy of God, and without any national (governmental) assistance, shall return to its original root, reflourish, and bear abundant fruit.' After having heard these prophetical words, the saintly King Edward opened his eyes, returned to his senses, and the vision vanished. He immediately related all he had seen and heard to his virgin spouse, Edgitha, to Stigard, Archbishop of Canterbury, and to Harold, his successor to the throne, who were in his chamber, praying around his bed."

This vision of our great and venerated monarch, St. Edward, has ever been very dear to the Catholics of England, and the interpretation given it by our Catholic ancestors is most important at this present epoch.

They have always believed that the evil spirits mentioned in it were the Protestant innovators, who pretended, in the sixteenth century, to reform the Catholic Church in England. The severance of the green tree from its trunk signifies the separation of the English Church from the centre of Catholic unity, from the root of the Catholic Church, from the holy Roman See, which has been for England, in a most special manner, the original root and source of her Catholicity. This tree, however, had to be separated from its life-giving root the distance of *three furlongs*. These three furlongs are understood to signify three centuries, at the end of which England shall return to its Roman Catholic Apostolic stem, without the help of human hands, and, being once more reunited to it, she shall bud forth flowers of virtue and abundant fruits of holy actions.

In corroboration of this ancient prophetical vision, we give here the prophecy of St. Malachy, Archbishop of Armagh. It was copied by the learned Benedictine Dom. Mabillon, from an ancient manuscript preserved at Clairvaux, and transmitted by him to the martyred successor of the saint, Oliver Plunkett. It is to the effect that his beloved native isle would undergo, at the hands of England, oppression, persecution, and calamities of every kind, during a week of centuries; but that she would preserve her fidelity to God and to his Church amidst all her trials. At the end of seven centuries she would be delivered from her cruel oppressors, who, in their turn, would be subjected to dreadful chastisements, and that Catholic Ireland would be instrumental in bringing back the British nation to that divine faith which Protestant England had, during more than three hundred years, so rudely endeavored to wrest from her. May God soon grant to that long-suffering nation, so noble, so Christian, a vengeance, that she may return good for evil.

CHAPTER IV.

PREVISIONS AND PREDICTIONS ABOUT ENGLAND, OF ST. PAUL OF THE CROSS AND OF DOMENICO SAVIO.

THE eighteenth century, the most disastrous for Catholic France, was eminently an epoch of great and holy men for Italy. In that century Italy was conspicuous for the birth and holy life of between fifteen and twenty illustrious servants of God, several of whom have already been solemnly canonized, others beatified, and more declared venerable by the Holy See, and at present under process of beatification in Rome. In this last class we find foremost the venerable Bishop of Macerata, Vincent Maria Strambi, a Passionist, who wrote the admirable life of St. Paul of the Cross, with whom he lived, and from which work we cull the following previsions and predictions of the holy founder of the Passionists, about England.

St. Paul of the Cross was born at the beginning of the year 1694, in the town of Ovada, at that time under the Catholic government of the Republic of Genoa.

From his earliest age Paul Francis began to practise the severest bodily mortifications and penances, which he heroically continued until the end of his long and laborious apostolic life. He from his childhood conceived a most tender devotion to the mysteries of Our Saviour's Passion, whence he derived the idea of a Religious Congregation, which, in subsequent years, he founded in company with his saintly brother, John Baptist Danei, after having obtained in Rome the blessing and the permission of Pope Benedict XIII.

Subsequent pontiffs formally approved the same Religious Congregation. St. Paul of the Cross was a person of most sincere and profound humility, a great lover of prayer, penance, and solitude ; yet ever full of an active zeal for the conversion and salvation of Christian sinners and deluded heretics. God communicated to him the gift of working miracles, which is continued at the present day through his sacred relics. He died at the head house of his Religious Congregation in Rome on the 18th of October, 1775, aged nearly eighty-two years. He was endowed with an eminent spirit of prophecy. Among his many predictions he foretold that about a hundred years after his death an ecumenical council should be held, when it would be found necessary, on account of the deplorable condition of human society, to define the existence of God, of the adorable Trinity, and of the incarnation of the eternal Word, etc. He distinctly foretold the re-establishment of the Society of Jesus. In one of the latest Lives of this great saint, published in Rome about the time of his canonization, in the year 1867, we learn that a letter of condolence was addressed by St. Paul of the Cross, founder of the Passionists, to the Superior General of the Society of Jesus in Rome, in the year 1773, in which letter, after expressing his cordial sympathy in the severe trial of the afflicted head of the illustrious society, and after exhorting him to resignation in the inscrutable and mysterious designs of God, St. Paul most clearly foretells the speedy restoration and formal re-establishment of the Society of Jesus, promising that it should again, and more than ever, flourish in holiness, zeal, and sacred learning. So far all this has been verified.

We must now pass to his prophetic previsions about England. During more than fifty years St. Paul of the

Cross almost continually prayed for the return of England to the Catholic faith. He often said that England was so deeply fixed in his mind and heart, that he could not forget it in his prayers. We must remark, however, that under the idea of England he embraced the United Kingdom of Great Britain and Ireland. He was often heard to say: *Poor England! poor England! once the island of saints, turned now into a den of heresy, I cannot forget to pray for that great nation. God, I believe, will be merciful to her.*

Whilst in prayer St. Paul had several times visions and revelations about the approaching reconversion of England to the Catholic faith. He saw in spirit his religious sons established in England, and working for the conversion and sanctification of souls in that nation. As we gather from the Appendix in the third volume of St. Paul's Life, the Passionists have been established in England since the year 1842, and possess now several monasteries in Great Britain and Ireland. It is well known that a certain Father Dominic, the first founder of the Passionists in England, a religious of profound learning and eminent virtue, highly esteemed by the late Cardinal Wiseman, received into the Catholic Church many converts from Protestantism, among whom were several members of the famous Oxford University, the most remarkable of them being the celebrated Dr. John Newman, the worthy superior of the Oratorian Fathers in Birmingham, Warwickshire. Several thousands of converts have since 1842 been received in the Church by Passionist missionaries in Great Britain and Ireland. Some of the congregations attached to their churches are mainly composed of converts from Protestantism.

We will close this chapter with another hopeful vision of the youthful prophet, Dominico Savio.

Dominico Savio was born April 2, 1842, and died March 9, 1857. The Rev. John Bosco, founder of the seminary of St. Francis de Sales, in Turin, Italy, wrote his Life, which was first published in the year 1859, and reprinted in 1860 and 1861.

This pious and truly virtuous youth, anxious to embrace the ecclesiastical state of life, entered the above-mentioned seminary in order the better to prepare himself for this sublime vocation. The stainless conduct of his life, his solid and fervent piety, rendered him a model of virtue to all his young companions in the seminary. Though but a boy fifteen years old, his holiness was already so extraordinary that, about the end of his short life, God elevated him in ecstasies, and illumined his beautiful and innocent soul with visions and revelations, which through humility he used to call *distractions*. In speaking with the zealous director of the seminary, Dominic often expressed to him his eager desire of seeing and speaking with the Pope before his own death, because he had something of great impartance to communicate to him. At last the same director asked Dominic what it was that he was so anxious to manifest to his Holiness the Pope? The pious youth answered, "If I could speak to the Pope, I would tell him that among all his great trials he would never cease to occupy himself with a special solicitude about England, because God prepares a great triumph in that kingdom for the Catholic religion." "But upon what foundation do you ground these assertions, my child?" "Well I will tell it to you, reverend sir, provided you do not mention it to any of my companions, lest they may laugh at me; but if you, sir, go to Rome, please to relate all to the Holy Father. You may know, then, that on the morning of the seventh day of September, 1856, whilst I was making my thanksgiving after holy communion, I was overtaken by a strong *distraction* (vision, ecstasy), during which it seemed to me to behold a most extensive plain full with people enveloped in a thick fog. They were moving about like persons, who, having lost their way in darkness, know not whither to place their feet. A person near me said, 'This country is England.' I was about asking other things, when I beheld the Sovereign Pontiff, exactly as I have seen Pope Pius IX. in large paintings. He wore a magnificent robe, and, holding in his hand a most brilliant torch, he kept advancing towards that immense multitude of people; as he came nearer, the fog was so completely dissipated by the bright light in the Pope's hand, that the people remained surrounded by as much light as when the sun shines at full meridian day. . . . . The friend near me explained that the bright light in the hand of the Pope was the Catholic religion, which will again enlighten the English people."

The Rev. John Bosco, mentioned above, went to Rome in the year 1858, on which occasion he related to the Sovereign Pontiff Pius IX. this holy youth's vision, which the Pope heard with much satisfaction.

This prophecy is in a fair way of being accomplished in England. Since the re-establishment of the Hierarchy, several hundred members of the Universities of Oxford and Cambridge, some of whom are eminent professors, have renounced Protestant error, and embraced Catholic truth. Many formerly Episcopal ministers are now zealous and learned Catholic priests and missionaries in England and Ireland.

There is scarcely any noble family in Great Britain without some near relative professing the Catholic faith and worshipping at a Catholic altar.

A fair calculation would show that, on an average, there have been a thousand converts made every month in England to the Catholic faith during the last twenty years.

The wisdom and prudent zeal of the Catholic episcopate and clergy of Great Britain, the enlightened piety and devotion of the English Catholic nobility, the large number of educated converts, the fervor and common-sense of the people, the calm energy and uncommon ability displayed by the Catholic press, and the compact union of the whole Catholic body, argue well for the future conversion of England to Catholicity.

CHAPTER V.

LETTERS OF ST. FRANCIS DI PAOLA.

THE following prophetical letters of St. Francis di Paola are mentioned by several authors worthy of confidence for their learning and virtues: Luke Montoya, a Spaniard, who wrote the Chronicles of the Friar Minims, of whom St. Francis di Paola was the founder; Francis Sachelli, an Italian, in his Latin essays; John James Courroisier, a French author, in his Treasure of Spiritual Works, Treatise IX. chapters 2 and 3; Vincent Fussari, Italian, *Prolegomena in Apocalypsim;* Father P. Morales, a Spaniard, in his Chronicle of Andalusia, text 5 and 12; Father P. Ivan de Moral, text 5 and 12; Father Cornelius a Lapide, in his celebrated commentaries on the Holy Scriptures, Apocalypse, chapter 17.

These letters were addressed by St. Francis to a certain Simeon de Limena, Lord of Montalto, in Calabria, Kingdom of Naples, who was a very pious Christian, originally from Spain, and a great benefactor to St. Francis and to his spiritual children. The extraordinary humility and holiness of St. Francis di Paola is well known by every Catholic. Through the miraculous intercession of St. Francis of Assisium, when his pious parents were advanced in years, he was born in Paola, near the sea in Calabria, midway from Naples to Riggio.

From his childhood Francis began to practise great bodily austerities, and at the age of fifteen he retired to a solitary cave. He was only twenty years old when the fame of his sanctity drew some companions to his solitary retreat, and they began the severe and contemplative religious Order of Minims, who abstain and fast continually during their life. The holy man was favored with an eminent spirit of prophecy. Among other instances, for three years before it happened, he several times foretold the taking of Constantinople by the Turks, which prophecy was verified May 24, 1453, under the personal command of Mahomet II.

He also foretold that Otranto, one of the most important places in, and the key of, the Kingdom of Naples, would fall into the hands of the same infidels, which, in fact, happened in August, 1480.

But he also promised the Christians, and especially the pious John Count, of Arena, one of the generals of Ferdinand I., king of Naples, certain success the following year, when, in reality, the Christian arms recovered that most important city, and drove the Turks completely out of Italy.

In the year 1482, our saint was called to Plessis,

near Paris, by Louis XI., king of France, who was in much trouble, and whose death St. Francis foretold. During the course of his long life he raised seven persons from death. He handled burning coals in his hands without receiving the slightest injury. He wrought innumerable miracles. He lived to be ninety-one years of age, and died April 2, 1508, in his new convent at Plessis, near Paris, where his body remained incorrupt in the church until the impiety of the Calvinist Protestants in 1562 dragged it through the public streets, and burned it at a fire which they had made from the sacred wood of a large cross and holy crucifix. (See Butler's Lives of Saints, 2d April.)

The original of the following letter is preserved as a precious relic by the respectable family Benedetti in the city of Spoleto, States of the Church:—

MY MOST ESTEEMED LORD, — Through the grace of the Holy Spirit, and through your merits, but not through my virtue, the spirit of prophecy is granted to me often to foretell most wonderful events in relation to the reformation of the Church of the Most High.

From your lordship shall be born the great leader of the Holy Militia of the Holy Spirit which shall overcome the world, and shall possess the earth so completely that no king or lord shall be able to exist, except he belongs to the Sacred Host of the Holy Ghost. These devout men shall wear on their breasts, and much more within their hearts, the sign of the living God, namely, the cross.

The first members of this holy Order shall be natives of the city of . . . . where iniquity, vice, and sin abound. But they shall be converted from evil to good; from rebels against God they shall become most fervent and most faithful in his divine service. That city shall be cherished by God and by the great monarch, the elect and the beloved of the Most High Lord. For the sake of that place all holy souls who have done penance in it shall pray in the sight of God for that city and for its inhabitants. When the time shall come of the immense and most right justice of the Holy Spirit, his Divine Majesty wills that such city become converted to God, and that many of its citizens follow the great Prince of the Holy Army. The first person that will openly wear the sign of the living God shall belong to that city, because he will through a letter be commanded by a *holy hermit* to have it impressed in his heart and to wear it externally on his breast.

That man will begin to meditate on the secrets of God about the long visitation which the Holy Spirit will make and the dominion that he will exercise over the world through the Holy Militia. O! happy man, who shall receive from the Most High the greatest privileges! He will interpret the hidden secrets of the Holy Ghost, and he shall often excite the admiration of men by his revealed knowledge of the internal secrets of their hearts. O, rejoice, my lord, because that Prince above other princes, and King over other kings will hold you in the greatest veneration, and, after having been crowned with three most admirable crowns, will exalt that city, will declare it free and the seat of the Empire, and it shall become one of the first cities of the world. I say nothing more. Kissing your hand, together with the inhabitants of . . . . whom I beg, when they shall see this letter, to receive it as a prophecy, I remain,

Perpetual servant,

FRIAR FRANCIS DI PAOLA.

From our house of PAOLA, 5th February, 1482.

Second Letter.

The original of this letter is preserved in the city of Montalto in Calabria :—

MY EXCELLENT LORD, — You and your consort desire to have children; you shall have them. Your holy offspring shall be admired upon earth. Among your descendants there will be one who shall be like the sun amidst the stars. He shall be a first-born son; in his childhood he will be like a saint; in his youth, a great sinner; then he will be converted entirely to God and will do great penance; his sins will be forgiven him, and he shall become a great saint.

He shall be a great captain and prince of holy men, who shall be called *the holy Cross-bearers of Jesus Christ*, with whom he shall destroy the Mahometan sect and the rest of the infidels. He shall annihilate all the heresies and tyrannies of the world. He shall reform the Church of God by means of his followers, who shall be the best men upon earth in holiness, in arms, in science, and in every virtue, because such is the will of the Most High. They shall obtain the dominion of the whole world, both temporal and spiritual, and they shall support the Church of God until the end of time. I say no more.

FRIAR FRANCIS DI PAOLA.

25th March, 1485.

Third Letter.†

MY EXCELLENT LORD, — O great treasurer of the Holy Spirit! O new Abraham upon earth! [After these words St. Francis gives a long and severe reproach to ecclesiastics for their covetousness, indolence, and want of charity and zeal for the spiritual welfare of the people; then he says:] Let the kings and princes in Christendom be ashamed of themselves, who live without charity. God has granted them means to lead a good life, and they are bad, having their hands shut up with the accursed lock of avarice; they are stingy in good works and prodigal in doing evil; they spend more than what they have in vanities and in useless things, in order to indulge their passions, oppressing their poor subjects. O wretched, unhappy men! Do you know what vanity is? Do you understand that your people are the creatures and subjects of the Most High God? They are men like you; children of Adam like you; they have been given to you as subjects, not that you might rob and maltreat them, but in order that you govern them with that diligence and care required in the shepherd towards his own sheep. O ye worse by far than ravenous wolves and worse than hungry lions! Be ashamed of your wicked actions, ye Christians by name, but without truth; you are worse than the infidels, O ye tyrants of the people of God! Woe to you!

God Almighty will exalt a very poor man of the blood of the Emperor Constantine, son of St. Helena, and of the seed of Pepin, who shall on his breast wear the sign which you have seen at the beginning of this letter (†). Through the power of the Most High he shall confound the tyrants, the heretics, and infidels. He will gather a grand army, and the angels shall fight for them; they shall kill all God's enemies. O my Lord! that man shall be one of your posterity, because you come from the blood of Pepin.

FRIAR FRANCIS DI PAOLA.

25th of April, 1485.

Fourth Letter.

MY EXCELLENT LORD AND BENEFACTOR, — From the beginning of the world, after the creation of man, and to the end of human generation, there have been and there shall be seen wonderful events upon the earth. *Four hundred years shall not pass* when his Divine Majesty shall visit the world with a new religious order much needed, which shall effect more good among men than all other religious institutions combined. This religious order shall be the last and the best in the Church; it shall proceed with arms, with prayer, and with hospitality. Woe to tyrants, to heretics, and to infidels, to whom no pity shall be shown, because such is the will of the Most High! An infinite number of wicked men shall perish through the hands of the Cross-bearers, the true servants of Jesus Christ. They shall act like good husbandmen when they extirpate noxious weeds and prickly thistles from the wheat-field. These holy servants of God shall purify the earth with the deaths of innumerable wicked men. The head and captain of these holy servants of God shall be one of your posterity, and he shall be the great reformer of the Church of God.

FRANCIS DI PAOLA.

From SPEZZANO, 13th of January, 1489.

Fifth Letter.

The original of the following letter is preserved in the city of Montalto in Calabria, Kingdom of Naples, and has been copied by John Baptist Francesco, a public notary: —

MY LORD AND BROTHER IN JESUS CHRIST OUR LORD, — May his Divine Majesty reign in every place, namely, in heaven, upon earth, and even in hell. How spiritually blind are those persons who, having no thought about the things of God, fix their end in earthly objects! Wretched men! by far worse than the very beasts which are guided by their senses, because they cannot have reason; but when men abandon the use of their reason, they become brutalized. Hence they shall ever be in confusion. Let, therefore, the princes of this world be prepared for the greatest scourges to fall upon them. But from whom? First from heretics and infidels, then from the holy and most faithful Cross-bearers elected by the Most High, who, not succeeding in converting heretics with science, shall have to make a vigorous use of their arms. Many cities and villages shall be in ruins, with the deaths of an innumerable quantity of bad and good men. The infidels also will fight against Chritians and heretics, sacking, destroying, and killing the largest portion of Christians. Lastly, the army, styled of the Church, namely, the holy Cross-bearers, shall move, not against Christians or Christianity, but against the infidels in pagan countries, and they shall conquer all those kingdoms with the death of a very great number of infidels. After this they shall turn their victorious arms against bad Christians, and shall destroy all the rebels against Jesus Christ. These holy Cross-bearers shall reign and dominate holily over the world until the end of time. The founder of these holy men shall, my lord, be one of your posterity. But when shall this take place? When crosses with the stigmas shall be seen, and the crucifix shall be carried as the standard. [Miraculous crosses have lately been seen in Germany, and several holy persons have now stigmas. One of these holy souls is in San Francisco.] May our blessed Lord Jesus Christ reign! *Gaudeamus omnes ; let us all rejoice* who are in the service of the Most High, because the great visitation and reformation of the world is approaching, when there shall be only one fold and one Shepherd.

25th of March, 1490.
F. FRANCIS DI PAOLA.

Sixth Letter.

MY EXCELLENT LORD, — The time is coming when his Divine Majesty will visit the world with a new religious order of holy Cross-bearers, who will carry a crucifix, or the image of our crucified Lord, lifted up upon the principal standard in view of all. This standard will be admired by all good Catholics; but at the beginning it will be derided by bad Christians and by infidels. Their sneers shall, however, be changed into mourning when they shall witness the wonderful victories achieved through it against tyrants, heretics, and infidels. Many wicked men and obstinate rebels against God shall perish; their souls will be plunged into hell. This punishment shall fall upon all those transgressors of the Divine commandments who with new and false doctrines will attempt to corrupt mankind and turn men against the ministers of God's worship. The same chastisement is due to all obstinate sinners, *but not to those who sin through weakness, because these being converted, doing penance, and amending the conduct of their life, shall find the divine mercy of the Most High full of kindness towards them.* O holy Cross-bearers of the Most High Lord, how very pleasing you will be to the great God, much more than the children of Israel! God will through your instrumentality work more wonderful prodigies than he has ever done before with any nation. You shall destroy the sect of Mahomet, and all infidels of every kind and of every sect. You shall put an end to all the heresies of the world by extinguishing all tyrants. You will remove every cause of complaint by establishing a universal peace, which shall last until the end of time. You will work the sanctification of mankind. O holy men! People blessed of the Most Holy Trinity! Your victorious founder shall triumph over the world, the flesh, and the Devil. *Laus Deo et omnibus Sanctis ejus. May God and all his saints be praised.*

FRIAR FRANCIS DI PAOLA.

7th of March, 1495.

Seventh Letter.

MY EXCELLENT LORD, — Let your soul rejoice! for his Divine Majesty manifests through you such wonderful signs and great miracles, according to what I, by God's will, have often and again written and foretold to you. One of your posterity shall achieve greater deeds and work greater wonders than your lordship. That man will be a great sinner in his youth, but like St. Paul he shall be drawn and converted to God. He shall be the great founder of a new religious order different from all the others. He shall divide it into three classes, namely: 1. Military knights; 2. Solitary priests; 3. Most pious hospitallers. This shall be the last religious order in the Church, and it will do more good for our holy religion than all other religious institutes. By force of arms he shall take possession of a great kingdom. He shall destroy the sect of Mahomet, extirpate all tyrants and heresies. He shall bring the world to a holy mode of life. There will be one fold and one Shepherd. He shall reign until the end of time. On the whole earth there shall be only twelve kings, one emperor, and one pope. Rich gentlemen shall be very few, but all saints. May Jesus Christ be praised and blessed; for he has vouchsafed to grant to me, a poor unworthy sinner, the spirit of prophecy, not in an obscure way as to his other servants, but has enabled me to write and to speak in a most clear manner. I know that unbelieving and reprobate persons will scoff at my letters and will reject them; but they will be received by those faithful Catholic souls who aspire to the possession of heaven. These letters shall infuse such sweetness of divine love in their hearts, that they will be delighted in perusing them often, and in taking copies of them, because such is the will of the Most High. In these letters it will be found out who belongs to our blessed Lord Jesus Christ and who does not, who is a predestinate or a reprobate. Much better will this be known through the holy sign of the living God. He shall be a saint of God who will take it, love it, and wear it. Nothing more occurs to me.

FRIAR FRANCIS DI PAOLA.

18th August, 1496.

Some will condemn St. Francis for announcing that the Holy Militia will kill such large numbers of men; but we must reflect that he speaks or writes as a prophet, namely, what was revealed to him by God, as he states. The prophets of the Bible and our Divine Lord made even more dreadful prophecies. Besides, menacing prophecies are generally conditional; the punishment is moderated in proportion as the sinner is converted. Moreover, the new religious Military Order so often foretold in these letters will be animated by the true spirit of Christianity, which is a spirit of charity and justice. They will not wage any unjust war, nor will they practise cruelties and barbarities even in just wars. They will fight because they shall be obliged to fight, for the defence of their just rights, for the rights of God and of religion, of conscience and of Christian society. The modern pagans, the Turks, heretics, and other sectaries and impious men, have already too long violated the rights of true Christianity, of justice, and of conscience. They will soon become even worse, and attempt more than ever to oppress the true believers, persecute them in every way in their power, and attempt to exterminate the Catholic religion, if they could. But God will not permit it, and he will in due time and very soon raise valiant defenders, who will be assisted by his holy angels in fighting the battles of the Lord God of Hosts. Their victory, in spite of all the malice and efforts of evil spirits and of wicked men, will be most certain and complete. God will be with his faithful servants. *If God be with us, who shall be against us?* (Rom. viii. 31.)

CHAPTER VI.

DAVID LAZZARETTI.

WE place the following important account immediately after the seven letters of St. Francis di Paola, because if its authenticity is realized, the prophetical predictions contained in these seven letters are in all probability about to be accomplished. However, whether David Lazzaretti is really or not the holy founder of the new religious order foretold in each of St. Francis's letters, yet the four hundred years fixed by the saint in his fourth letter have arrived, or at least are very near. That letter is dated January 13, 1489; we are now in the year 1873. But the saint prophesied that *four hundred years should not pass before the new great religious order should be established.* Before its establishment the founder, elected by God and prophecied by St. Francis, must be converted in his youth, do much penance, be very poor, and full of a burning zeal for the welfare of the Catholic religion. Now all these coincidences we will find in David Lazzaretti.

The following particulars are literally translated from *Derniers Avis Prophétiques*, by Victor C. de Stenay (*Un Sauveur inattendue*, "An Unexpected Saviour," p. 251): —

From divers sources, both French and Italian, we have learned that a young Italian, under the assumed name of David Lazzaretti (the youthful Lazarus, or resuscitated), shall have to play a great *rôle* in the approaching future events of France and Italy. He is a native of Tuscany. In his early youth he joined the Garibaldians, and fought with them against the Pope's troops at the battle of Mentana. It seems that he on that occasion was mortally wounded, but shortly after miraculously cured in body and converted to God, like St. Paul, in an extraordinary manner. The blessed Virgin Mary, St: Peter, St. Michael the Archangel, and Manfredi Pallavicini appeared to him. The prince of the apostles impressed on his forehead a royal crown, and *a star visible to the eyes of all men.*

Since that time, namely, 2d of November, 1867, this extraordinary young man has been leading an hermitical and penitential life in the cave of St. Angelo della Rupe Santa, near Montorio Romano in Sabine, not far from and between Rome and Terni. His good works begin already to bear their fruits; for he reclaimed to a good life more than three hundred young men, who are preparing to defend the Church at the price of their blood when the hour fixed by Divine Providence shall arrive. David Lazzaretti is highly esteemed by ecclesiastical authority. He has written a beautiful pamphlet, and published also some surprising prophecies about himself. In one of his visions he was commanded to rebuild the ancient and ruined Monastery of Saint Angelo, which has to become the asylum of great saints. Having gone to that place he found the monastery in the state shown him in his vision. Aided by the good people of the neighborhood, he began the work of reconstruction, which is already far advanced. But Lazzaretti had to return to Tuscany in order to build a grand church at Monte Labro in Archidosso, province of Grossetto, next to the States of the Church. At Montorio Romano, David Lazzaretti is considered a holy man sent by God to deliver Italy from the yoke which so heavily presses upon her, as Moses was sent to the Israelites to deliver them from Egyptian bondage. All seem to agree that the salvation of Italy has to come forth from the cave of St. Angelo della Rupe Santa (namely, *Saint Angel of the Holy Rock*). About two years ago, this privileged young man discovered, very unexpectedly, the grave and the mortal remains of a son of King Pepin. Here we quote the words of a letter written upon this subject, dated December 5, 1871: "A dead person appeared to him (to David) in the cavern, wherein he was doing penance, and, pointing down to a certain spot, said to him: *Dig in this spot, but beware; thou shalt die if thou excavate without the presence of witnesses.* He invited witnesses, among whom there were many priests. In their presence he dug up the earth and found human bones. During all this time the dead person was present. As soon as the bones were discovered, the apparition said: *My mission is now accomplished; read, there on the sepulchral stone.* All the persons present read the words: *Filius Pepini;* Pepin's son, or, the son of Pepin. Then the dead person continued, addressing David Lazzaretti: '*Thou art my descendant; thou shalt be king of France;* thou shalt be conducted to the banks of the Rhine by the Emperor of Russia, who shall say, "Frenchmen, behold your king!" Thou shalt conquer all Germany, Greece, Italy, and Spain. Thou shalt convert the Musselmen. In Germany all the soldiers dressed in white habits with a cross on their breast shall triumph through prayer, without drawing their swords; they shall have over them invisible and well-disciplined hosts (of angels fighting for them).'"

From all this it appears that David Lazzaretti is a descendant of King Pepin. God likes to prepare his great and extraordinary works in secret. He envelops them in mystery. The veil will be removed when his divine providence judges best. Thus the pretended wisdom of statesmen is confounded, and all their prearranged plans are completely upset and rendered useless, and often turned against their most sanguine expectations. O, when will men acknowledge that *there is no wisdom, there is no prudence, there is no counsel against the Lord!* (Prov. xxi. 30.)

To return to our extraordinary youth, David Lazzaretti; some well-informed persons think that the Duke of Normandy had a truly legitimate son from a lady who may have been suspected by some persons, but to whom the Duke, on account of his known piety, must have been married according to the laws of the Church. It is well known that the Duchess of Angouleme, having about the end of her life grave remorses of conscience in relation to the Duke, her brother, commissioned some trusty persons to place in the hands of the Pope some most important papers relative to this subject. If David Lazzaretti is the legitimate son of Louis XVII., his holy and penitential life renders him doubly worthy of being the precursor of Henry V., as an honorable reparation to the memory of his royal father. In fact, the prophecy of Blois, and others which will be read in this book, announces the advent to the throne of France of a young monarch not expected by any person. The following are the words of the prophecy of Blois: *The king who shall reign will not be the one expected by many. The true savior of France shall be a person unexpected by her.*

We shall corroborate this prediction by another remarkable prophecy, which seems to agree in a striking manner with these statements about David Lazzaretti. This prophecy was made in the twelfth century. It was published in the *Liber Mirabilis* (the marvellous book), in the year 1524. It was most probably made by William, Bishop of Marsico Nuovo, because with some variations it is found among the prophecies of this Neapolitan bishop, as it can be seen in the marvellous book of the hermit Theodore. It is divided into three titles, as follows: —

1. *A Good Prayer shall be computed as Treasure for the Poor.*

"There shall be a man who will live in a cavern in a most frugal manner, and he shall continually be in tears and groans, and in a total detachment from everything, when a star shall appear." (This star may be the one miraculously impressed on the forehead of David Lazzaretti, as we have stated above; or the next Pope, whose title shall be *Lumen in Celo; Light in Heaven*.)

2. *Charity.*

The sceptre shall unexpectedly and as by enchantment be restored to a man of the name De N, (Normandy, or son of the Duke de Normandie?) Heaven shall have announced this event, for a voice from on high, coming from an invisible being, shall cry aloud: *Make haste to go to the West.* [France is west of Italy.] *You will find there a man who is my friend. Lead the just into the royal mansions. Meek and ingenuous, able above all to read the future, he shall find the road to the empire.*

3. *Reign of Concord.*

"Behold here the man of the mysterious race (of Pepin and Constantine) who, coming from his obscure cavern in complete poverty, goes to begin a brilliant life, the truest image of an edifying life."

Is not this a coincidence of surprising exactitude? We wish, however, to use every possible circumspection in interpreting and applying these details of an event so extraordinary and so wonderful, because the correspondents may have been led into some mistake and mixed in their narrative some exaggeration. Let us have a little more patience, and impending future events will soon remove the veil from the eyes of expectant humanity.

We give here some extracts from a letter written by David Lazzaretti and addressed to the Romans. It has relation to visions seen by him on the 20th of March, 1871. This writing is very extraordinary. We translate it from the Italian: "Ah Rome! ah Romans! I am shedding tears over your impending calamities, as Jeremias on the walls of Jerusalem was weeping for the terrible events of the future. Ah Rome! Rome! I look on thee from the summit of these mountains, and I tremble. I am terrified, and weep on thy account. I have many things to announce to thee of the evils and calamities thou shalt have to suffer; but for the present moment I cannot, because . . . . I shall only say that Heaven is irritated on account of thine . . . . and the people cry for justice. The days already announced by me are not distant," etc. Seven great personages, who seemed to be the seven exterminating angels of the seven capital sins, appeared to David Lazzaretti. One of them uttered the following words: "My Creator and my Master, our swords are ready; we attend the number of the victims. Our legions are in order. Hell is roused against them; its fury is terrible; the clamor of the population is universal; the wicked ask for vengeance; the just entreat for peace and pardon; and amidst these two clamors resounds a confused multitude of voices deafening heaven and earth and exclaiming, Justice! justice!! justice!!! My Creator, my Lord, what must we do? A voice severe and terrible, like thunder before a horrible and impending storm, answered the angel's request: Go! go!! go!!! against those who insult my name, despise my holiness, profane my faith, falsify my religion, violate my law, abuse my worship, deform my truth, and despise my clemency. Go! go!! go!!! against the wicked, who are the enemies of my justice and of my law. Let them be exterminated from the number of the living. Let those who ask for blood pay with blood. Let vengeance be executed on those who demand vengeance. Let justice be done to those who cry for justice. Go! go!! yes, go! my wrath shall be appeased through justice. Justice, therefore! yes, justice!"

The same angel, then turning himself towards the seer, said to him: "Man of .... continue in the way of thy mission; be free in thy works and affectionate towards the whole world. Proclaim, yes, proclaim all that has happened to thee, and spread thy writings among all nations. Announce to the Romans our visit to this holy place (*the cave of St. Angelo della Rupe Santa, near Montorio Romano in Sabine*), in order that through their instrumentality all distant nations may come to know it. I announce to thee that within a short time Rome shall lose its prestige and shall weep for the loss of her .... (Pope?). Her splendor shall be eclipsed for a short time. Proclaim, yes, proclaim all this, and join to it the tidings of thy arrival. Because a day will come when thy writings will be shown to the people, who, trembling and confused, shall be surprised at them, for they shall recognize them as the process of their wickedness foretold beforehand by God's command."

Whether David Lazzaretti shall be the great personage foretold by St. Francis di Paola and by the holy hermit Theodore, we know not. A few years more, and the truth will be better understood. It is a remarkable fact, however, that the providential advent of a similar personage is announced by many prophetical predictions, which can be more fully read in their proper places in this volume. The fact is, that almost all the principal prophecies more or less explicitly announce this advent. (See Chapter XIV., page 208.)

CHAPTER VII.

PROPHETICAL PREVISIONS AND PREDICTIONS OF THE VENERABLE BARTHOLOMEW HOLZHAUSER.

THE Venerable Bartholomew Holzhauser is considered one of the most enlightened commentators of the Apocalypse. His interpretation is evidently the work of Divine inspiration. Having once been asked where he could have received such extraordinary lights for the interpretation of so difficult a book, the humble servant of God with tears in his eyes answered: *I am nothing but a little child, whose hand and pen his teacher holds and guides to make him write.* Our best guaranty for the prophecies of Holzhauser is the exact realization of his predictions referring to events already come to pass.

Bartholomew Holzhauser was born in Longanau, near Augsburg, in the year 1613, and died at Bingen, near Mayence, on the 20th of May, 1658. He founded a religious congregation of regular priests in the year 1640, which was approved by Pope Innocent IX. In the year 1658, he announced that within a short time Catholic priests would, under pain of death, be prohibited during one hundred and twenty years to say mass in England and in the English American Colonies. In fact, in 1658 this impious and cruel prohibition was proclaimed in England and only revoked in the year 1778, exactly one hundred and twenty years after its promulgation. The same royal decree was extended to the American Colonies in the year 1663, and lasted until 1783, again one hundred and twenty years' duration. So, likewise, more than one hundred and thirty years before the event, he had foretold in the most minute details the French Revolution of 1789, all of which has literally been realized. Let these few but striking instances suffice to enhance our confidence in his Apocalyptic interpretations. This venerable man divides the periods and the duration of the Church from Jesus Christ until the end of the world into seven ages or seven different epochs. He founds this seven-fold division on the seven churches of Asia, the seven candlesticks, the seven stars, the seven seals, seven spirits, seven trumpets, seven plagues of the Apocalypse, and also on the seven days of creation mentioned in the first chapter of Genesis. According to his statement, the first age or special epoch of the Church begins from Jesus Christ and lasts until the first persecution under the cruel pagan emperor, Nero; the second, from Nero to Constantine the Great; the third, from Constantine till Charlemagne; the fourth, from Charlemagne to Charles V., the pontificate of Leo X., and the heresy of Martin Luther; the fifth age, from Luther to the Great Pope, *Papa Angelicus*, and the Great Monarch; the sixth will open at the death of these two great men, and shall last till the last persecution of Antichrist;

the seventh will introduce the elect to the eternal sabbath.

We are at present more immediately concerned with the fifth age of the Church. According to the interpretation of Holzhauser, this age shall soon come to an end. During this epoch, he says, faithful Catholics shall be persecuted and oppressed by heretics and by bad Catholics. Everywhere shall be experienced deplorable calamities and terrible wars. Kingdoms shall be disorganized, thrones upset, monarchs killed. Men will conspire to proclaim republics, and finally the Church of Christ and his sacred ministers shall be despoiled of their property.

Are these the predictions of prophecy, or the faithful records of history? Observe that the predictions were made by the Venerable Bartholomew Holzhauser about three hundred years ago. They have been literally verified, the last portion of them under our own eyes. Now that, like Thomas, we have seen and touched, shall we believe? Let us now pass to his more hopeful and consoling promises for the immediate future.

At the sixth epoch of the Church, all unexpectedly shall, through the all-powerful hand of God, be effected such a wonderful change as to surpass all human imagination and expectation. There will be a great and holy pope, and a powerful monarch, who will come as the envoy of God to put an end to disorder. He will subject everything to his power, and will manifest a great zeal for the welfare of the true Church of Jesus Christ. All heresies shall be banished to hell, whence they issued; the Turkish Empire shall be broken up, and all nations shall come to and worship their God in the true Catholic and Roman faith. Then true love, concord, peace, and perfect happiness will reign supreme upon earth.

That powerful monarch will then be able to consider almost the entire world as his own inheritance. With God's special assistance he will free the earth from the presence of wicked men, will repair all ruins and banish all evil. It is he who will help to carry to a happy conclusion, after having passed through many tribulations, a general council that shall be the greatest and the last of all. He will use all his authority to have all its decrees executed. The God of heaven will bless him, and will put everything in his hands. (Interpretation of the Apocalypse, Latin edition of Bamburg, 1784, Tom. I. page 184, and Tom. II. page 6.)

CHAPTER VIII.

PROPHECY OF MARY LATASTE, A RELIGIOUS OF THE SACRED HEART.

MARY LATASTE was first a poor shepherdess and then became a lay sister among the Ladies of the Sacred Heart. On account of the great holiness of her life she deserved to receive, from the year 1832 to 1843, very extraordinary heavenly lights, visions, and revelations from God. She died in the year 1847. By order of her spiritual director she wrote many of these divine revelations, which were scrupulously examined by the Rt. Rev. Bishop of Aire, and allowed by him to be published in three volumes by Ambrose Bray. (Second edition, 1866.) We begin with a letter written by her to her confessor on the 20th of November, 1843, which has relation to France and to the Great Monarch.

"MONSIEUR LE CURÉ, — In this letter I write to you what Jesus Christ has said to me after receiving the Holy Communion. 'My daughter, I am the Master of my own word: I say all that I wish to say, when I wish, and to whom I wish, and nobody has any right to question me in this way.' 'Why, Lord, do you speak in such or such manner? Why do you use such words?' 'I know how to turn everything to my glory and to the economy of my providence in behalf of one particular soul as well as towards the entire universe. To-day I will speak to you about your country. Listen. I am the First King and the First Sovereign of France. I am the Master of all nations; in a particular manner I am the Master of France. When she is faithful in listening to my voice, I give her prosperity, eminence, greatness, and power above all other nations. When they are faithful in hearing my voice, I bless her population more abundantly than all other people of the earth. I have chosen France, to give her to my Church as her daughter of predilection. As soon as she bowed down her head under my yoke, France became the hope of my pontiffs, and very soon after their defence and their support. They gave to her the well-merited title of *First Daughter of the Church.* Now you know that all which is done to my Church I consider as done to myself. To the honor and glory of your country, I say that, during some ages, France has defended and protected my Church; she has been my instrument and the indestructible and visible rampart which I have given to my Church for protection against her enemies. From high heaven I will protect her, her kings and their subjects. What great men has she produced! It is I who have given her such men, who shall forever be her glory. My generosity is not exhausted for France.

My hands are full of graces which I should like to bestow upon her. *Why has she failed in her duty to me? Is it again required; shall it then be necessary for me to take the scourge of my justice?* What spirit of insane license has replaced in her heart the only spirit of true liberty, that comes from heaven, and which is subordination to the will of God? . . . . What spirit of arid and cold egotism has been substituted in her heart instead of that spirit of fervent charity from heaven, which is the love of God and of man? What spirit of unjust manœuvre, of trickery, and of deceitful policy has been substituted in her heart in place of the nobility of her conduct and of the straightforwardness of her word, — conduct and word formerly directed by truth, descended from heaven, which is God himself? I see yet, and shall ever find in the *kingdom of France*, men submissive to my will, men inflamed with charity, men friends of truth; but at this present hour their number is small. [Reflect it was in November, 1843.] I have raised to her kings, but she has chosen others according to her fancy. Has she not seen before, does she not perceive, that I use her will to punish her misconduct and to force her to raise her eyes up to me? Does she not feel herself humbled before the nations of the earth? Injustice struts with uplifted head, and appears invested with authority; she has no opposition, and acts as she lists. Impiety is making preparations to lift her haughty and proud forehead at a time which she does not believe distant, and which she is determined to hasten with all her might. *But in truth,* I tell you, *impiety shall be crushed, her projects shall be dissipated, her designs reduced to naught at that very moment when she will suppose them accomplished and forever executed.* O France! France!! . . . . how ingenious thou art both for irritating and for appeasing the justice of God! If thy crimes make the chastisements of Heaven fall upon thee, the virtue of charity will cry towards Heaven, *Mercy! O Lord, pity!* It will be permitted thee, O France, to behold the judgments of my irritated justice at a time which will be rendered manifest to thee. [Here Sister Mary Lataste announces the future apparition of La Salette.] But thou wilt also recognize the judgments of my compassion and of my mercy, and thou shalt say, *Praise and thanksgiving, love and gratitude to God, forever in time and during all eternity.* Yes, at a breath, which shall proceed from my mouth, the thoughts, projects, and labors of the impious shall disappear as smoke before the wind. What has been chosen shall be rejected; what has been rejected will be reassumed. What has been loved and esteemed shall be detested and despised; what has been hated and despised will again be esteemed and loved. Sometimes from a tree felled in a forest nothing more remains than the trunk; but a sprout comes forth in springtime, and in the course of years it develops and grows up into a magnificent tree, the honor of the forest. Pray for France; pray much and never cease from praying. *France shall not perish.*'"

In the year 1842, Sister Mary Lataste wrote the following prophecy to her spiritual director: —

"Behold what Jesus said to me after the Holy Communion: 'Afflictions shall come over the earth. Oppression shall reign in the city which I love, and where I have left my heart. She shall be in mourning and desolation, surrounded on every side by her enemies, like a bird caught in the net. *During three years and a little more, this city shall appear overcome.* But my Mother will come down to that city (Rome); she will take the hand of the *old man* (Pius IX. ?) sitting on the throne, and will say to him : Lo! the hour is come; rise up; behold thy enemies! I make them disappear, one after the other, and they shall disappear forevermore. Thou hast given me glory both on earth and in heaven. Behold, men venerate thy name, venerate thy courage, venerate thy power; thou shalt live, and I will live with thee. Dry up thy tears, old man; I bless thee (amen, amen).' "

Sister Mary adds : " Peace shall return to the world, because the blessed Virgin Mary will breathe over the storms, and shall quell them. Her name will be praised, blessed, and exalted forever. Prisoners or captives shall recover their liberty; exiles shall return to their country, and the unfortunate or unhappy shall be restored to peace and happiness. Between the most august Mary and her clients there will be a mutual exchange of prayers and graces, of love and affection. From the east to the west, from the north to the south, all shall proclaim the holy name of Mary; Mary conceived without original sin, Mary, queen of heaven and earth, amen."

This prophecy was written twelve years before the dogmatic definition of the Immaculate Conception by the reigning glorious Pontiff, Pope Pius IX. May he live, and Mary live with him. May he soon behold, like holy Simeon, the salvation of the Lord brought to him and to all his devoted and faithful children, in the virginal arms of Mary Immaculate.

CHAPTER IX.

VISIONS OF ELIZABETH MORA.

COMPILED from the process of her beatification, and from her Life, published in Italian, with the approbation of Monseigneur Villanova Castellani, Archbishop of Petra. This Life has been translated into the French language, and edited in Paris, 1869, by Sarlit.

Biographical Sketch.

Elizabeth Canori was born in Rome, from respectable parents, on the 21st of November, 1774, and in due time she was married to Christopher Mora, an advocate in the Roman Court, from whom she had several children. She had much to suffer from these, and more especially from her husband. But she made such good use of these trials that she rapidly advanced to the highest degree of Christian perfection. In the year 1820, Elizabeth joined the third order of the discalced or barefooted Trinitarians, and five years later, on the 5th of February, being fifty years of age, she died in Rome, in great odor of sanctity. Then, according to her prediction, her husband, Christopher Mora, was converted so entirely to God that he became a priest, and died a Minor Conventual Friar of St. Francis. From the process of the beatification of Elizabeth, introduced in Rome, we learn that this great servant of God wrought many miraculous cures, and that it was she who freed the young Count John Maria de Mastai Ferretti, the present Pope Pius IX., from epilepsy, which had so far prevented his admission into the ecclesiastical state. God had chosen Elizabeth as a victim of propitiation for his Church, capable of arresting the punishments of Divine justice, provoked by the iniquities of mankind. We give here an instance of the power of this voluntary expiation and intercession in behalf of sinners, which is very important to observe at the present time, when, more than ever, we are in great need of such heroic devotion. On the 24th of January, 1819, this venerable servant of God was, during her prayer, warned by God to keep herself ready for a severe combat, which she should have soon to endure for the Church, for the Pope, and for sinners. God then permitted great numbers of demons to assail Elizabeth, and to torment her in a thousand horrible ways. Her extreme sufferings deprived her of sight; she was unable to open her mouth; her palate was torn to pieces; her cheeks were burned; her head was nearly severed from the trunk; and her whole body was, as it were, penetrated by a kind of infernal fire: the anguish of her soul was inexpressible. She was reduced to terrible agony. God, however, did not cease to console her interiorly. He commanded an angel to bring her the Holy Communion every day, and our Lord appeared to her eyes under the figure of a consecrated Host. In this manner Elizabeth was more and more encouraged to offer herself, with generosity of soul, as a holocaust, in order to suspend the effects of God's justice against sinners. This heroic servant of God had an extreme want of these heavenly comforts; without them she should have died under these terrible attacks of the infernal spirits, who went so far as to nail her body to a cross, and pierced her heart with a lance. This made her fall into a swoon, which was supposed mortal by her attendants. During this agony our Blessed Lord appeared to his generous spouse, radiant with Divine light, detached her with his own hands from the cross, and instantly cured her of all her wounds. The most holy Virgin Mary also visited her; then St. Peter, St. Paul, and other saints. She found herself, as it were, swallowed up in an ocean of heavenly delights. On this occasion, among other things, our Blessed Lord said to Elizabeth: "Thy sacrifice has done violence to my irritated justice. I suspend the punishment, and give free scope to my mercy. Christians shall not be dispersed, nor shall Rome be deprived of her Pontiff. I will reform my people and my Church; I will send zealous priests, and my spirit shall renew the face of the earth. I will restore fervor to religious Orders, and give to my Church a new pastor, filled with my spirit, who, through his zeal, shall sanctify my sheep." These are words and promises of high importance. We learn from them that holy souls, through their prayers and voluntary self-immolations, can appease the wrath of God, and turn away the calamities that our innumerable prevarications deserve, as our Lord revealed to Mary Lataste, in the following expressions: *My daughter, it is enough sometimes for a soul to present herself before God with a holy fear and trembling, and to address her supplications to him, in order to arrest his indignant arm, already lifted up to chastise an entire nation.*

We shall now give a symbolic prophecy, very threatening against the wicked, but, at the same time, most consoling for good Christians, because it announces the future triumph of the Church, after the fearful punishments of its enemies.

Prophetic Vision of Elizabeth Mora.

"On the Feast of St. Peter, 29th of June, 1820, whilst I was praying," our venerable Elizabeth says, "for the wants of the Church and the conversion of sinners, amongst whom I am the first, I was ravished in spirit, and drawn very near to God. Through an infinite light I was so intimately united to him that I lost all sentiments of myself. The sweet impressions of the love of God replenished me with an inexpressible joy and satisfaction. My soul, however, remained calm in these tokens of Divine kindness. Then it seemed to me to behold the heavens opening, and St. Peter, prince of the Apostles, coming down, surrounded with great glory and by a numerous escort of heavenly spirits, singing canticles. St. Peter was dressed in his pontifical robes, and held in his right hand the pastoral staff, with which he used to draw upon the earth an immense cross; at the same time the angels sang these words of the Psalmist, *Constitues eos principes super omnem terram,* — You will constitute them princes over the whole earth.

"After this the holy Apostle touched with his staff the four extremities of the cross, from which instantly sprung up four beautiful trees loaded with blossoms and fruits. These mysterious trees had the form of a cross, and were surrounded by a splendid light. Then I comprehended in the depth of my soul that St. Peter had produced these four symbolic trees to the end that they may serve as a place of refuge to the little flocks of the faithful friends of Jesus Christ, and in order to preserve them from the fearful punishment which shall convulse the whole earth. All good Christians shall then be protected under these trees, together with all those religious persons who shall have faithfully preserved in their hearts the spirit of their order. I say the same thing in relation to the secular clergy and to all other persons of every class who shall have kept in their heart the Catholic faith, — they shall all be protected. But woe, to those religious who do not observe their rule! thrice unhappy they! for they shall all be struck by that terrible punishment. I say the same to all secular clergy, and to all classes of people in the world who give themselves to a life of pleasure, and who follow the false maxims of modern ideas, which are opposed to the holy precepts of the gospel. These wretched people, who through their scandalous conduct deny the faith of Jesus Christ, shall perish under the weight of the indignant arm of God's justice. Not one of them shall be able to escape the punishment.

"I beheld those good Christians, who had sought a refuge under those mysterious trees, in the form of beautiful lambs confided to the care and vigilance of St. Peter, their good shepherd, testifying to him the most humble and most respectful obedience. As soon as St. Peter, the prince of the Apostles, had gathered the flock of Jesus in a place of safety, he reascended into heaven, accompanied by legions of angels. Scarcely had they disappeared, when the sky was covered with clouds so dense and dismal that it was impossible to look at them without dismay. On a sudden there burst out such a terrible and violent wind, that its noise seemed like the roars of furious lions. The sound of the dreadful hurricane was heard over the whole earth. Fear and terror struck not only men, but the very beasts.

"All men shall rise one against the other, and they shall kill one another without pity. During this sanguinary conflict the avenging arm of God will strike the wicked, and in his mighty power he will punish their pride and presumption. God will employ the powers of hell for the extermination of these impious and heretical persons who desire to overthrow the Church and destroy it to its very foundation. These presumptuous men in their mad impiety believe that they can overthrow God from his throne; but the Lord will despise their artifices, and through an effect of his almighty hand he will punish these impious blasphemers by giving permission to the infernal spirits to come out from hell. Innumerable legions of demons shall overrun the earth, and shall execute the orders of Divine justice by causing terrible calamities and disasters; they shall attack everything; they shall injure individual persons and entire families; they shall devastate property and alimentary productions, cities and villages. Nothing on earth shall be spared. God will allow the demons to strike with death those impious men, because they gave themselves up to the infernal powers, and had formed with them a compact against the Catholic Church.

"Being desirous of more fully penetrating my spirit with a deeper sentiment of his divine justice, God showed to me the awful abyss; I saw in the bowels of the earth a dark and frightful cavern, whence an infinite number of demons were issuing forth, who under the form of men and beasts came to ravage the world, leaving everywhere ruins and blood. Happy will be all true and good Catholics! They shall experience the powerful protection of the holy Apostles, St. Peter and St. Paul, who will watch over them lest they may be injured either in their persons or their property. Those evil spirits shall plunder every place where God has been outraged, despised, and blasphemed; the edifices they profaned will be pulled down and destroyed, and nothing but ruins shall remain of them.

"After this frightful punishment I saw the heavens opening, and St. Peter coming down again upon earth; he was vested in his pontifical robes, and surrounded by a great number of angels, who were chanting hymns in his honor, and they proclaimed him as sovereign of the earth. I saw also St. Paul descending upon the earth. By God's command, he traversed the earth and unchained the demons, whom he brought before St. Peter, who commanded them to return into hell, whence they had come.

"Then a great light appeared upon the earth, which was the sign of the reconciliation of God with man. The angels conducted before the throne of the prince of the Apostles the small flock that had remained faithful to Jesus Christ. These good and zealous Christians testified to him the most profound respect, praising God and thanking the Apostles for having delivered them from the common destruction, and for having protected the Church of Jesus Christ by not permitting her to be infected with the false maxims of the world. St. Peter then chose the new pope. The Church was again organized; religious orders were re-established; the private families of ordinary Christians, through their great fervor and zeal for the glory of God, became like the most exemplary religious communities. Such is the glorious triumph reserved for the Catholic Church; she shall be praised, honored, and esteemed by all men. All men shall become Catholics, and shall acknowledge the Pope as Vicar of Jesus Christ. Amen."

CHAPTER X.

PROPHECY OF BLESSED BOBÔLA, S. J.

THE *Civitta Cattolica*, 1864, related the following recent prophetical prediction, the authenticity of which was attested by a person worthy of confidence, that heard it from the Polish religious to whom the prophecy was made:—

"In the year 1819, the Rev. Father K——, a most zealous Dominican preacher, was most strictly forbidden by the Russian schismatical government to publish any writing, to preach, or even to hear confessions, under penalty of exile to Siberia. He was most afflicted in being thus deprived of every opportunity and means of working for the spiritual welfare of souls. One evening, about nine o'clock, before going to rest, this holy religious opened the window of his cell in the monastery wherein he lived, and looking up towards heaven he made with great fervor the following prayer: 'O glorious martyr of Jesus Christ, Blessed Andrew Bobôla! you who so many years since foretold the liberation and restoration of our Poland, you who see our masters determined to force her to become through schism an enemy of God, ah! do not allow such a scourge and humiliation to fall upon her. Obtain, holy martyr, from the omnipotence of God, that our common Catholic country may be delivered from her schismatic Protestant yoke.' Having after this prayer shut up the window and prepared to lay down on his humble bed, the holy martyr appeared to him and said: 'Behold, I

am the person to whom you have addressed your prayer; open again the same window and you will see. . . . . '
The good religious, surprised and somewhat terrified, opened the window, when, to his great amazement, the enclosed grounds and little garden attached to the monastery had disappeared, but in their stead he saw an immense plain. Then the blessed martyr, resuming, said to him: 'You behold now the fields of Pinsko, where I had the glory of suffering martyrdom for the faith of Jesus Christ. . . . . Now, looking again in the same direction, you will learn what you wish to know."
The Rev. Father K—— once more turned his eyes towards the place indicated, and beheld that vast field covered with Russian, Turkish, French, English, Austrian, and Prussian armies, and others which he could not well discern, all of them fighting in a most furious manner one against the other. Not being able to comprehend the meaning of this vision, Blessed Bobôla explained it to him in the following words: 'When the war which you see shall end, then the kingdom of Poland shall be re-established, and I shall be acknowledged its principal patron. In token of the reality of this vision and of the realization of this prophecy, behold my hand.' In saying this the blessed martyr placed his hand flat upon the little table in the cell, and disappeared.

"Amazed beyond expression, the pious religious was attempting to make some short prayer in thanksgiving to God for the favor received, and being entirely restored to his senses he looked immediately on the table and really beheld the impression of the martyr's hand. With sentiments of lively devotion, he kissed it several times, after which he quietly retired to his needed rest. As soon as he awoke on the following morning, his first impulse was to look again for the miraculous impression, which he found just the same as on the preceding evening, and this more than ever convinced him of the reality of the vision of the previous night. Then, having gathered in his room all the religious of the monastery, he showed to them the miraculous sign of the hand, and related to them all that had happened to him the evening before. Other persons have been informed of these wonderful events by letter, and I, who relate these facts, heard them in person in Polock, where I was about that time."

CHAPTER XI.

PROPHECY OF RODOLPHUS GEKNER.

TAKEN from his Works printed in Augustburg in the year 1623; chapter entitled "The Waves of the Mystic Bark," page 310.

"Before the middle of the nineteenth century seditions shall arise in Europe, especially in France, Switzerland, and Italy. Republics will be proclaimed, monarchs will be killed, high and zealous ecclesiastics will be murdered, and religious persons will have to leave their monasteries and convents. Famine, pestilence, and earthquakes shall destroy many cities. Rome shall by wicked men be deprived of her sceptre. The Church of God will first be subject to pay tribute, then she will be despoiled of her temporalities. Some time after the Pope shall be no more. [This as well as other prophecies seems very clearly to indicate a long vacancy in the holy Roman See.] A great prince of the North with a most powerful army will traverse all Europe, uproot all republics, and exterminate all rebels. His sword, moved by Divine power, will most valiantly defend the Church of Jesus Christ. He will combat in behalf of the true orthodox faith, and shall subdue to his dominion the Mahometan Empire. A new pastor of the universal Church (*Pastor Funalis*) will come from the shore (of Dalmatia) through a celestial prodigy, and in simplicity of heart adorned with the doctrines of Jesus Christ. Peace will be restored to the world." (The famous English doctor, John Cumming, a Protestant minister, has translated this prophecy in one of his books.)

CHAPTER XII.

PROPHECY OF MAGDALENE PORSAT.

MAGDALENE PORSAT is a humble, illiterate, and aged country maid. She has been a domestic servant above fifty years in the family Labbe, in the town of St. John de Bournay, department of Isere, France. She speaks about future events with the authority and exactness of a learned divine. She in a special manner announces great earthquakes. Magdalene has been favored with divine revelations since the year 1843, which she has invariably expressed in the same words.

Mr. Laverdant, one of the editors of the *Memorial Catholique*, in the year 1866 received from the mouth of Magdalene many of her predictions, which he published, with some commentaries, in the above-mentioned monthly review, in 1866 and 1868. The following are the most important passages : —

"Listen, my children, to what Mary our Mother charges me to announce to you.

"Behold the end of time! Behold the end of evil and the beginning of good. What is going to happen is not an ordinary event. It is a grand epoch which is going to commence. It is the third (era of the world). [Some authors divide the reign of perfect peace upon earth in three epochs. 1. That of God the Father; 2. That of God the Son; 3. That of the Holy Ghost. The first was from the creation of Adam until the universal deluge; the second, from the birth to the death of the Incarnate Word; the last will be the epoch of the Holy Ghost during the pontificate of the angelic Pope and of the great future monarch of France. Various prophecies announce this event.] Since the Father, who has created us, in order that we may know, love, and serve him; since the Son, who has redeemed us; behold now the Father and the Son to console us, send to us the triumphant spirit with Mary his spouse. This is a grand miracle.

"Mary comes from Heaven. She comes accompanied by a legion of angels. The elect living upon earth should through spiritual electricity (great fervor) elevate themselves in order to go forward before the messengers of God. Behold the host of the Lord! Many holy women, few St. Johns. Behold the armor of God! No gun or musket, no club or truncheon, no bolt, no watch-dog, no material force, no human means. [This shows how perfect order, security, honesty, and peace will be upon earth.]

"Different Customs in a Different Era.

"It is now twenty-six years since I announced to you the seven crises, the seven wounds and sorrows of Mary which should have to precede her triumph and our cure, namely : 1. Inclemencies of seasons and inundations; 2. Diseases to animals and plants; 3. Cholera over men; 4. Revolutions; 5. Wars; 6. *An universal bankruptcy;** 7. Confusion.

"The preceding evils have been mitigated through Mary's intercession, who detained the arm of her Son, Jesus. Behold now the sixth calamity, the *commercial crisis*. Commerce marches to its ruin, because the axle, confidence, is shattered. [Business men and commercial nations should take notice of this prophecy, but they will be the very last persons to do it.] There will be no respite between the sixth and seventh crises; the passage shall be rapid. The year 1798 upset France only; that which is coming shall cause the revolution of the whole world. The seventh crisis shall come to parturition. [*La septieme crise aboutira a l'enfantement.* It may mean that it shall go to the last extremity of confusion. We interpret it that it will extend to the birth of Antichrist, or arrive at the last extremity of disorder in everything upon earth, including religious affairs.] Men shall believe that all is lost and annihilated. Immense trouble shall be over the agitated sea of time. Whoever is not on the bark of Peter shall be ingulfed. The bark goes up and down. [Here Magdalene with her hands makes a movement like that of a vessel agitated by billows.] Peter, have confidence. The ark comes out of the storm, and a calm ensues. *Pius IX. is the last pope of the Church oppressed. Cross of the cross. To him sorrow, but also joy.* After him

* See page 58.

comes deliverance. *Lumen in Celo.* Light in Heaven. This is Mary's eye. [Beautiful idea.] In the Church, Christians will imagine that all is lost. Mary arrives. Behold there is confusion; confusion even in the sanctuary. Notwithstanding, it is to the Catholic priests that one shall have to go for absolution and blessing."

Some person having found fault with Magdalene for saying that *Pius IX. is the last pope,* she replied, *that Pius IX. was the last pope of an epoch.* "Do you think that Mary will come to destroy the work of her Son? The Pope holds the place of God upon earth; so does the bishop in every diocese, and the parish priest in every parish. Behold the representative of Jesus Christ, as the good and religious mother is the image of Mary. Go to your pastors who have been appointed by God. But woe! woe! to mercenaries who go to the side of the world! Look at that field where among bad weeds and every kind of damaged wheat there are some fine ears; that is a figure of how human society is now seated in wickedness. What should be done with it? Good souls should not be allowed to perish. The sound ears are good souls. Well! Mary comes to harvest the elect from the earth. . . . .

"A grand event shall have to take place in order to terrify the wicked to their advantage. After this, Mary, all powerful, shall change all men into good wheat. All shall be good. The Pharisees (the hypocrites) will be the last (to be converted); the great brigands (great sinners) will arrive beforehand. The Jews who have refused to receive Jesus Christ in his humiliation will acknowledge him at the glorious arrival of Mary.

"The dove (the peace and grace of God through Mary) comes to us from heaven, wearing on her breast a white cross, sign of reconciliation, and waving a sword of fire, symbol of love. She seats herself on a throne of solid gold, figure of Noah's ark; for she comes to announce the end of a deluge of evils. Behold, she comes, our Mother! The Church prepares everything for the glorious arrival of Mary. The Church forms for her a guard of honor to go before the angels. The triumphal arch is nearly accomplished. The hour is not far distant. It is Mary in person! But she has her precursors, — holy women, apostles, who shall cure the wounds of the body as well as the sins of the heart. Holy women, images of Mary, shall have power to work miracles. After them comes Mary to prepare the place for her Son in his triumphant Church. Behold the immaculate conception of the kingdom of God that precedes the arrival of Jesus Christ! It is the mansion of God upon earth, which is going to purify and prepare itself to receive the Emmanuel. Jesus Christ cannot come into this hovel of the world. It is necessary that God should send his spirit to renew the face of the earth by means of another creation, to render it a worthy mansion for the God made man. Behold here, after the fire from below (of the petroliers), for burning and changing everything. Behold here the fire from above! the love of God comes to embrace and transfigure the world. I see the earth rendered level; its valleys are raised; its mountains are lowered; there is nothing more than gentle hills and beautiful vales (images of the Christian virtues regenerating fallen humanity).

"Since I am as I am, I see nothing else before us but union and universal fraternity. All men are in reciprocal love. One helps the other. They are all happy. (*Deo gratias et Marie immaculate.*)"

CHAPTER XIII.

PROPHETICAL ANNOUNCEMENTS ABOUT THE POPES, ATTRIBUTED TO ST. MALACHY, ARCHBISHOP OF ARMAGH, IRELAND.

ST. MALACHY was born in Armagh, Ireland, in the year 1094. He was successively abbot of a famous monastery in Benchor, Bishop of Connor, Archbishop of Armagh, and Primate of all Ireland. After having greatly improved the spiritual condition of his flock by his learning, fervent zeal, and holy example, he renounced his archbishopric and returned to his See of Connor. Four years later, namely, in 1139, he went to Rome, to give a statement of the affairs of his diocese to the Pope. In his way through France he paid a visit to the holy Abbot of Clairvaux, St. Bernard, with whom he contracted a most intimate friendship. In the year 1148, St. Malachy left Ireland again with the intention of meeting in France the holy Pope Eugene III., the illustrious disciple of St. Bernard. But the pontiff had returned to Rome before his arrival. St. Malachy, before proceeding to Italy, went a second time to see his beloved friend St. Bernard, in whose arms he died on the 2d of November, 1148, in the fifty-fourth year of his age, and was buried in the Chapel of our Lady of Clairvaux. On this occasion St. Bernard preached twice the panegyric of St. Malachy, and remarked that his name well expressed the angelic purity and great holiness of his life. He calls him an angel *and a prophet*, and the faithful imitator of the prophet of the Bible in his sanctity, purity, *and prophetic spirit*.

It is universally believed that this great Irish prelate and saint wrote the remarkable and short prophetical predictions whereby he indicates some noticeable trait of all the future popes from Celestine II., who was elected in the year 1130, until the end of time.

The authenticity of these prophecies is proved at great length by the learned Father Menestrier in his treatise on the prophecies of St. Malachy. They are also approved by Moreri in his Biographical Dictionary, under the word *Malachia*, and by Sandini in his "Lives of the Roman Pontiffs"; also in the Elements of History of the Abbé Vallemont, published in 1702; and Cornelius A. Lapide, "Comment. in joanem," Capt. X. No .16, mentions it.

For the sake of brevity we confine ourselves to copying the mystical titles of the popes of the present century, beginning, however, with Pope Pius VI., who was elected February 15, 1775.

1775. *Peregrinus Apostolicus. Apostolic Pilgrim.* The exile, peregrinations, and death in France of Pope Pius VI., whose family name was Braschi, are well known.

1800. *Aquila rapax. Rapacious Eagle.* Pius VII., Chiarormonti, had a black eagle in his coat of arms. Moreover, the eagle of Napoleon seized first his temporal dominions, then his person. He also was swiftly carried into exile. But the victory of Waterloo over the eagle of Napolen left him at liberty, and he returned to Rome and to the Pontifical States in the month of May, 1814.

1823. *Canis et Coluber. Dog and Serpent.* Leo XII., Della Genga, like these two animals, was watchful, faithful, and prudent.

1829. *Vir Religiosus. Man of Religion.* Pius VIII., Castiglioni, was a most pious and religious Pope.

1831. *De Balneis Etruriæ.* Gregory XVI., Capellari,

a native of Belluno, a Camaldolese religious from Camaldoli in Tuscany. *De Balneis Etruriæ* literally means *from the baths of Tuscany*.

1846. *Crux de Cruce. Cross from the Cross.* Different but all well-suited interpretations can be given to this mysterious title. The present great and holy Pope Pius IX., John Maria Mastai Ferretti, a native of Sinigaglia, may be considered *Crux de Cruce*, if we, like the ancient and learned Eutimius, take the *cross* as a symbol of glory. *Gloria Appellatur Crux.* For he was raised to the pontifical throne among the general acclamations of the world, and his pontificate has already been the longest of any Pope, and his long reign has been rendered illustrious by his holy life and glorious actions. In fact, he restored the Catholic Hierarchy in England in 1850, and in Holland 1853. He with great solemnity defined, in 1854, the dogma of the Immaculate Conception of the Blessed Virgin Mary. In the year 1862 he canonized the Japanese Martyrs. He promulgated the famous Syllabus, 1864. He celebrated the eighteenth centenary of St. Peter in 1867, canonizing at the same time twenty-seven holy martyrs and confessors. On the eighth day of December, 1869, Pope Pius IX. in person opened the Vatican Ecumenical Council, in which the dogma of Papal Infallibility was proclaimed *Urbe et Orbe plaudente*. On the 18th of July, 1870, in the same year, he proclaimed St. Joseph Patron of the Church. On the 16th of June, 1871, the Catholic world celebrated the jubilee, and sang the *Te Deum* in thanksgiving for his having reached the twenty-fifth year of his pontificate. Finally the immortal Pius IX. surpassed the years of St. Peter in Rome on the 23d day of August, 1871. All this is very glorious for him. If, then, we interpret the *cross* for *glory*, no Pope had a more glorious reign that our present most Holy Father, Pius IX. *May the Lord preserve him, and give him life, and make him blessed upon earth, and deliver him not into the hands of his enemies. Amen! Amen!!*

The cross upon earth, however, is inseparable from great sufferings. Pope Pius IX. has had during his long pontificate to bear a large and heavy cross. He was exiled to Gaeta from November 25, 1848, until the 12th of April, 1850. Despoiled of Bologna and the Legations, June, 1859, and of the Marches and Umbria, September, 1860, which formed more than two thirds of the pontifical earthly dominions. Finally, on the memorable twentieth day of September, 1870, the usurping and sacrilegious government of Victor Emmanuel, violating their faith with God and with men, shelled Rome, shivered with cannon-balls the gate which bore the name of the Pope, hence called *Porta Pia*, through which the worst scum of Europe entered, took possession of the capital of the Christian world, and have since defiled the Holy City by their presence, by their wickedness, by their sacrileges, by their oppressions and persecutions.

We should remark here that all these painful crosses have been heaped upon the shoulders of the Venerable Pontiff by the hands of a scion of the old ducal family of Savoy, the King of Sardinia, on whose flag there is a cross. Hence it is literally true that the cross of Savoy and of Sardinia has been so far the cross of Pius IX. *Cross from the cross.* O, how the former religious dukes of Savoy and truly Catholic kings and pious queens of Sardinia would blush at and thoroughly condemn and detest the criminal connivance to the impious designs, and royal sanction to the sacrilegious usurpations of modern antichristian sectaries and bloody carbonari, given by one of their successors to a throne hallowed by their virtues, but dishonored by his conduct. Finally, some are of opinion, grounded upon certain predictions, that the present Pope, like St. Peter, shall be crucified, and thus receive the glorious crown of martyrdom, and from the cross pass to everlasting glory. *Crux de cruce.*

In a prophecy of a holy Italian Bishop of Marsico Nuovo, called Anselm, who lived in the twelfth century, he says: *He who wears a long beard* (Garibaldi) *shall in a special manner be detested for having by his words excited his followers to murder the Pope, whose name is Io. obi. John.* Pius IX.'s name is John Maria de Mastai Ferretti. We pass now to the successors of Pius IX. as indicated by St. Malachy, according to whom only eleven popes remain.

  I. *Lumen de Celo,* — Light from Heaven.
 II. *Ignis ardens,* — Burning Fire.
III. *Religio depopulata,* — Religion depopulated.
 IV. *Fides intrepida,* — Intrepid Faith.
  V. *Pastor Angelicus,* — The Angelic Pastor.*

---

* *Papa Angelicus*, the Angelic Pope, who is so frequently mentioned in these prophecies, deserves some special attention. It seems that this future Pope, who is now living, is a native of Dalmatia (see prophecy). He is described as being a learned, humble, and self-denying Franciscan religious of Friar Minors. This is expressly foretold by the Venerable Fra. Bartholomew da Saluzzo, whose long prophecy in odd Italian poetry Pius VI. so highly esteemed as to have it enclosed in a silver urn, which is preserved as a precious relic in Rome. In relation to this holy person, at the present moment living in obscurity, and unknown to the world, Fra. Bartholomew says : " Blessed friar of the Minorites, the Lord, after freeing thee from thy afflictions, will give thee great honor and glory. Fear not; thou shalt be endowed with very great courage, and pusillanimity shall fly from thee. Bear all thy trials with humble resignation, for the sake of the Lord. Reflect that he suffered more than thou, and he will communicate his power and strength to thee."

Rodolphus Gekner, another prophetical seer, calls him *Pastor*

VI. *Pastor et Nauta,* — Pastor and Sailor.
VII. *Flos Florum,* — Flower of Flowers.
VIII. *De Medietate Lune,* — From the Half of the Moon.
IX. *De Labore Solis,* — From the Labor of the Sun, or Eclipse of the Sun.
X. *Gloria Olivæ,* — Glory of Olive.
XI. *Petrus Romanus,* — Peter of Rome.

We must observe that St. Malachy does not mention the last Pope as a distinct person from the preceding one, whom he styles *Glory of Olive.* He merely says, "During the last persecution of the Church, Peter II., a Roman, shall reign. He shall feed the flock in many tribulations, at the end of which the City of the Seven Hills (Rome) will be destroyed, and the awful Judge shall judge his people."

According to St. Malachy, then, only ten, or at most eleven, popes remain to be in future more or less legitimately elected.

We say more or less legitimately elected, because out of those future popes it is to be feared that one or two will be unlawfully elected as anti-popes. It is suspected that the one designated *Ignis Ardens* — *Burning Fire* — shall be the first anti-pope, who will be unlawfully elected in opposition to the *Lumen de Celo,* — *Light from Heaven,* — the legitimate successor of the present Pope. Besides some predictions announcing this deplorable event, many powerful and influential persons in Europe are at present agreed and determined to use all their efforts to elect an anti-pope, in order to produce a schism in the Church, and to have a man who will favor their impious designs against the Catholic religion. In some reliable French

---

Funalis, or Pope girded with a cord like the Friar Minors. John de Vatiguerro, another prophet, foretells that he will, like the Friar Minors, go about with bare feet, preaching to the people.

and Italian Catholic papers, as the Paris *Univers*, and *La Voce della Verita* of Rome, it has been asserted that the government of Berlin, under the arch-schemer Bismarck, has made overtures on this subject to some European governments, and especially to that of Victor Emmanuel in Italy. It is known that the old apostate Doellinger, with his associates in Germany, and the apostate ex-Friar Hyacinthe Loyson, and a few others in France, with Gavazzi and others in Italy, are engaged in preparing the way to the approaching advent of an anti-pope. It is said that they have *in petto* a certain cardinal, who, since the occupation of Rome, has given much cause of uneasiness to the Holy Father Pius IX., the august prisoner of the Vatican. Moreover, we should take notice that St. Malachy, immediately after mentioning *Burning Fire*, speaks of the *Depopulation of Religion*, which seems a consequence of it.

Finally, according to the predictions of Holzhauser (page 175), there will be another anti-pope contemporaneous with Antichrist, who will greatly help him in his persecution against the true Church and religion of Jesus Christ. It is supposed that this last anti-pope will be that mentioned by St. Malachy, under the designation of *De Medietate Lune*, — *From the Half of the Moon.* If, therefore, we admit that *Petrus Romanus*, or Peter the second of this name, coincides with that called *Gloria Olivæ*, — *Glory of Olive*, — only ten popes remain; and if from these ten popes we subtract two anti-popes, their number is evidently reduced to eight. Now by calculation it is found that the average number of years of the popes on the chair of St. Peter is *seven*, rather less than more. In fact, to the present year, or rather to 1846, there have been two hundred and fifty-six popes. From this we may conclude how long this world is likely to last. But this subject will be more fully examined in the last part of this book, where we shall speak about the last judgment, the coming of Antichrist, and the end of time.

We must conclude, however, that, whatever the future events may be, Catholics can afford to wait for them with firm and calm confidence in the wisdom, power, goodness, and promises of God in behalf of our Holy Church, against which the gates of hell could never prevail in the past, and shall not be able to prevail in the future. When the number of the elect shall be accomplished, time indeed will end; but a glorious eternity will begin for them. May we find ourselves in their happy company in heaven.

We place here some prophetical words which his Holiness Pius IX. addressed to General Kanseler and his pontifical staff officers on the 27th of last December, 1872, Feast of St. John the Evangelist, the patron saint of the Pope. About the end of his Address, his Holiness said:—

"The conclusion I draw from this is, that the Revolution must perish, and that it is the very sword of our enemies that will deliver us from its grasp. It will be slain by its want of principles, by its abuse of power, by the injustice of its proceedings, by the breach of Porta Pia, by a host of causes I need not enumerate, especially to you, who, living in the city, are fully cognizant of all these facts.

"Let us hold this as certain, that the Revolution will be slain by its own arms, the very arms which it now wields against truth, against justice, against all that is holy and sacred on this earth. But when and how will it perish? *Domine Deus Israel, respice.* God knows it.

"We must imitate Judith, prostrating ourselves before

God, and imploring him to aid us by his grace and power, to grant us the consolation we need, and crown the fond hopes of our heart. We must pray with fervor and with faith; we must pray without intermission; and the suicide of the Revolution will come to pass when we least expect it.

"As of yore God promised to the ancient Jerusalem, he has also promised to the modern Jerusalem, this city of Rome, which belongs to him, that, after justice shall have performed its course, he will again appear amongst us in all the splendor of his mercy. These are the prayers I offer to-day, not for myself, — for I have but a short time to live, — but I offer them for the Church, for you, for so many millions of souls, spread over the whole face of the earth, having the same faith and hope, and firmly united with me in their eager desire that these prayers may be realized.

"Now I bless you in your persons, in your families, and in your business; but receive a special benediction, by which I beseech Heaven to grant you new courage, and a firm confidence that you will one day be able to pay your respects *to me*, in a manner suited to your rank as honorable soldiers, Christian warriors; that you can present yourselves before me clothed in your uniforms, and armed with the sword, which constitutes your glory, and which in your hands would be employed to re-establish peace and maintain the rights of law and order."

Benedicto Dei, etc.

CHAPTER XIV.

PROPHECY OF THE ABBOT MERLIN JOACHIM.

MERLIN JOACHIM, on account of his prophetic spirit surnamed the *Prophet*, was born in 1130, in the town of Celico near the city of Cosenza, Kingdom of Naples. In his youth he was page to Roger, King of Sicily; but some years later he became a Cistercian monk in the Monastery of Corazzo, of which, on account of his great knowledge and eminent virtue, he was soon elected prior and abbot.

But with the permission of Pope Lucius III., in the year 1185, Joachim retired to the solitude of Casemara, where he occupied himself in writing commentaries on the Holy Scriptures. He returned to his Monastery of Corazzo in 1187; but having been ordered by the Pope to continue his learned biblical commentaries, he asked and obtained permission to renounce his abbatial dignity, and withdrew to Flora, in Calabria, where he established a new monastery with a rule similar to that of Citeaux. He died in 1202, when he was seventy-two years old, leaving a great number of works which were printed in Venice in a large folio volume in the year 1516. Dom Gervais, Monk of La Trappe, wrote his Life in two volumes, which he published in 1745. In the Bollandists many details can be found about this holy and learned monk. We give here only some extracts from his prophetic writings.

I am rejoiced at what has been said to me. After many prolonged sufferings endured by Christians, and after a too great effusion of innocent blood, the Lord shall give peace and happiness to the desolated nation. A remarkable Pope will be seated on the pontifical throne, under the special protection of the angels. Holy and full of gentleness, he shall undo all wrong, and through his amiable virtues he shall recover the states of the Church, and reunite the exiled temporal powers. He shall be revered by all people, and shall recover the kingdom of Jerusalem. As the only Pastor he shall reunite the Eastern to the Western Church, and thus one only faith will be in vigor. The sanctity of this beneficent Pontiff will be so great that the highest potentates shall bow down before his presence. This holy man shall crush the arrogance of religious schism and heresy. All men will return to the primitive Church, and there shall be one only pastor, one law, one master, — humble, modest, and fearing God.

The true God of the Jews, our Lord Jesus Christ, will make everything prosper beyond all human hope, because God alone can and will pour down on the wounds of humanity the oily balm of sweetness. Excellent man! When a monster shall appear to thee in the sky, thou shalt find a ready escape towards the east, and after nine years thou shalt render thy soul to God.

The heavens proclaim the glory of God, and the faithful are in joy and happiness, because the Lord has vouchsafed to be merciful to them. He shall invite his elect to the banquet of the Lamb, where melodious canticles and harmonious concerts will be heard.

The power of this Pontiff's holiness will be so great as to be able to check the fury and impetuosity of threatening waves. Mountains shall be lowered before him, the sea (in some places) shall be dried up, the dead shall be raised, the churches shall be reopened and altars erected. (From this we learn that this great Pope will be elected during some terrible persecution against Catholics.)

At that time a handsome monarch, a scion of King Pepin, will come as a pilgrim to witness the splendor of this glorious pontiff, whose name shall begin with R. . . . . A temporal throne becoming vacant, the Pope shall place on it this king whose assistance he shall ask. (See David Lazzaretti, page 168.)

It should be known that there will be two heads, one in the East and the other in the West. (Does this mean two emperors, or an anti-pope in the East?) This (true) Pope shall break the weapons and scatter the fighting hordes. He will be the joy of God's elect. This angelic Pope will preach the gospel in every country. Through his zeal and solicitude the Greek Church shall be forever reunited to the Catholic Church. At the beginning, in order to obtain these happy results, having need of a powerful temporal assistance, this holy Pontiff will ask the co-operation of the generous monarch of France. Before, however, being firmly and solidly established in the holy See, there will be innumerable wars and violent conflicts, during which the sacred throne shall be shaken. But through the favor of Divine clemency, moved by the prayers of the faithful, everything will succeed so well that they shall be able to sing hymns of thanksgiving to the glory of the Lord.

This holy Pope shall be both pastor and reformer. Through him the East and West shall be in everlasting concord. The city of Babylon shall then be the head and guide of the world. Rome, weakened in temporal power, shall forever preserve her spiritual dominion, and shall enjoy great peace. During those happy days the angelic Pope shall be able to address to Heaven prayers full of sweetness. The dispersed nation shall also enjoy tranquillity. But six years and a half after this time the Pope will render his soul to God. His death will be illustrated by miracles. The end of his days shall arrive (take place) in an arid province, situated between a river and a lake near the mountains. . . . .

A man of remarkable sanctity will be his successor in the Pontifical chair. Through him God will work so many prodigies that all men shall revere him, and no person will dare to oppose his precepts. He shall not allow the clergy to have many beneffces. He will induce them to live by the tithes and offerings of the faithful. He shall interdict pomp in dress, and all immorality in dances and songs. (There is an urgent need of such interdict.) He will preach the gospel in person, and exhort all honest ladies to appear in public without any ornament of gold or precious stones. After having occupied the holy See for a long period of time he shall happily return to the Lord.

His three immediate successors shall be men of exemplary holiness. One after the other will be models of virtue, and shall work miracles, confirming the teaching of their predecessors. Under their government the Church shall spread, and these Popes shall be called the *Angelic Pastors*.

CHAPTER XV.

ADDRESS OF THE CATHOLICS TO HIS HOLINESS POPE PIUS IX.

WE cannot close this Second Part better than by copying the following grand Address from the "New York Freeman's Journal" of the 5th of April, 1873. The Holy Father gave audience, in the hall of the Consistory, to an international Catholic deputation, comprising one hundred and sixty-three gentlemen, bearing some of the noblest names in Europe, come hither to renew, in the name of the Catholics of their respective nationalities, the homage of their devotion, and more especially to protest regarding the iniquitous crime against the Catholic Church proposed by the Piedmontese government in the imminent law of suppression of all religious corporations. All nations were represented. Austria by thirty persons, headed by Prince Alfred de Lichtenstein; England by seventeen individuals, comprising the Duke of Norfolk, the Earl of Denbeigh, etc.; Belgium by twenty persons, including Count de Hemptinne, Count d'Ursel, Count de Robiano, Senator de Cannart de Hamale, Monseigneur Moreau d'Audry, Dean of the Chapter of Liege, Canon Bethune of Bruges, and others. America was represented by Mr. T. James Glover of New York, presiding over the deputation; Dr. Dean of Boston; Dr. Gartner, Vicar-General of Milwaukee; Mr. Milmore; and by three other gentlemen, names unknown to us. Of the remaining number, seventeen were from France, fourteen from Germany, thirty-eight from Italy, five from Spain, three from Switzerland. Ireland was also represented, but the number of persons is not given. (The Correspondence de Geneve mentions the Count de la Poer and the Chevalier Errington as the representatives of Ireland.) The deputation was accompanied and introduced by eleven representatives of the *Society for Catholic Interests*, presided over by Duke Salviati Borghese, who generously placed an apartment in his palace at the disposition of the members of the deputation during their stay in Rome, to serve as their place of meeting. At midday the Pope entered the hall, attended by Cardinals Barnabo, De Luca, Monaco, Pitra, and Sacconi; by several foreign bishops, including "the Bossuet of the nineteenth century," Monseigneur Pie, Bishop of Poitiers; by the prelates of his court, and by many distinguished Roman gentlemen. His Holiness having ascended his throne, a noble and earnest Address was read by Prince Alfred de Lichtenstein, amid signs of approval from his colleagues.

"Most Holy Father, — When, by the most infamous violation of the rights of nations, the capital of your States was invaded, the authors of that execrable outrage affirmed that they sought only to combat against your temporal realm; and they protested that they would hold themselves honored in respecting your spiritual power, in protecting the Church and the free exercise of your authority over the fold Catholic.

"These hypocritical assurances could deceive those only who love to be deluded. It was very soon evident that the guards were jailers; the protectors, oppressors.

"Since that time we have ceased not to point out to our respective governments, that the unity of Italy served but as a pretext to reduce the Church to a state of servitude; that the injury wrought against your throne affected likewise whomsoever was invested with legitimate authority; and that in the attack directed with infernal cunning and violence against your independence, the independence of all was imperilled.

"And how frequently have our persecutors justified our fears and confirmed our apprehensions and our previsions by their iniquitous proceedings!

"Now they are meditating new and more atrocious misdeeds; they are preparing to lay a sacrilegious hand upon the very heart of the Church; since to that most noble seat of life, namely, the heart, may rightly be be compared the religious orders, — inexhaustible nursery of saints, of apostles, of doctors; sacred hearths, whereon is fed the flame of charity, of zeal, and of science; marvellous fountains, whence springs purer and more vivid the blood of Christ to circulate through the veins of the Church, whereof you are the august head.

"These orders also form around your holy throne a cohort of intrepid defenders; they are the impregnable bulwark and the massive columns which uphold the temple of the Lord.

"But with enemies who so rage against yourself, Holy Father, and against them, all conciliation is impossible. The war waged by similar foes is in nowise to be feared; peace with them is alone to be dreaded. Undoubtedly they would be well content to be enabled to conclude with you a perfidious compromise; they ardently desire the establishment of a tacit agreement, a sort of system of reciprocal toleration. They hope that through lassitude you will be reduced to accept their *modus vivendi,* — their mode of existence.

"However, that compact between the despoiler and him who is spoliated, between the executioner and his victim, never will be, never could be, but a dream. Good sense demonstrates it; and your indefatigable voice, Most Holy Father, so teaches it, as you have never wearied, under whatsoever circumstances, in raising it with ever-increasing energy against each fresh attempt of your oppressors; nor have you suffered the world for one single moment to imagine the Supreme Shepherd in connivance with the ravenous wolf which so cruelly ravages his flock. No, no; Peter living in your person will be ever admirable in his heroic firmness against Herod. Your children joyfully applaud your courage, and beg of the Lord to be prodigal towards you of succor proportionate to the perils which surround you, and to the always increasing violence of the furious struggle.

"If all the signs of the times do not deceive us, this struggle is approximating towards the climax; the persecutors will erelong have filled their measure; and God, whose justice is slow because sure, reserves to them in an approaching future the chastisement which awaits traitors, — the treachery of accomplices.

"In so far as the human eye may scrutinize the future, we certainly perceive that terrible trials await us. But we contemplate them fearlessly.

"Comforted by God's grace, encouraged by your heroic example, we will endure those trials unflinchingly, and we shall end by conquering together with you, Holy Father.

"Meanwhile, rest assured, Most Holy Father, that if governmental Europe has culpably abandoned you, the Catholic people feel themselves, for that very reason, all the further called upon to press around you. The defection of their political chiefs teaches them still more potently their duty to assume in their stead the place of honor beside your prison.

"That post they retain through love, and they will there remain with still greater constancy than hitherto. Light is diffusing itself among souls, and the faithful daily better understand the spirit of supreme wisdom which inspired you when you crushed by your anathemas the perverse doctrines which were the poisoned germ whence issued all the misfortunes of Europe and of the world. The *Syllabus* and the memorable *Encyclical* which accompanied it will henceforward be to the eyes of true believers the pharos which shines through the darkness of the tempest, and the standard of salvation which all must defend to avoid perishing.

"It is precisely because of these hopes and these fears, towards which tend the hearts of the true children of the Church, that we have determined to come to prostrate ourselves at your sacred feet, O Most Holy Father! solemnly to attest to you all the horror inspired in us by the new crime soon to be perpetrated near to your Apostolic See against the religious orders, which are the best defenders of the same.

"The comfort of our voices will not be wanting to them; they are already assured of the support of your arm; and when the entire Christian family, both father and children, raise towards Heaven the cry of protest and of prayers, God will hearken to them, and celestial ire will be ready to strike the guilty and to avenge the spouse of Christ and his Vicar."

The Holy Father replied in a magnificent discourse, twice interrupted by the enthusiasm of his auditors. The Pope himself was visibly affected. His apostolic benediction given, Pius IX. descended from his throne, made the circuit of the room, speaking to each person, and presented every member of the deputation with a large bronze medal of the category, struck in commemoration of the Ecumenical Council of the Vatican.

THIRD PART.

THE LAST JUDGMENT.

"He hath prepared his throne in judgment. He shall judge the world in equity; he shall judge the people in justice. The Lord shall be known when he executeth judgment." — Ps. xi. 8, 17.

CHAPTER I.

NECESSITY OF A GENERAL JUDGMENT.

IT is a dogma of Christian faith that at the end of time mankind shall be summoned to a general judgment. *We must all be manifested before the judgment seat of Christ, that every one may receive the proper things of the body according as he has done, whether it be good or evil.* (2 Cor. v. 10.) Both the Old and New Testaments are full of similar texts.

From these words of St. Paul we learn four articles of Christian belief. We learn first that at the end of the world there shall be a general judgment for all men. *We must all be manifested before the judgment seat.* The next word in the text points out to us the second article of our faith, and reveals the divine character of our judge. *We must all be manifested before the judgment seat of Christ.* The rest of the sentence contains the two other articles of our belief. In the last judgment men shall be divided into two large but unequal sections, namely, the elect and the reprobate. The elect shall be placed at the right hand of the Divine Judge, the reprobate shall be thrust to the left. The elect shall appear in great and immortal glory; the reprobate shall have to endure the most horrible confusion. *We must all be manifested before the judgment seat of Christ, that every one may receive the proper things of the body according as he hath done, whether it be good or evil.*

Three classes of men assume to deny, or affect to ignore, the Christian dogma of a future general judgment. These are the proud infidel, the sensual epicurean, and the earthy materialist.

The proud infidel denies the very existence of a personal God in order to deify his own human intellect; or, by one of the greatest extravagances of the human mind, he makes God equal to himself and to all nature by his pantheistic absurdities. His pretended scientific oracles are his only dogmas. He cannot stoop to have them reprobated as criminal impieties by a Divine Judge, who shall have to condemn his proud spirit to the fiery dungeon of eternal infamy. The crowd of these self-conceited spirits is rapidly increasing every day upon the earth, and they are very active in propagating their maxims of impiety, which subvert and corrupt every sound principle of natural and Christian morality.

Hence we have in the second place a larger number of carnal and sensual epicureans, whose god, according to the expression of St. Paul, is their belly, and Venus is their worship. This earth is their heaven, and all their coveted happiness consists in the gratification of their senses. They never think of any other eternity than that which they expect somehow to secure during their life of pleasure upon earth. What wonder if these carnal men hate the very thought of a general judgment, and of the final destruction of their earthly elysium!

As the pride of spirit naturally sinks into flesh, so the

flesh, through her own weight and innate propensity, soon buries itself, like a mole, into the earth, and produces the earthly and material man.

It is proper here to remark, that as the Eastern or Byzantine heresies were the offspring of proud spirits, so the Northwestern heresies of the sixteenth century were generated by carnal men, and these during this last century have deeply buried themselves into the earth.

More than at any other epoch of human existence, man is now of the earth earthly. He lives and vegetates upon the earth. The soul of the majority of modern society scarcely ever can rise above the chimney of a factory, the funnel of a steamboat, the stack of a railway engine, or the shelves and counters of stores and banks. All their modern speculations are upon the earth, from the earth, and for the earth. It seems that the majority of men have become grave-diggers, preparing for the universal funeral of humanity.

Such are in America those gigantic speculations founded upon centuries of future commercial progress, and the intended developments of new coveted sources of wealth. Men multiply and cherish in their heads their grand railway schemes from the Atlantic to the Pacific Oceans, their ship-canals, their future Western cities, their city lots and town lots, their lines of steamboats to the East Indies, China, and Japan, and, in fine, their universal republic, speaking one language, covered by one large flag, with a remodelled constitution, when, *to the sole exception of one creed*, every man and woman of every size, shape, and color will be president; when everybody will command, and no one will be obliged to obey.

Europe is no less active. Prussia has her greedy hands full; yet she is preparing to bore the rocky Alps, in order to cast through the long tunnel a covetous look to sunny Italy, to the placid Adriatic Sea, and to the recent Suez Canal. Austria shyly turns her sad eyes towards Athens and Constantinople. Russia directs her slow but steady march towards China, Persia, and Hindostan. England and France are watching all these ominous movements, training their armies, and constructing their iron-clads.

Man cannot run very fast upon this earth, because its mud sticks heavily to his feet. Much time will be required before all these vast projects can be accomplished.

Can, however, these vast and ambitious undertakings be attempted without challenging the most strenuous opposition? But strong opposition causes delay, and delay demands an increase of time; and will this necessary time be allowed by Him who regulates the motion of the sun and moon? But why should the sun or the earth be kept turning on its worn axle? The ever-increasing spots on the face of the sun proclaim to the keen eye of the distant astronomer that it is getting old and wrinkled. Our cold winters demonstrate that it has lost much of its youthful fire, and, if it has any left, it must be the fitful heat of a strong fever. Mother Earth, in her old age, too heavily loaded with big factories, large stores, cumbersome shops, heavy theatres, thick prisons and jails, and hooped round about with iron rails and telegraph-wires, is evidently flagging in her movements. Yet our material men of progress are determined to keep these worn-out creatures in perpetual motion for thousands of years to come, in order that their pet commercial speculations may succeed, and through them the memory of the God of justice may be more completely erased from the mind and heart of humanity.

O man of the earth, is God obliged to prolong the

duration of time that by its abuse thou mayest go farther from him in eternity? Thou hast been created for heaven and not for the earth, for God and not for thyself. All creatures were made to help thee to know, love, and serve thy Maker during time, that thou mayest deserve to enjoy him during a happy eternity. But in thy ingratitude and impiety thou disownest thy Divine Creator, and, as much as it is in thy power, thou pervertest every creature against the end for which thou and they were intended by God. This is the first and principal cause why the angel of the Apocalypse, standing with the left foot on the agitated waters of time, and with the right foot on the solid rock of eternity, swears by the immortal and eternal God, *that time shall be no more.* (Apoc. x. 6.)

Before the end of time, however, whether we believe in it or not, whether we are willing or unwilling, prepared or unprepared, we shall all, all without exception, be summoned to a general judgment.

Two grand events have, more than any other, ever excited the hopes and the fears of humanity. These are the first and the last coming of Jesus Christ upon earth. The first on account of the necessity all men have of believing in him if they wish to obtain eternal life; the second on account of the danger we shall incur of being eternally condemned by him for our want of faith, and fidelity in his Divine love and service. Faith, hope, and charity shall most certainly receive from Jesus Christ the blessing of everlasting bliss and glory; as impiety and wickedness shall hear and feel the curse of his eternal reprobation. *He hath prepared his throne in judgment; he shall judge the world in equity, he shall judge the people in justice. . . . . The Lord shall be known when he executeth judgment.* (Ps. xi. 8, 17.)

God has decreed to summon all men to a general judgment in order that he may have a most fit opportunity to justify and triumphantly vindicate the conduct of his divine providence, so often and so publicly blasphemed by impious and wicked men.

Proud and haughty man, unable to comprehend the secret designs of Divine Wisdom, impiously presumes to call the conduct of the Almighty to the bar of his human reason, and often proceeds so far in his blasphemy as to *say in his heart*, and even with his tongue, *There is no God.* (Ps. xiii. 1.) Many, however, who profess to believe in the existence of God, do not hesitate to deny his universal providence, or to impeach his divine justice. Hence it is not only just, but it is necessary, that God should challenge to a public judgment all those impious men, who durst arrogate to themselves the authority of pronouncing judgment against Him. *The Lord shall be known when he executeth judgment.*

In this general assembly God will demand from all men and from each individual a strict account of all public benefits and private gifts and graces received from his divine goodness. *Redde rationem villicationis tuæ,*— *Give an account of thy stewardship.* (St. Luke xvi. 2.)

God will ask satisfaction for all the sins and crimes committed by all obstinate sinners against his divine law, and for the scandals given to their fellow-men.

Justice demands that God should make a public and solemn defence of his calumniated and persecuted friends and servants, and that the malice and hypocrisy of the wicked should be publicly unmasked and exposed to universal and eternal execration. *Then shall the just stand with great constancy against those that have afflicted them, and taken away their labors. The wicked, seeing it, shall be troubled with terrible fear, and shall be amazed at the suddenness of the unexpected salvation of the just.* (Wisd. v. 1.) Lastly, all angels, good and bad, all men, just and sinners, elect and reprobate, all, all shall be summoned to the presence of the awful Judge before whose divine majesty every knee shall have to bow in profound adoration, when upon the prostrate and silent multitude our Sovereign Lord and God, Jesus Christ, from his high throne of glory and power, will pronounce the irrevocable sentence of eternal doom, calling his elect to everlasting happiness, and sending the unhappy reprobate to never-ending misery. *We must all be manifested before the judgment seat of Christ, that every one may receive the proper things of the body according as he has done, whether it be good or evil.* (2 Cor. v. 10.) *Understand these things, you that forget God; lest he snatch you away and there be none to deliver you.* (Ps. xlix. 22.)

CHAPTER II.

NATURE OF THE GENERAL JUDGMENT.

WE do not intend to write a theological treatise on the general judgment, but will copy the description of it given in various portions of the Holy Scriptures. We shall make use of the Rt. Rev. Bishop Hay's "Sincere Christian," Chap. VIII., *Office and Dignities of the Redeemer*, Quest. 40: "The general judgment is one of the most important truths revealed by God to man. He has been pleased to give a most minute and awful description of everything concerning it.

"The great day of the Lord is near, says the Prophet

Sophonias; it is near and exceeding swift; the voice of the day of the Lord is bitter; the mighty man shall there meet with tribulations. That day is a day of wrath, a day of tribulation and distress, a day of calamity and misery, a day of darkness and obscurity, a day of clouds and whirlwinds, a day of trumpet and alarm against the fenced cities and against the high bulwarks. And I will distress men, and they shall walk like blind men, because they have sinned against the Lord; their blood shall be poured down as earth and their bodies as dung. (Soph. i. 14.)

"Behold the day of the Lord shall come, a cruel day, and full of indignation and of wrath and fury, to lay the land desolate and to destroy the sinners thereof out of it. For the stars of heaven and their brightness shall not display their light; the sun shall be darkened in his rising, and the moon shall not shine with light; and I will visit the evils of the world, and against the wicked for their iniquity; and I will make the pride of infidels to cease, and I will bring down the arrogance of the mighty. For this I will trouble the heaven, and the earth shall be moved out of her place. For the indignation of the Lord of hosts, and for the day of his fierce wrath. (Isai. xiii. 9.)

"Immediately after the tribulation of those days the sun shall be darkened, and the moon shall not give her light, and the stars shall fall from heaven, and the powers of heaven shall be moved. (Matt. xxiv. 22.)

"The heavens departed like a book folded up; and every mountain and the islands were moved out of their place; and the kings of the earth and the princes, and the tribunes, and the rich men, and the strong men, and every bondman, and every freeman, hid themselves in the dens, and in the rocks of the mountain; and they say to the mountains and to the rocks, Fall upon us and hide us from the face of Him that sitteth upon the throne, and from the wrath of the Lamb. For the great day of their wrath is come, and who shall be able to stand? . . . . (Apoc. vi. 14.)

"Our God shall come manifestly, our God shall come and not keep silence; a fire shall burn before him and a mighty tempest round about him. (Ps. xlix. 3.) Clouds and darkness are round about Him, justice and judgment are the establishment of his throne; a fire shall go before him, and shall burn his enemies round about. His lightnings have shone forth to the world; the earth saw and trembled; the mountains melted like wax at the presence of the Lord of all the earth. (Ps. xcii. 2.)

"The day of the Lord shall come as a thief, in which the heavens shall pass away with great violence, and the elements shall be melted with heat, and the earth and the works that are in it shall be burnt up. (2 Peter iii. 10.)

"The day of the Lord cometh, because it is nigh at hand; a day of darkness and of gloominess, a day of cloud and whirlwinds. . . . . Before the face thereof a devouring fire, and behind it a burning flame. The land before it is like a garden of pleasure, and behind it a desolate wilderness; neither there is any one that can escape it. . . . .

"*General Resurrection.* — *The Lord himself* shall come down from heaven with commandment, and with the voice of an archangel, and with the trumpet of God. (1 Thess. iv. 15.) And he shall send his angels with a trumpet and a great voice, and they shall gather together his elect from the four winds, from the farthest part of the heavens to the utmost bounds of them.

(Matt. xxiv. 31.) At the sound of the angelic trumpet the sea gave up the dead that were in it, and death and hell gave up the dead that were in them. (Apoc. xx. 13.)

"The hour cometh wherein all that are in the graves shall hear the voice of the Son of God, and they that have done good shall come forth unto the resurrection of life, but they that have done evil unto the resurrection of condemnation." (St. John v. 28.)

Appearance of the Divine Judge. — Immediately after the general resurrection all mankind shall be assembled together in the valley of Jehoshaphat, within sight of Mount Calvary, that, where Jesus Christ underwent the greatest excess of his humiliations and sufferings, there he may appear in the full splendor of his majesty and glory, according to what was foretold by his holy prophet Joel.

"I will gather together all nations, and I will bring them down to the valley of Jehoshaphat . . . . for there I will sit to judge all nations round about. (Joel iii. 2, 12.) Then shall appear the sign of the Son of Man in heaven, and then all the tribes of the earth shall mourn, and they shall see the Son of Man coming in the clouds of heaven with great power and majesty. (Matt. xxiv. 30.) Jesus Christ shall be received from heaven with the angels of his power in a flame of fire, yielding vengeance to them who know not God and who obey not the gospel of our Lord Jesus Christ. (2 Thess. i. 17.) Behold the Lord cometh with thousands of his saints to execute judgment upon all, and to reprove the impious for all the works of their ungodliness whereby they have done impiously, and for all the hard things which ungodly sinners have spoken against God." (Jude, 14, 15.)

The awful Judge being seated on the throne of his

glory, the terrible separation shall be made of the good from the bad. At present the kingdom of Christ upon earth is likened in the gospel to a barn floor wherein the good grain and chaff are mixed together in one heap; to a field in which the wheat and the tares grow up together till the harvest; to a net cast into the sea and enclosing all kinds of fish, both good and bad; and to a flock composed both of sheep and goats. In this life, the just and unjust, saints and sinners, the children of God and servants of Satan, are mixed together in one body and can scarcely be distinguished one from the other.

"But at the great day, the Judge, whose fan is in his hand, will thoroughly cleanse his floor, and gather his wheat into his barn, but the chaff he will burn with unquenchable fire. (Matt. iii. 12.)

"When the Son of Man shall come in his majesty, and all nations shall be gathered together before him, he shall separate them one from the other, as the shepherd separates the sheep from the goats, and he shall set the sheep on his right hand, but the goats on the left. (Matt. xxiv. 31.)

At present, by a particular dispensation of Divine Providence, the elect of God, who are the righteous, are too often confounded with the wicked and with hypocrites. God's saints, who are meek and humble of heart, far from being honored and respected, as they deserve, are often despised and insulted. God's servants who are poor in spirit, instead of being relieved and comforted, are abandoned and neglected by the proud and wealthy sinner. But it will not always be so. In the great accounting day the scene shall be entirely changed. On that great day of strict justice the godly shall be separated from the wicked, the elect from the reprobate, and placed by the good angel at the right hand of the Divine Judge in great honor and glory. All their virtues and all their acts of piety shall be manifested to men and angels, and 'they shall be enriched with eternal treasures, which rust cannot destroy, fire cannot burn, and no thief can take away from them. So admirable will be their exaltation, that their enemies, the wicked reprobates, "who oppressed, persecuted, and afflicted them in their mortal life, seeing their great glory, shall be troubled with great fear, and shall be amazed at the suddenness of the unexpected salvation of the elect. Repenting and groaning for anguish of spirit, they shall be forced to say: 'These are they whom we had sometimes in derision and for a parable of reproach. We fools esteemed their life madness, and their end without honor. Behold! how they are numbered among the children of God, and their lot is among the saints! Therefore we have erred from the way of the truth; and the light of justice hath not shined unto us, and the sun of understanding hath not risen upon us. We wearied ourselves in the way of iniquity and of destruction, and have walked through hard ways. But the way of the Lord we have not known. What hath pride profited us, or what advantage hath the boasting of riches brought to us? All these things have passed away like a shadow. We also being born, forthwith ceased to be, and have been able to show no mark of virtue, but are consumed in our wickedness.' (Wisdom v.)

"The wicked shall see and shall be angry; he shall gnash with his teeth and pine away. (Ps. xci. 10.) There shall be weeping and gnashing of teeth, when you shall see Abraham, and Isaac, and Jacob, and all the prophets in the kingdom of God, and you yourselves thrust out. (Matt. xiii. 28.)

The separation being accomplished, the final judgment shall immediately follow. "I saw a great white throne, and Jesus Christ sitting upon it, from whose face the earth and the heavens fled away, and there was no place found for them; and I saw the dead, great and small, standing in the presence of the throne, and the books were opened, and another book was opened, which is the book of life, and the dead were judged by those things which were written in the books, according to their works. (Apoc. xx. 11.)

"We shall all stand before the judgment seat of Christ, ... and then every one of us shall render an account to God for himself. (Rom. xiv. 10.) The Lord will come, who will bring to light the hidden things of darkness, and will make manifest the counsel of hearts. (1 Cor. iv. 5.) There is not anything secret that shall not be made manifest, nor hidden that shall not be known and come to light. (St. Luke viii. 17.)

"Then shall the King say to them that shall be on his right hand, 'Come, ye blessed of my Father, possess the kingdom prepared for you from the foundation of the world.'

"To those unhappy wretches at his left hand the Divine Judge, with a frowning countenance and a thundering tone of voice, will say, 'Depart from me, ye cursed, into everlasting fire, which was prepared for the devil and his angels.' These two sentences shall be immediately executed. The reprobates shall go into everlasting punishment, but the elect into life everlasting (Matt. xxv. 34), where these shall shine as the sun in the kingdom of their Father." (Matt. xiii. 14.)

CHAPTER III.

SIGNS OF THE APPROACHING GENERAL JUDGMENT.

"I will show wonders in heaven and on earth, blood and fire and vapor of smoke." — Joel ii. 30.

GOD willeth not the death of the sinner, but that he be converted from his evil ways and live. Hence, before inflicting his severest punishments on the wicked, God, as a kind and loving father, warns him in time. If the sinner repent, he is forgiven. If he remain obstinate, he must and shall be punished. Sacred history is full of these facts. King David and the Ninevites become guilty of grievous crimes, they are warned by God, they repent, do penance, and are forgiven.

Through his holy prophets God invited to repentance the sacrilegious King Nabuchodnosor, the wicked Baltassar, and the impious Antiochus; they obstinately rejected the offer of God's mercy, hence they had soon to experience the severity of his divine justice. Again our merciful Lord sent his holy servants and even his angels to forewarn the vicious inhabitants of Sodom and Gomorrha who, blinded by carnal passion, continued obstinate in their crimes, and were in consequence destroyed by fire. The Lord of mercy and of justice, before destroying the famous city of Jerusalem the first time, sent many of his prophets to call to repentance its wicked inhabitants. The zealous warnings of the holy servants of God were despised, the prophets were persecuted and put to death. So much malice and obstinacy had to be punished. The city and the Temple were destroyed by

Nabuchodnosor, many thousands of the people massacred or led into captivity with King Sedecias. (4 Kings, xxv.) The city of Jerusalem and the Temple of God were rebuilt. Religion and piety flourished for a time among the Jews. But fervor cooled and iniquity soon abounded in that fickle nation. God, as usual, sent prophetical warnings, which were unheeded. When behold! awful visions of terrible warriors were seen by all fiercely fighting in the air during forty days and nights. Soon after this the traitor Jason and the impious King Antiochus took the city by storm, massacred the people, and profaned the sacred Temple.

After having sent in vain many of his holy prophets, the great Son of God came down from heaven in person for the conversion and salvation of the Jewish nation. He assumed human nature, was born, and lived among his people during more than thirty years. He went from place to place, preaching everywhere, working numberless miracles in their behalf, inviting all sinners to faith and repentance. In order more effectively to facilitate the conversion of his beloved nation, our merciful Saviour chose twelve Apostles and seventy-two disciples, and sent them to every part of Palestine, preaching to all the necessity of penance to avoid the wrath to come. *Except ye do penance, you shall all likewise perish.* These holy messengers of mercy, on account of their external poverty, and simple, unpolished manners, were despised by the Jewish people. Our Divine Redeemer went often to Jerusalem, and in the most affectionate and earnest way exhorted the people to avert the most awful impending punishments by a sincere and prompt repentance and penance. In case of refusal our blessed Lord repeatedly and distinctly foretold to them the utter destruction of the city, and the complete dispersion of the whole nation. But these perverse and wicked men, instead of being converted, filled up the measure of their iniquities by condemning to the death of the cross the Author of Life, the Divine Redeemer, and Saviour of mankind.

The most wicked of crimes deserves the severest punishment. *Heaven and earth may pass away, but our Lord's words cannot fail.* A few years after the death and resurrection of our Divine Saviour, a long and appalling comet in the shape of a sharp sword appeared suddenly in the sky, with its red, fiery point directed against the sinful city of Jerusalem. This awful vision continued for a long time.

Whilst from the sky the comet announced to the guilty city the wrath of the God of heaven, other prodigies were taking place within its walls upon earth. One day terrible voices were heard by all the inhabitants of Jerusalem proceeding from the Temple, and crying aloud, *Migremus hinc! migremus hinc!! Away from this place! away from this place!!* These unearthly sounds were heard from every part of the city; they drew immense crowds of terrified spectators near the Temple; when behold! in the sight of all, a large, thick gate of solid brass was by an invisible power thrown suddenly open, and the voices were heard louder than ever repeating, *Away from this place! away from this place!! Migremus hinc! migremus hinc!!*

In spite of all these numerous and extraordinary warnings of Divine mercy, the Jews remained obstinate in their sins and superstitions. In punishment of this the inhabitants of the city were starved to death by the pagan Roman armies, Jerusalem was destroyed by fire, and the rest of the Jewish people have ever since been scattered through every Christian nation, to serve as a living example and a salutary warning to all obstinate sinners and impious unbelievers.

As the general judgment will be the last and the most terrible of all punishments inflicted upon a sinful humanity by the God of justice, we should be certain that it will be announced by many striking and unmistakable forewarnings. *I will show*, God says,—*I will show wonders in heaven and on earth, blood and fire and vapor of smoke; the sun shall be turned into darkness, and the moon into blood, before the great and dreadful day of the Lord doth come.* (Joel ii. 30.)

Many other signs are mentioned in the Scripture, and some are taught by tradition. These manifold signs are divided into two classes. Some of these signs are more remote, some are more immediate. We shall consider first the more important remote signs of the general judgment, which will form the subject of the next chapter.

CHAPTER IV.

REMOTE SIGNS OF THE GENERAL JUDGMENT.

THROUGH his great and holy servant, Moses, God informs every believer in revelation that he created this vast universe in six days, and *that on the seventh day God ended his work which he had made, and he rested on the seventh day, and sanctified it.* (Gen. ii. 2, 3.)

Because time is getting shorter every hour, we will not lose a single moment of it in speculative discussions about the meaning and duration of these six mysterious days of creation. We proceed then at once to the fourth day, when God said: *Let there be lights made in the firmament of heaven to divide the day and the night, and let them be for signs and for seasons, and for days and years.* (Gen. i. 14.) In these Divine words God himself informs us that the sun and the moon are to give us signs and seasons, days and years. We have no difficulty in admitting that they give us seasons, days, and years. God, however, in the very first place affirms that they are also *signs* indicating some future event more important than days, seasons, and years. What, then, can be this future event of general and paramount importance? Both revelation and tradition will assist us to discover it.

The royal prophet says: *A thousand years in thy sight, O God, are as yesterday, which is past.* (Ps. lxxxix. 4.)

St. Peter, the first infallible pope, more fully explains these words in reference to the last general judgment. *Behold*, he says, *this is the second epistle I write to you, my dearly beloved, in which I stir up by admonition your sincere mind, that you may be mindful of those words, which I told you before from the holy prophets, and of your Apostles, of the precepts of the Lord and Saviour; knowing this first, that in the last days there shall come scoffers with deceit, walking according to their lusts, saying: Where is his promise, or his coming? For, since the fathers slept, all things continue so from the beginning of the creation.* (Are not these last days approaching? Are not these scoffers amongst us at present? Are you, reader, one of them?) *But be not ignorant, my beloved, of this one thing, that one day with the Lord is as a thousand years, and a thousand years as one day. . . . . The day of the Lord shall come as a thief, in which the heavens shall pass away with great violence, and the elements shall be dissolved with heat, and the earth and the works that are in it shall be burnt up.* (2 Peter iii.)

One day with the Lord, then, is as a thousand years, and a thousand years as one day. It is the common interpretation that each of the six days of creation is equivalent to one thousand years for the future existence of human generations. Now God employed six days in the creation of this world; this world, then, shall last only six thousand years; the Sabbath, or seventh day, representing eternity.

The learned Cornelius A. Lapide, in his erudite commentaries on the Bible, in the second chapter of Genesis and twentieth chapter of the Apocalypse, attests that it is a common opinion among Jews and Gentiles, among Latin and Greek Christians, that this world shall last only six thousand years.

Many of the Jewish rabbis, or doctors of the Jewish law, derive this tradition from the very first verse in the first chapter of Genesis, where the Hebrew letter, *Aleph*, which signifies thousand, is found six times. Hence, in their famous Talmud, we read: *The world shall last six thousand years, and then it shall be destroyed. This world lasted two thousand years in the law of nature, two thousand years in the law of Moses, and shall last two thousand years in the law of the Messiah.* (Talmud, Tom. IV. tract. 4; Malvenda, Lib. II. chap. 21.)

Among the Gentiles, this was the opinion of Hydaspes, Mercurius Trismegistus, and of the famous Sibyls. (A. Lapide in Apoc. xx. 4.)

Christian writers have taught the same opinion from the beginning of Christianity. This belief is clearly and distinctly expressed in the epistle attributed to the Apostle St. Barnabas, which, though not admitted as canonical by the Church, yet all must acknowledge that it is very ancient, and witnesses to the belief of the primitive Christians during the apostolic age.

St. Ireneus, who may be considered a writer of the apostolic times, commenting on the above-quoted words, — *one day with the Lord is as a thousand years, and a thousand years as one day*, — says, that as God created this world in six days, so it is destined to last six thousand years; because each day mentioned in the history of creation is prophetical of a thousand years. In proof of his opinion, St. Ireneus wisely remarks, that the Hebrew text in the first and second verses of the second chapter of Genesis literally says: *So the heavens and the earth were consummated, and all the furniture of them. And on the seventh day God consummated his work which he had made.* (St. Iren. *advers.* Heres., Lib. V. c. b. 25 and 28.)

A little reflection will make it clear that these Divine words have two distinct meanings; one historical, the other prophetical; one is a date of the past, the other is a sign of the future; the first states the time of the world's creation, the second foretells the epoch of the world's consummation.

Our Divine Redeemer's words to his Apostles seem to confirm this interpretation: *Behold, I am with you all days, even unto the consummation of the world.* (Matt. xxviii. 20.) This word *consummation* literally agreeing with the prophetic words of Genesis, which fix the duration of the world to six thousand years, when it shall be *consummated* or destroyed. The words of the Latin vulgate, *perfecit* and *complevit* translated into the English *finished* and *ended*, are not in substance very different from the Hebrew text; but this last is more expressive in what we call its prophetical signification.

Upon the above-mentioned words of the royal Psalmist and of St. Peter, St. Jerome says: *I believe that in this place thousand years are commonly taken for a day, because this world having been made in six days, it is believed that it will last only six thousand years.* (Epist. ad Cyprian supr. Ps. lxxxix.) Remark here, that St. Jerome affirms as a well-known fact that *this belief was common among the faithful in the fourth century.* St. Jerome is not a small authority.

The same belief is affirmed by St. Gaudentius, the learned and holy Bishop of Brescia and great friend of St. Ambrose, both Fathers of the Church.

"We expect," he says, "that truly holy day of the seventh thousand years, that shall come after those six days, or six thousand years of time, which, being finished, shall begin that holy rest for all true saints and for all those faithful believers in the resurrection of Jesus Christ." (Tract. 10.)

Our limits do not allow any more extracts. For those who desire to examine many more Fathers and doctors of the Church, we will here supply a pretty long list of them: St. Cyprian, Lib. IV. Epist. 5; St. Ambrose, Comment. 2 Thess. 11; the famous book of St. Hypolitus, De Antichristo; St. Hilary, Can. in 17 Matt.; St. Augustine, De Civit Dei, Lib. XX. chap. 17; Lactantius Firmianus, Lib. VII. chaps. 14 and 15; St. Anastatius Sinaita, Lib. XVII. in Hexamer; St. Justin ad ortodox, Quest. 71; St. Germanus, Patriarch of Constantinople, St. Cyril; the ancient writer, Q. Julius Hilarion; Cassiodorus, St. Isidore, Victorinus, Rabanus, Bellarmine, Genebrardus, etc., and many others, who, to use the words of Q. Julius Hilarion, unanimously affirm: *Summa completa annorum sex millium fiet resurrectio. At the end of six thousand years shall take place the general res-*

urrection. Our kind critics will please pay some attention to these numerous and grave authorities before they disapprove what we here state.

From all the above-mentioned authorities we learn, then, that the six mystic days of creation are intended to signify the six thousand years of the world's duration. The seventh day, which, to the exclusion of the other six days, God has in a special manner blessed and sanctified, must be taken for the happy eternity of the blessed saints, for the holy sabbath of everlasting rest, for the blissful duration of perpetual peace, and perfect happiness to the elect of God, who will behold him face to face, praise, love, adore, and glorify him forevermore. Amen!

Assuming now as pretty certain that this world shall last only about six thousand years, because such is the common opinion and expectation of humanity, how many years more, it may be asked, still remain to the end of this world? The solution of this question depends on the settlement of another. This is the exact epoch of the birth of the Messiah. Now the majority and most reliable portion of Christian writers agree that Jesus Christ, our Divine Redeemer, was born in Bethlehem, of the ever-blessed and immaculate Virgin Mary, some years after the four thousand years *from man's creation.*

The truly learned and pious Suarez evidently inclines to this opinion. How many years after he does not expressly state, but he seems to incline to from twenty to thirty years. (Suarez, De Incarnat., Quest. 1, Art. 3, disput. 6, sect. 1.) In the same place he mentions grave and learned Christian authors who by chronological calculations conclude that our Divine Saviour was born many years later. Alban Butler is of the same opinion. (See 15th October note in "St. Teresa's Life.")

But let us take between twenty and thirty years. In this supposition we have the balance of only about a hundred years. We are writing this in 1873. From these remaining one hundred years, however, we must subtract a considerable portion of time. This truth cannot be controverted by any Christian. Our Divine Lord and Saviour, Jesus Christ, has most clearly and emphatically foretold this event in the following words: At the end of the world *there shall be great tribulations, such as has not been from the beginning of the world until now, neither shall be; and unless those days had been shortened, there should no flesh be saved; but for the sake of the elect, those days shall be shortened.* (St. Matt. xxiv. 22.) Here our Divine Lord evidently speaks of the last years of time, as every candid reader can see by attentively perusing this chapter. The same warning is repeated in the Gospel from St. Mark, xiii. 20.

The famous tiburtine Sibyl, or pagan prophetess of Tivoli, not far from Rome, who, a few centuries before the birth of Jesus Christ, made so many wonderful prophecies about him and about subsequent events, whose predictions have been highly esteemed by many holy and learned Fathers of the Church and other Christian writers,—this famous Sibyl, I say, has distinctly foretold that at the end of the world *the years and months, the weeks and days and hours, shall be shortened.**

This shortening of time having been made an important subject of a special prophecy of our Divine Lord, who ever was so cautious about announcing the end of time, we must conclude that a considerable number of years shall be abbreviated. *And unless those days had been shortened, there should no flesh be saved; but for the sake of the elect those days shall be shortened.*

We must observe that this abbreviation of time at the

* See page 266.

end of the world will be made for two highly important objects. First, to shorten the extreme and terrible afflictions and tribulations which all men then living shall have to endure; and, secondly and principally, to free the elect from the malicious deceits and cruel persecutions of Antichrist, and of his fanatical followers, and secure the eternal salvation of his faithful, suffering servants. Now all this seems to require the shortening of a goodly number of years. We are strongly inclined to opine that from ten to twenty years shall be subtracted. Hence, this world is doomed to utter destruction in much less than a century from the present date of 1873..

Reader, do not condemn this opinion without serious consideration. It has not been advanced lightly. The writer has heard learned and grave bishops and priests strongly advocating it. He has with attention perused different works on this subject, and matured his opinion by many years of serious reflection. We beg you to do the same; then, if you have more substantial facts and conclusive arguments to prove the contrary, we shall all be very glad to receive them from you, or from anybody else. We have been studiously careful to conform to the wise and prudent decree of the Lateran Council, held under the great and learned Pope Leo X., which in its twelfth session forbids, *especially in preaching*, to pretend to announce *the exact time of Antichrist; and to fix with certainty the day of the general judgment,* — *tempus prefixum Antichristi, aut certum diem judicii.*

We do not pretend to fix either the day, week, month, or year. Moreover, with our whole mind and heart we submit in anticipation all that we write in this book, or in any other way, to the infallible judgment of the Church, and especially of the holy Roman See. Standing on this venerated rock of Peter, we are determined not to pay any attention to the sneers, ridicule, sarcasms, and offensive epithets of any superficial and prejudiced writer or speaker. We are a travelling Pellegrino, having no lasting city here below.

CHAPTER V.

TWO OTHER IMPORTANT SIGNS OF THE APPROACHING GENERAL JUDGMENT, — APOSTASY FROM FAITH, AND THE ABOLITION OF THE ROMAN EMPIRE.

ACCORDING to St. Paul's doctrine and the general interpretation of the Fathers of the Church, apostasy from the faith and the abolition of the Roman Empire will be two of the principal signs of the general judgment.

The Apostle says: *Let no man deceive you by any means; for, unless there come a revolt first, and the man of sin be revealed, the son of perdition. . . . . And now you know what withholdeth that he may be revealed in his time. . . . . The mystery of iniquity already worketh. Only that he, who now holdeth, do hold, until he be taken away.* (2 Thess. xi. 3.) See also Chap. IX., page 256, on Antichrist.

The revolt or falling off mentioned by St. Paul is explained in two ways: —

First. — *The falling off* from the Christian faith. This is the interpretation and opinion of St. Augustine, Venerable Bede, St. Anselm, St. Thomas of Aquin, Liranus, Estius, etc.

Our Divine Redeemer says: *Will not God avenge his elect, who call to him day and night? . . . . I say to you he will quickly avenge them. But yet, when the Son of Man cometh shall he find, think you, faith on earth?* (Luke xviii. 7, 8.) Thanks be to God, there is faith yet among true Catholic believers. But, in the first place, not all those who bear the name of Catholic have real Catholic faith. Moreover, in comparison to the rest of mankind, true, practical Catholics are a very small minority. Besides, we must reflect that the faith and law of the gospel was not only intended for mere individual men, but for entire nations. Nations are governed and represented by their recognized civil superiors. When these publicly and formally apostatize, the whole nation must be considered as an apostate. So we find in the Old Testament, that when the Jewish kings fell off from the worship and law of God, the whole nation was considered guilty, and severely punished. When the high-priests and Jewish magistrates crucified Jesus Christ and persecuted his Apostles, the whole nation was abandoned by God, and expelled from the Land of Promise.

With scarcely any exception, every government in Christendom has, by its impious laws, antichristian maxims and conduct, apostatized from the true faith of Jesus Christ. According to our Saviour's prophetical words, these apostate nations will, at the end of the world, hate and persecute his Church. *Then shall they deliver you up to be afflicted, and shall put you to death, and you shall be hated by all nations, for my name's sake.* (Matt. xxiv. 9.) But when has this practical apostasy been more general than at the present time? When has this fiendish hatred and persecution been more universal against the head and body of the Church of Jesus

Christ than at the present moment? Now, according to the infallible words of our Divine Master, this general hatred against truth and persecution of his Church upon earth must be taken as a sign of the approaching universal judgment.

Second Sign. — The second sign mentioned above by the Apostle St. Paul, many of the Fathers understand to refer to the abolition of the Roman Empire. This is the opinion of Tertullian, Lactantius, St. Cyril of Jerusalem, St. Jerome, who says that *it is the common opinion among Christian writers;* St. Ambrose, or an ancient commentator on the Pauline Epistles ; St. John Chrysostom, St. Augustine, St. Prosper, St. Primatius, Theophilatus, Eucomenius, Aimon, St. Rupert, and innumerable other ancient authors. St. Augustine says: *Nulli dubium est eum* (S. Paulum) *de Antichristo ita dixisse. There is no doubt that St. Paul in these words spoke of the abolition of the Roman Empire at the coming of Antichrist.* St. Ephrem Syrus says: *Ubi romanorum imperium fuerit impletum omnia consummari oportebit;* namely, *when the Roman Empire has been abolished, the world shall be destroyed.*

But the Roman Empire has been abolished by the first Napoleon at the beginning of this present century; therefore, according to the common opinion of the Fathers of the Church, and of many other learned writers, the coming of Antichrist and the general judgment cannot be very far from the present time.

The first reason in proof of this conclusion is because the Apostle St. Paul teaches that these two great events shall be very near one to the other. His words are : *And now you know what withholdeth, that he (Antichrist) may be revealed in his time,* namely, the existence, through God's will, of the Roman Empire. Hence St.

Paul adds: *Only that he who now holdeth* (the imperial sceptre) *do hold until he be taken away. And then that wicked one shall be revealed.* (2 Thess. xi. 3.) The second reason is because this is the common doctrine of the Fathers of the Church and of other learned writers, who believe that these two events shall be contemporaneous, or nearly so. More recent grave authors, as Bellarmine, Becanus, Lessius, A. Lapide, are of the same opinion. The fact is, that scarcely any author, ancient or modern, opines differently.

In order more fully to elucidate this important point, we will give here a brief sketch of the Roman Empire since the third century of Christianity.

At the end of the third century and the beginning of the fourth, under Maximian and Diocletian, the Roman Empire was divided into two, namely, the Western and Eastern Empires. These two persecuting and cruel emperors were immediately followed by Constantius Florus, father of Constantine, as Emperor of the West, and by Galerius, Emperor of the Eastern Empire, the capital of which was Antioch, whilst Rome remained the capital of the Western Empire. After Constantius and Galerius came Constantine and Licinius. The ambition of the latter made him fight against Constantine for supremacy, but he was completely defeated and killed; and thus, through God's special providence, the vast Roman Empire was happily reunited in Constantine, justly styled the Great. At his death the Empire was again divided among his three sons, Constantine, Constantius, and Constans; and after some years once more reunited in the unworthy person of the impious apostate, Julian; followed soon by the more worthy emperor, Jovian; and after his death divided again, under the Eastern and Western emperors, Valens and Valentinian. In the year 476, at the death of Augustulus, the Roman Empire was again united in the person of the Emperor Zeno, who resided in Constantinople. The Eastern Empire continued until the year 1453, when Constantinople was taken by the Turks under Constantine IX., and has been held by them till the present time. But they shall not keep it much longer. In the West the Roman Empire, after different trials and various changes, was fully and solemnly re-established by Charlemagne in the year 800, and in his successors it has continued ever since, until the beginning of the present century. During seven centuries, namely, from the eighth till the middle of the fifteenth, these two empires coexisted and recognized one another. When the Eastern Empire fell under the infidel and carnal Turks, the Western Empire continued to exist.

We must observe that at the re-establishment of the Empire of the West, in the year 800, under Charlemagne, the Eastern Empire had many possessions in Western Europe, and especially in Italy, all of which passed, with every legitimate title and right, and with the full consent of the Eastern emperor, Nicephorus, to Charlemagne and his successors, who was solemnly consecrated Roman Emperor by the Supreme Pontiff, St. Leo III., on Christmas day, 800, in St. Peter's, Rome.

We must moreover add, that the non-residence of the emperor in Rome did not in any way invalidate his title of Roman Emperor. It was through a special direction of God's holy providence, *which effects everything mightily and ordereth all things sweetly,* in behalf of his holy Church and of the Supreme Pontiff, that since the fifth century, and before, no Roman emperor has ever fixed his imperial throne in Rome. Rome has been chosen by Jesus Christ as the seat and centre of his universal spiritual dominion over the earth. *Roma per sacram beati Petri sedem caput orbis effecta latius presideret religione divina, quam dominatione terrena.* (St. Leo the Great, Serm. 1, in Nativ. Apost.)

Constantine the Great was the first to leave Rome to the Pope, when he went to found his imperial throne in Byzantium, which he called Constantinople, after his own name. The following emperors either continued to reside in the same city, or at Aix-la-Chapelle in France, or in Vienna in Germany. Thus the Roman Empire continued until the year 1806, when the proud Napoleon Bonaparte obliged Francis II. to renounce the title of Roman Emperor and to take that of Emperor of Austria. Hence, instead of Francis II. as Roman Emperor, he has been since known as Francis I., Emperor of Austria.

Napoleon was not satisfied with this act of tyranny. Helped by Luther's and Calvin's heresies, he easily abolished throughout all Germany the Electoral Princes, whose long-established right and duty was to elect the Roman Emperor. This was more completely effected by the arbitrary and haughty Napoleon with the Ecclesiastical German Electors, whose earthly possessions were sacrilegiously confiscated. Moreover, all these high-handed deeds were confirmed by the European half-infidel powers, united in the famous Congress of Vienna, in the year 1815. It is then evident that, since at least this last date, the Roman Empire has been entirely abolished both in fact and in name.

The Catholic Church also since that time no longer recites on *Good Friday* the ancient customary prayer for the Roman Emperor, the name of whom has also been taken away from the canon of the mass. But, as we have stated above, according to St. Paul's doctrine as understood and explained by the almost unanimous consent of the Fathers, the fall of the Roman Empire must soon be followed by the advent of Antichrist, the universal judgment, and the end of the world.

We are, therefore, forced to conclude that these awful events should be expected much sooner than too many persons wish to believe. . . . . God is not obliged to await for the modern invention of the *plébiscite*, or ballot-box, to execute his eternal decrees, and often threatened punishments against a faithless and sinful world. When his own time is arrived, God asks no advice from any man. He acts, and what God does is always the best.

CHAPTER VI.

MORE SIGNS OF THE APPROACHING GENERAL JUDGMENT.

THOUGH the majority of men obstinately refuse to believe that this earth, the cherished object of all their affection, and the centre of their happiness, has soon to be destroyed by a universal conflagration, and time has to be forever swallowed up in eternity, yet every reflecting mind must see that the conduct of the generality of mankind, in divers ways, imposes upon God the necessity of putting an end to the propagation of a perverse and godless generation. The vast majority of men either never care to learn, or have completely forgotten the end of their creation. We beg to be allowed to repeat a most essential and fundamental maxim of Christianity. Man has been made for eternity, he has been created for God. God has provided him with every means most effectively to obtain this glorious end. God has endowed man with reason, he has enlightened reason with revelation, has confirmed and strengthened revelation through the incarnation of his coeternal and consubstantial Son, *the Word made flesh.* This Divine Redeemer has, during nineteen centuries, established and most completely organized his infallible Church, in order that she may teach, guide, protect, and help mankind in the attainment of his final end. But perverse man has obstinately rejected or maliciously abused all these Divine gifts and favors, and his obstinacy and malice is rapidly increasing more and more sensibly every day. With what show of reason can we then expect God to prolong the duration of time and the continuation of his gifts, when these, through man's perversity and malice, are turned to God's dishonor, and to his own deeper condemnation and more severe eternal punishment? In such state of humanity it is an effect of God's wisdom and goodness to cut off the very root of the evil tree by putting an end to the duration of time. When time is universally abused, time should be suppressed.

But we should not attempt to preach to those who refuse to listen. Let us come back to plain and practical proofs. We have said that man's malice imposes upon God the moral necessity of putting an end to human generation. In fact, in order to preserve humanity upon earth, during hundreds and thousands of future centuries, as many expect, we absolutely need healthy and strong parents. This natural principle nobody can venture to contradict. Now, look at the rising generation of modern youths, and decide how strong and healthy their physical constitution appears to be. Their general training at home, in the public schools, in many non-Catholic colleges, academies, and universities, does not tend to improve them morally or physically. They have scarcely arrived at the age of reason, when they have already learned precocious malice, and contracted vicious habits of dissipation, which render them in their youth thin, pale, sickly walking skeletons. Is it from these dry bones that we can expect future healthy, strong, and virtuous fathers and mothers ? Let us proceed.

Every law, natural and positive, human and divine, requires a legitimate marriage to give us the necessary supply of honorable and hopeful children. The very law of nature demands that children should be well trained at home by the sound and virtuous maxims, and still more by the good example, of their legitimate parents. Hence, again, the natural obligation that the marriage contract should be for life. Nature abhors divorce. True Christianity has confirmed, sanctified, and elevated this natural law through a great sacrament, and ever inexorably condemned divorce.

If, in one single exception, the Divine Legislator allows divorce, yet he strictly forbids either party to marry again during the natural life of the other. His Divine words admit no human interpretation : *Whosoever shall put away his wife (except it be on account of adultery), and shall marry another, committeth adultery, and he that shall marry her that is put away committeth adultery.* (Matt. xix. 3.) *What, therefore, God hath joined together, let no man put asunder.* (Matt. xix. 6.)

Human laws in favor of divorces have no validity with God and his Church. His divine law is very wise ; it checks lust and promotes the principal end of matrimony. The hope of divorce leads to infidelity ; whilst both hope and fear of divorce is opposed to an increase of family.

But is now the Christian law of the inviolable unity and indissolubility of marriage faithfully observed in nominal Christian nations, both in Europe and America? Ah! alas! almost all Protestant governments, and too many so-called Catholic, liberal, modern governments, have pretended to legalize divorce, or rather adultery, and rendered it very easy and too frequent in practice, so far as to scandalize the very pagan nations of the earth. Is it these apostate nations that expect to last for an indefinite number of future ages? Are they not, on the contrary, doing all in their power to oblige the sovereign God of heaven and earth to cut them off soon from the land of the living?

But, abstracting now from the antichristian and vicious law of divorce, do all the young people who marry, and marry with the solemn promise, and under the admitted law of union for life, — do they all enter into the marriage life with the full and firm determination to observe the Divine law given by God to Adam and Eve, and more solemnly repeated by him to Noah and his wife, and to their three married sons, *to increase and multiply and fill the earth* with legitimate, virtuous, and useful children? We must be permitted to ask this important question, because it necessarily bears upon our subject, though we are not able to answer it. Various reliable statistics, however, both in Europe and America, have from well-authenticated facts answered it with such a cry of horror, that it must force the offended God of nature to deal with humanity as he did at the memorable epoch of the universal deluge, and afterwards with the corrupted and demoralized inhabitants of Sodom and Gomorrah.

We shall not mention the barbarity of the Chinese and other unnatural parents, pagan by profession or by practice, who expose their newly born infants as food to their vilest domestic animals, or who destroy them in body and soul before they are allowed to see the light of day. We cannot defile these pages by stating the facilities afforded even by legal enactments, and by too many high examples of depravity, to what essentially destroys the very source and principle of human life. But we are justified in asserting that mankind has conspired in imposing upon a just God the necessity of shortening the time, and removing the opportunity for the commission of so many crimes that cry aloud to Heaven for a speedy universal punishment.

This is the proper place for mentioning another sign given by our Divine Lord and Judge, indicating the approach of the end of the world. This is the thoughtless incredulity of carnal men, their greediness for sensual pleasures, the almost general levity of mind manifested in relation to the most serious and sacred concerns of life, and especially in everything relating to the marriage state. As at the present time no event can create in society a more lively nor a more brief excitement than a marriage, so no subject is more frequently spoken of with disgusting frivolity among young and old, men and women, than marriage. Listen, then, to the opportune warnings of our Divine Saviour. *As it was in the days of Noe, so shall also the coming of the Son of man be. For, as in the days before the flood they were eating and drinking, marrying and giving in marriage, until the day that Noe entered the ark, and they knew not till the day came, and took them all away; so also shall the coming of the Son of man be.* (St. Matt. xxiv. 37–39.)

The perversion of public justice, honesty, and equity

upon earth is another clear sign and powerful motive for the hastening of the final general judgment. *Love justice, you who are judges of the earth.* (Wisd. i. 1.) *Justice exalteth a nation, but sin maketh a nation miserable.* (Prov. xiv. 33.) *All bribery and injustice shall be blotted out. .... The riches of the unjust shall be dried up like a torrent, and shall pass away with a noise like a great thunder in a storm.* (Eccli. xl. 12, 13.)

A kingdom is translated from one people to another, because of injustice and wrongs and injuries and divers deceits. .... (Are not these very frequent in this world, Old and New?) *There is not a more wicked thing than to love money, for such a one setteth even his own soul to sale.* (Eccli. x. 8, 10.)

When a unanimous and universal shout of indignation is heard over the whole earth against the perversion of judgment and justice by those very governments and officials who should proclaim, uphold, protect, and defend these fundamental rights of humanity, we shall conclude with the words of the wise man: *I saw under the sun in place of judgment, wickedness, and in place of justice, iniquity; and I said in my heart, God will judge both the just and the wicked, and then shall be the time for everything.* (Eccles. iii. 16, 17.)

Another general sign of the dissolution of society and of the end of the world is the almost universal insubordination of mankind. Human governments are in rebellion against God and his Holy Church; and as an inevitable consequence people are dissatisfied with and rebel against these governments. Subjects refuse obedience and homage to their superiors; inferiors aspire to dominion and command. Liberty or rather license and independence is the mad clamor of the day. Civil and social disorder is general and supreme. Human society cannot last long in this wretched condition. We are arrived at the latter days foretold by our Divine Master, *when iniquity abounds and the charity of many has grown cold.* (Matt. xxiv. 12.) (See again the small remaining number of future Popes, page 204.)

CHAPTER VII.

AN OBJECTION ANSWERED.

THE objection, which some urge against the approach of the general judgment, because the gospel is not actually received by all nations, not only has no force, but becomes an additional argument in favor of its speedy arrival. It is true that our Divine Redeemer commanded his Apostles, and in them and through them his Holy Church, *to teach all nations, and to preach the gospel to all creatures.* Moreover, in the twenty-fourth chapter of St. Matthew, he says, *This gospel of the kingdom shall be preached in the whole world for a testimony to all nations; and then shall the consummation come.*

But the opinion of Christian authors is divided whether this has to be understood of the simultaneous existence of the Catholic Church in every part of the earth, or of the opportunity successively offered by authorized Christian missionaries to all nations for hearing the gospel, and learning its tenets and maxims. No person acquainted with Catholic history can deny that this opportunity has been over and over again offered to the world. St. Paul, the Apostle of the Gentiles, testifies that the gospel was preached by him and by his fellow

Apostles to the principal nations of the earth, *and bore fruit.* (Col. i. 6.)

Since Christianity began, the fervid zeal of the true and legitimate successors of the Apostles braved in every century all manner of dangers and obstacles to carry the good tidings of the gospel of Jesus Christ to every corner of the known world.

In conformity with the meaning of his beautiful Christian name, *Christopher Columbus,* the immortal Italian navigator, undertook the grand discovery of the New World in order to bring to it the olive branch of peace, by planting upon every hill and mountain the saving cross of Jesus crucified. The most ardent desire of his truly noble, catholic soul was not to obtain human fame, wealth, and glory; but to procure the extension of Christ's spiritual kingdom in the conversion and salvation of unknown millions of men.

Catholic missionaries answered immediately Columbus's invitation. Whilst Italian zeal and genius, supported by Spanish faith, opened the ocean-way to the far west, Portuguese enterprise rounded the African Cape of Good Hope to convey the light of the gospel and the hope of eternal salvation to the more populous nations of the East. As soon as the apostate Luther began in Germany to extinguish with his foul breath the lamp of faith, St. Francis Xavier, the greatest apostle of modern times, was successfully engaged with his zealous Jesuit companions in spreading the light of Catholic truth and the flames of Christian charity among millions of sincere converts from paganism in India, Japan, and China.

During the last four hundred years, the intrepid and accomplished Spanish, Portuguese, and French missionaries have been the most zealous apostles of the faith, and the brave pioneers of true Christian civilization in the eastern and western continents, and in the southern archipelagoes. In this present century Celtic faith and generous Irish devotion has planted the cross of salvation upon thousands of Catholic churches, convents, and schools in America and Australia.

If the world is not yet entirely converted to Christianity, the blame is not on the head nor in the conscience of the Catholic Church. Greek schism and Protestant heresy shall soon have to answer at the bar of the dreaded tribunal of Jesus Christ for their obstinate war against Catholic faith and zeal. Russian ambition and tyranny, Russian diplomacy and intrigue, have during centuries paralyzed the energy and thwarted every effort of Catholic charity in the conversion of the Greek heretic and of the Mahometan infidel. The bitter Calvinism of Holland fired the torch of persecution in the East and West against the Catholic faith, and its sordid love for lucre made it to trample under foot in Japan the cross of Jesus Christ, which Xavier planted with his sweat, and his companions and disciples watered with Catholic blood.

Ah! wretched Protestantism shall have to answer for the loss of faith and for the persecution of Christianity in Japan and elsewhere.

English schism and heresy have squandered their treasures and abused their great temporal power, not only in persecuting the faith in Great Britain and Ireland, but also in banishing the true religion of Jesus Christ from their vast American possessions, and from their more populous and richer Indian Empire. Their long-deserved punishment, however, is approaching from the North!

If China, Cochin China, Tonquin, and Corea have most stubbornly refused to receive the true saving faith of the gospel, and cruelly persecuted and massacred Catholic bishops, missionaries, and religious who brought it to them, they have only themselves to blame and condemn.

During the last hundred and fifty years infidel sectarianism has from its dark conventicles endeavored to conjure up the dying spirit of Luther and Calvin, and has slyly thrown across the path of Catholic zeal every obstacle that human malice could invent and suggest to oppose the progress of true Christianity. Its influence for evil was first manifested in Portugal through Pombal; it has since spread through Spain. At the present moment it is very active in both countries. But Don Carlos, the legitimate king of Catholic Spain, supported by legions of brave volunteers, is determined to fight for his religion, for his God, for his country, and for his rights. Jesus Christ and victory are with him. Hence the universal clamor of sectarian infidelity against his just cause. Hence the studied suppression, by the infidel press and telegraph, of every fact favorable to his noble undertaking.

But, unhappily, Portugal and Spain are not the only countries that have suffered and continue to suffer from the baneful venom of the sneaking serpent of concealed sectarianism. It has been from this masked enemy that our missionary labors for the conversion to Christianity and to genuine civilization of the red man of America and of the negro of Africa have been rendered comparatively barren. The impiety of the French Revolution, the Freemasonry of King Louis Philippe and of the late Emperor Louis Napoleon, and of their respective governments, after banishing from France and from Northern Africa the white flag of the most Christian dynasty of Catholic France, did officially forbid and oppose in every way the conversion of millions of Africans to the faith and religion of St. Cyprian and of St. Catherine, of St. Monica and of St. Augustine. It is from these polite and smooth sectarians, raised to civil offices and dignities by too credulous and too confiding Catholic voters in this and other countries, that our political rights and just claims for our religion and schools have constantly been and will ever be refused. It is the same antichristian spirit and agency that imprisons at this present time the Pope in the Vatican at Rome, that persecutes Catholic bishops, priests, and religious in Italy, in Germany and Switzerland, and cripples them in the Austrian Empire. *Let, then, God arise, and let his enemies be scattered, and let them that hate him flee from before his face. As smoke vanisheth, so let them vanish away; as wax melteth before the fire, so let the wicked perish at the presence of God. Arise, O God! and judge thy own cause.* (Ps. lxvii. 2, 3.)

In what we have written so far in this chapter we have briefly but energetically endeavored to prove that if Christianity is not professed by mankind upon earth, it has not been through the neglect of the Catholic Church. Paganism and infidelity, schism and heresy, the four savage beasts revealed to the Prophet Daniel, and to St. John in the Apocalypse, have obstinately opposed the preaching of the gospel to the nations of the world. Our Divine Redeemer, though most anxious for the conversion of mankind, yet ordered his Apostles to shake the very dust of the earth from their feet in condemnation of those cities and nations that refuse to listen to their words of faith and salvation. When men stubbornly shut their eyes to the light of eternal truth, they cannot blame God or his Church if they fall into the bottomless abyss. However, we believe that *the mercy of God is above all his works. God willeth not the death of the wicked, but that he may be converted and live.*

Hence, with many sincere and devout Catholics, we hope in the general and actual conversion of the vast majority of mankind to the Catholic religion before the end of the world. In the whole course of this work, and especially in the Second Part, we find solid grounds for this hope, and well-authenticated promises from God that this glorious event will soon take place. *This our hope is laid up in our bosom.* (Job. xix. 27.)

From several prophetical predictions contained in this book we distinctly learn that the conversion of mankind to true Catholic Christianity will be effected in about twenty years from this date, 1873. (Read next chapter.) But then we must remark that, according to the interpretation given to the above-quoted words of our Divine Redeemer (twenty-fourth chapter of St. Matthew, verse 14), *this gospel of the kingdom shall be preached in the whole world for a testimony to all nations, and then shall the consummation come.* St. Jerome, Suarez, and the generality of Christian authors conclude that this last general conversion of mankind will be a most certain sign of the imminent destruction of the world. *Then shall the consummation come.* (See A. Lapide in chapter 24, Matt. verse 14.) This will also appear from the next chapter.

CHAPTER VIII.

PROPHECY OF AN OLIVETINE MONK.

IN the year 1720, whilst some Italian laborers were digging near the city of Viterbo, about forty miles from Rome, they found a grave containing an entire incorrupt body, dressed in the habit of an Olivetine monk, holding in his right hand a well-preserved manuscript, that nobody could remove from his grasp. The news of this discovery having been immediately communicated to the abbot of a neighboring monastery, he hastened to the spot indicated in company with several of his religious, and in their presence and that of many other persons he commanded the dead monk, in virtue of holy obedience, to give up the paper, which was immediately done. The abbot, having opened it, read in it the following predictions, which were faithfully copied, the original being forwarded to Pope Clement XII. in Rome, where it was also copied by several high ecclesiastics and other persons. It is from one of these authentic copies that we publish the following translation:—

I. From the year 1760 to 1770, America shall be on fire. This prophecy has relation to the American Revolution.

II. From the year 1770 to 1780, great earthquakes on the Rhine.

III. From the year 1780 to 1790, faith shall pass away.

Faith was poisoned in France and other neighboring

countries by the impious writings of Rousseau, Voltaire, Diderot, D'Lambert, and similiar apostles of infidelity.

IV. From the year 1790 to 1800, the Church of God shall bleed.

During the first French Revolution more than ten thousand ecclesiastics and religious persons were massacred in France in those ten years.

V. In the year 1800, the Pastor shall not exist.

Pius VI. was captured by the French revolutionary government, brought as a prisoner to Valence in the Delphine in France, where he expired on the 29th of August, 1799. After seven months, Pius VII. was elected in the city of Venice, March 14, 1800.

VI. From the year 1860 to . . . . God's wrath over the whole earth.

VII. For the year 1890. All nations come and adore God.

Here is again foretold the universal triumph of the Catholic religion, of which we treat in the Second Part of this book.

VIII. From the year 1940 to 1950, the victim and the sacrifice shall cease.

This is a clear and evident prophecy of the frightful persecution of Antichrist, when Catholics shall not be allowed to celebrate publicly the holy sacrifice of the mass, which, however, will most certainly continue to be offered up in secret until the end of the world; because our Divine Lord has promised to be with his Church till the consummation of time. (St. Matt. xxviii. 20.)

IX. From the year 1950 to 1980 shall be the abomination and desolation.

Jane le Royer, in her predictions (page 111), announces what is very natural, that many precursors, false prophets, and members of infernal secret societies, worshippers of Satan, shall impugn the most sacred dogmas and doctrines of our holy religion, shall persecute the faithful, shall commit abominable actions; but the real and extreme abomination and desolation shall more fully be accomplished during the reign of Antichrist, which will last about three years and a half.

St. Bridget of Sweden says: "In the year 1980 the wicked shall prevail; they will profane and sacrilegiously defile the churches, by erecting in them altars to idols and to Antichrist, whom they will worship, and will attempt to force others to do the same." This, strictly speaking, is called *the abomination of desolation*, foretold by our Lord Jesus Christ in these words: *When you shall see the abomination of desolation standing where it ought not.* When you shall see idols, and especially the man of sin, standing in person or in his statues or images in Christian temples, receiving Divine honors, *then in those days shall be such tribulations as were not from the beginning of the creation which God created until now, neither shall be. And unless the Lord had shortened the days, no flesh should be saved; but for the sake of the elect, whom he hath chosen, he hath shortened the days. And then if any man shall say to you: Behold, here is Christ; or, Lo, he is there, do not believe. For there will rise up false Christs and false prophets, and they shall show signs and wonders, and seduce, if it were possible, even the elect. Take you heed, therefore; behold, I have foretold you all things.*

But in those days, after that tribulation, the sun shall be darkened and the moon shall not give her light, and the stars of heaven shall be falling down, and the powers that are in the heaven shall be moved. And then they shall see the Son of Man coming in the clouds with great power and glory. And then shall he send his angels, and shall gather together his elect from the four winds, from the uttermost part of the earth to the uttermost part of heaven. Now of the fig-tree learn ye a parable. When the branch thereof is now tender, and the leaves are come forth, you know that summer is very near; so you also, when you shall see these things come to pass, know ye that it is very near, even at the doors. Amen. I say to you that this generation shall not pass until all these things be done. Heaven and earth shall pass away, but my words shall not pass away. But of that day or hour no man knoweth. Take ye heed: watch and pray; for you know not when the time is. (St. Matt. xxiv.)

CHAPTER IX.

ABOUT ANTICHRIST.

A TREATISE about Antichrist cannot be expected in this book. We will give only a sketch of what is more certain, and more commonly admitted by Catholic authors, about this horrible monster of humanity, the son of perdition, the man of sin, the most audacious and the most wicked enemy of Jesus Christ, and the most cruel persecutor of his Holy Church. St. John says that *the number of his name is 666* (Apoc. xiii. 18); that is to say, his name shall be found composed of Greek letters, which will enigmatically give this number. He is moreover called *Antichrist* on account of his excessive hatred against Jesus Christ. St. John of Damascus says: *Everybody who denies the incarnation of the Son of God, and that Jesus Christ is true God and perfect man, such person is Antichrist.* But in a more special and principal manner he will be known as *Antichrist who shall come about the end of the world.* (Lib. IV. De Fide, chap. 27.) A great number of Fathers and doctors of the Church affirm that his parents will be Jews of the tribe of Dan. (See Suarez, Quest. 59, Art. 6, Disp. 54, seer 11.) Suarez, after St. Jerome, St. Ambrose, Sulpitius, Severus, etc., says that Antichrist shall be born of Jewish extraction, and will profess the Jewish religion; not through real devotion, but through hypocrisy, in order more easily to persuade the great majority of that mysterious race to receive him as their Messiah. He will have two important objects in doing this. In the first place, he will thus mimic Jesus Christ; in the second place, he will thus obtain the enthusiastic support and the wealth of the Jews, and through this material advantage be able to open the way to his ambition for high dignities and human power. The opinion of these Christian writers is derived from the following words of the New Testament. Our Divine Lord and Saviour said to the Jews: *I am come in the name of my Father, and you receive me not. If another* (Antichrist) *shall come in his own name, you will receive him.* (St. John v. 43.) St. Paul also says: *He whose coming is according to the working of Satan, in all power and signs and lying wonders, and in all seduction of iniquity to them that perish, because they receive not the love of truth* (Jesus Christ) *that they may be saved; therefore God* (in punishment of it) *will send them the operation of error* (Antichrist), *to believe a lie.* (2 Thess. ii. 9, 10.) Our Divine Lord and Saviour Jesus Christ was born from the Jewish race, and, preaching to them the truth, confirmed it with many incontestable miracles, yet they obstinately refused to believe in him or in his doctrines. Antichrist shall be born from the same people, who will allow themselves to be deceived by his satanic power, signs, and lying wonders, and will enthusiastically receive him as their long-expected Messiah. Thus we see how obstinacy in error leads men to greater crimes and to final reprobation. *Because they receive not the love of truth, that they may be saved; therefore God sent them the operation of error to believe a lie.*

St. John Damascene says, *that Antichrist shall be an illegitimate child under the complete power of Satan; and that God, knowing his incredible future perversity, will allow the Devil to take a full and perpetual possession of him from his very sinful conception.* (Lib. IV. chap. 27.) This holy Father, with St. Cyril of Jerusalem, affirms that though Antichrist will from his childhood have the most wicked and cruel dispositions, yet, inspired by a preternatural precocious malice, he will practise the most consummate hypocrisy, deceiving the Jews and all his followers. In proportion as he shall advance in age, knowledge, vice, and power, his ambition will become excessive. He will not only strive for universal dominion over men upon earth, but, as St. Paul teaches, *he will oppose and be lifted up above all that is called God, or that is worshipped;* namely, Antichrist will oppose all that is duly or unduly worshipped, and be lifted up by his satanic pride and ambition above all that is called God, not allowing men to worship any other being but himself, as if he were the only God. *So that he sitteth in the temple of God, showing himself as if he were God.* (2 Thess. ii. 4.) *He shall speak words against the High One, and he shall crush the saints of the Most High, and shall think himself able to change times and laws.* (Daniel vii. 5.)

St. Cyril of Jerusalem teaches that Antichrist will exceed in malice, perversity, lust, wickedness, impiety, and heartless cruelty and barbarity all men that have ever disgraced human nature. Hence St. Paul emphatically calls him *the man of sin, the son of perdition, the wicked one, whose birth and coming is through the operation of Satan, in all manner of seduction of iniquity.* (2 Thess. ii.) He shall through his great power, deceit, and malice succeed in decoying or forcing to his worship two thirds of mankind; the remaining third part of men will most steadfastly continue true to the faith and worship of Jesus Christ. But in his satanic rage and fury, Antichrist will persecute these brave and devout Christians during three years and a half, and torture them with such an extremity of barbarity, with all the old and his newly invented instruments of pain, as to exceed all past persecutors of the Church combined. He will oblige all his followers to bear impressed upon their foreheads or right hands the mark of the beast, and will starve to death all those who refuse to receive it. (Apoc. xiii. 16.)

Henoch and Elias will appear in person to oppose Antichrist. They will greatly strengthen the courage of the persecuted Christians, and convert to the faith of Jesus Christ the majority of the Jewish followers of Antichrist. This unexpected disappointment will make him blaze with incredible fury against these holy men, upon whom, after the most strenuous efforts, he will, at the end of three years and a half, succeed in inflicting a most cruel death. Finally, *our Lord Jesus Christ in person shall kill him with the spirit of his mouth and shall destroy this human monster of pride,* impiety, wickedness, and cruelty, *with the brightness of his coming.* (2 Thess. ii. 8.)

Here we shall now make a few extracts from the Tiburtine Sibyl, and from the holy bishop and martyr, Bemecobus. The Tiburtine Sibyl lived at Tivoli, near Rome, during the reign of King Tarquin. She was highly honored as a holy virgin by the pagan Romans. She foretold the divine birth, the life, passion, death, and glorious resurrection of our Lord and Saviour; also his spiritual reign over the whole world, his second coming at the end of time, and the general judgment. Several holy fathers of the Church have praised and quoted her prophecies. The following are her words about Antichrist:—

A prince of iniquity shall come forth from the tribe of Dan, who will be called Antichrist. Child of perdition, full of arrogance, and of an insane malice, he shall work upon earth a number of prodigies in order to support his erroneous doctrines. Through his magical arts he will surprise the good faith of many persons. At his command fire shall come from above.

At that time the years shall be shortened as well as the months, the weeks, and the days and hours. God will shorten, not the measure or duration, but *the number of those terrible days.*

For the sake of God's elect, Antichrist shall be killed upon Mount Olivet by Michael (the Archangel). Then the dead shall rise. (See page 239.)

From a very old prophecy translated from the Hebrew and Greek into Latin by the holy bishop and martyr Bemecobus, who, according to St. Jerome, was Bishop of Patina in Lycia, we extract the following details about Antichrist:—

Antichrist, the son of perdition, will be born in Corozain will be brought up in Bethsaida, and shall begin to reign in Capharnaum, according to what our Lord Jesus Christ said in the gospel. *Woe to thee Corozain . . . . Woe to thee Bethsaida . . . . and thou Capharnaum, that art exalted up to heaven, thou shalt be thrust down to hell.* (Luke x. 15.)

Antichrist shall work a thousand prodigies on earth. He will make the blind see, the deaf hear, the lame walk, the dead rise, so that even the elect, if possible, shall be deceived by his magical arts. Swollen with pride, Antichrist shall enter in triumph the city of Jerusalem, and will sit on a throne in the temple to be adored as if he were the Son of God. His heart being intoxicated with arrogance, he will forget his being a mere man, and the son (bastard) of a woman of the tribe of Dan. He shall seduce many credulous persons through his deceitful errors. . . . .

Elias and Henoch will attack him boldly in the presence of the people, and shall convict him of imposture and lies. Then the Jews of all the tribes of Israel will be converted to the faith of Jesus Christ, and shall suffer martyrdom for his sake. In consequence of this Antichrist shall be seized with rage, and will put to death the two saints of God, and all those who have believed them.

Then the Son of God, our Lord Jesus Christ, shall come in person. He shall appear on the clouds of heaven surrounded by legions of angels, and shining with glory. He will put to death Antichrist, the beast, the enemy, the seducer, and all his followers. This shall be the end of time and the beginning of the general judgment.

Those who wish to study this subject more deeply and extensively can find plenty of materials in Genesis xlix., but more in the Prophecy of Daniel, the Epistles of St. Paul (especially 2 Thess. ii.), and the Apocalypse. Among the Fathers, see Lactantius, St. Jerome, St. John Chrysostom, St. Irenæus, Hyppolitus, and, more recently, the Dominican Malvenda, the Jesuit Francis Suarez, Pereyra, Lessius, Acosta, Da Baeza, etc.

But because these works cannot be had by all and many could not read them, so we would strongly recommend the perusal of the "General History of the Christian Church".... chiefly deduced from the Apocalypse by the Rt. Rev. Charles Walmesly, an English Catholic bishop, under the name of Signor Pastorini. It is an admirable book in the English language, much adapted to the present time. D. and J. Sadlier & Co. have given the first American edition, 1865.

CHAPTER X.

THE LAST PROPHECIES AND RECENT FACTS ABOUT ANTICHRIST.

1. *St. Hildegarde.*

AS an introduction to this chapter, we will give a revelation made by God to St. Hildegarde, which is taken from her own work entitled *Scivias*, written by this great saint about the year 1152:—

"God has employed six days in the creation of this world and rested on the seventh day; these six days represent the six first ages of the world. As God crowned all his works on the sixth day (by the creation of man), so in the sixth age of the world he has manifested new prodigies. The world is entering the seventh age, which indicates the end of time.

"My Son" (God said to the saint), — "my Son came upon earth when the day of time's duration was at the period which corresponds in the ordinary day to the hours of none and vespers, namely, between three and six o'clock, when to the heat of the day succeeds the coolness of evening. In short, my Son appeared on this earth after the first five epochs of the world, when this was already verging to its decline.

"The son of perdition, Antichrist, who shall reign only a very short time, shall come at the end of the day of the world's duration, at the period which corresponds to the moment when the sun has disappeared beyond the horizon; that is to say, he shall come at the last days of the world." (R. P. Renard, "Life of St. Hildegarde.")

2. *Sister Bertine.*

From a person well informed, of solid judgment, and endowed with every qualification to guarantee the incontestable authenticity of his information, we have recently learned (1872) that Sister Bertine, a holy religious, who died in the year 1850, at St. Omer, France, during her life was favored with heavenly revelations relative to the coming of Antichrist and the end of the world.

Sister Bertine was a religious of eminent sanctity. She was born in February, 1801. At the age of twenty-two she was impressed with the sacred stigmas of our Lord Jesus Christ, which were visible every Friday, and on all the principal Feasts, during the last twenty-nine years of her life. Her sincere and profound humility and the childlike candor of her evangelical simplicity were so great that all her religious sisters were filled with admiration and holy edification at her saintly conduct. This good sister was deeply mortified whenever marks of respect and veneration were shown to her, which were due to the extraordinary gifts which she received from God, and to the eminent holiness of her life. In order to shun these manifestations of esteem, she studiously kept herself concealed, avoided visits, and entreated her religious superiors to employ her in the lowest and hardest labors of the house. Her religious sisters unanimously believed that good Sister Bertine had ever preserved unsullied the white robe of her baptismal innocence. She died more through excess of Divine love than through physical pain, on the 25th of January, 1850, aged forty-nine years and ten months.

Sister Bertine had often foretold that she should not become old. The bishop of the diocese gave orders that a juridical information should be taken about the stigmatization of this great servant of God, and the ecclesiastical commission pronounced the stigmas to have been the effect of Divine operation. There is not the least doubt that Sister Bertine was one of those extraordinary souls through whom God is pleased to manifest the riches of his divine power, wisdom, and goodness. We shall now pass to some of her revelations about Antichrist. Sister Bertine said to some of her sisters: "Antichrist shall appear very soon. You shall not see him, nor those who shall immediately succeed you, but those who shall come after shall live under his dominion. (We must observe here that this prophecy was made about thirty years ago.) At the arrival of Antichrist no change shall be made in this house; everything shall go on in the regular order; the religious exercises of the community, domestic labor, the employment in the sick wards (the establishment in St. Omer is a large hospital), in fact, everything shall go on as at the present day; when, all of a sudden, our sisters will learn that the man of sin has arrived. This event will take place about the end of this present century, or at the beginning of the next. The last king of France shall die during a great battle at the time of Antichrist, and his body will be deprived of burial."

Sister Bertine moreover stated that she had seen the holy patriarch Enoch, one of the two just men who shall have to fight against Antichrist, and sustain the faithful during their severe trials at the end of the world. "He was dressed," she said, "like a missionary, ready, as it were, to start for his great approaching difficult mission; the end of the world, however," she added, "shall not be during this century, but between 1900 and 1950."

3. *Veronica Nucci.*

On the 29th of May, 1853, the Blessed Virgin Mary appeared to a poor and lowly shepherdess, twelve years old, called Veronica Nucci, born 26th of November, 1841, in the small village of Ceretto, diocese of Pitigliano, in Tuscany, Italy. She became a Franciscan nun when very young. In a short time she arrived at a sublime degree of religious perfection. Veronica died on the ninth day of November, 1862, aged twenty-one years. Her Life, full of edification, especially for young people, was published in the "Annals of Holiness," one volume, in the year 1869.

A few months before her death, the most holy and immaculate Virgin Mary appeared to Veronica, and said to her: "If sinners do not correct their evil ways, my Son is going to put an end to the world. *Dost thou, Veronica, prefer to die in three or four months, or to live to see the end of this world?*" Veronica promptly answered: *Blessed Lady, I prefer to die.* She did die.

In these words the most holy Virgin Mary offered to her favorite angelic shepherdess the privilege of choosing either to die soon, or to continue to live until the end of the world; therefore, the end of the world cannot be beyond the ordinary age of an old person at our present time, namely, beyond eighty or ninety years of age, beginning to count from November, 1841, when Veronica was born. This interpretation will be found fully corroborated by many of the predictions published in this book, but especially in those of Holzhauser, D'Orval, Sister Bertine, etc. Some of these predictions mention that the end of the world shall come about the year 1921, when Veronica should have been about eighty years old.

4. *The Curé d'Ars and Mary Lataste.*

The venerable Monsieur Vianney, Curé d'Ars, near Lyons, France, one day, with his habitual childlike simplicity, said : *They may intend to canonize me, but they shall not have the necessary time.* From these words L'Abbé Curicque concludes that the venerable servant of God knew that the approach of the general judgment was so near that the period of time ordinarily required for the whole process of a beatification and canonization should not be allowed by God. Moreover, our Divine Lord said to Mary Lataste : "I will very soon let my day appear. It will come when, in despite of all my previous signs in heaven and upon earth, men will least think of it."

Never in any age of the world have so many signs and wonders been seen in the heavens and upon the earth as during the last thirty years. During this comparatively short period of time, we have seen the two wonders of the Tyrol in the person of the bedridden, suffering Addolorata, and of the heaven-ravished ecstatic. In France, we have had the apparition of La Salette, and the revelation made to Melanie and Massimin, and the still more wonderful apparition of Lourdes to Bernardette Soubirous ; also the less known apparition at Pontmain Mayenne to the children of that village in France ; that made to the young woman, Zoe Tonare, in Lorraine, on the 10th of June, 1870, and several times repeated since to her who is destined soon to be a second Joan of Arc against Prussia and in behalf of France ; that of

Pouillé, near Ancenis (Loire Inferieure), to Eugenie Prudhomme, during the three days of 13th, 15th, and 16th of February, 1872. In Italy there have been so many miraculous motions of the eyes of sacred pictures and statues of the Blessed Virgin Mary, particularly in Taggia.

There are at present those living prodigies of Palma Maria Addolorata and David Lazzaretti, of whom we have spoken in this volume, pages 106 and 168.

In Belgium there is the wonder of Bois de Haine, diocese of Tournay, in the person of Louise Lateau, aged twenty-three years.

In Poland, on the 2d of February, 1871, warriors were seen publicly in the air by many persons in the village De Golaze, in the Duchy of Posen. In Germany, the *Deutsche Volksblatt* of Stuttgart, capital city of Wurtemberg, relates the appearance of a similar vision, which took place on the 29th of July, of the same year, and which was confirmed on the 26th of August, by a correspondent in the *St. Galler Volksblatt*. These two wonderful visions represented a great army headed by an emperor, who directed from Germany his victorious march towards the south; but, when he attempted to assail a great rock (that of St. Peter), was crushed to death and disappeared. We must also mention here the apparition of many crosses in the window-glasses of several cities in the Duchy of Baden during the autumn of 1872, and lately the hundreds of times repeated apparitions in divers forms on the summit of a mountain near Kruth, in Alsace, which were first seen last year, in the month of July, and still continue at the present time (April, 1873), as we learn from the truly Catholic German weekly, *Volks Zeitung*, of Baltimore. These public events have been witnessed by many thousands of persons of every age, class, creed, and condition of life.

They cannot be denied by any reasonable person; they must therefore be admitted as signs and wonders of the approaching general judgment.

5. *Antichrist already born.*

The following extraordinary facts about Antichrist, without vouching for them, are translated from *Derniers Avis Prophetiques*, "Last Prophetical Warning," several times quoted in this book. These extracts are made under the paragraph, *Prophetie inedite sur l'Antichrist et la Fin du Monde*, page 269,—"Inedited Prophecy about Antichrist and the End of the World." We give them as they are. We are neither able nor obliged to vouch for them.

We may remark, however, that in the supposed revelation of the Blessed Virgin Mary, made to Melanie of La Salette, no less striking announcements are made about Antichrist and his impious brothers. (See page 81.) We should also remember that in prophetical language, both in holy Scripture and in hagiography, impious and cruel persecutors of the Church of Jesus Christ are called Antichrists. The person announced in the following details may be one of these, if not the real Antichrist. We pass now to the translation.

During the month of May, 1871, a poor boy about twelve years old was in an extraordinary manner directed to a preparatory ecclesiastical seminary in France to begin his studies for the ecclesiastical state. It has been revealed to him by the Blessed Virgin Mary, that one day he shall be ordained priest, and that he shall have to combat against Satan and Antichrist. A missionary priest, in relation to this boy, writes the following lines: "Some day I shall speak to you about an apparition of the Most Holy Virgin Mary to a boy twelve years old, whom she directed to become a priest in order to fight against Antichrist, *who is already born.* The details of this apparition are highly interesting. But prudential motives counsel silence for the present."

At the beginning of April, 1870, this wonderful little child foretold the war between France and Prussia, the defeat at Sedan, the declaration of the Paris Republic, and other imminent events.

6. *More about Antichrist.*

In the French religious periodical, "The Rosary of Mary," the following correspondence from Geneva was published last year, 1872. The writer, who styles himself a *Frenchman who loves France,* is a gentleman connected with the *highest circles of the political world.* He is endowed with a solid, enlightened, and prudent judgment, and his soul is profoundly religious. The following are his words: —

"Many commentators of the sacred Scriptures believe that the end of the world is near at hand. A well-informed gentleman has stated to have read a revelation made in the year 1860, at the time of the massacre in Syria, and more especially in the city of Damascus, in which it was announced that those bloody murders were committed at the instigation of the demons, in order to celebrate the birth of Antichrist, which took place in the same year.

"Moreover, there is an extraordinary French lady of eminent and solid virtue who has been for some years employed in divers important and difficult missions to several sovereigns in Europe, and more especially to the Pope. In arriving or passing through any country, the language of which she did not previously know, she is by a special gift of God enabled to understand well what the people say to her, and she can make herself fully understood by them. When commissioned to treat on important affairs, which require secrecy, during her journey, she knows whither and to whom she is sent, but she totally forgets the subject of her mission until she is introduced to the personage to whom she has to speak. Her mission ended, she again loses the remembrance of it. This lady solemnly declares, that passing through a certain city, and having to stop at some hotel, she saw a woman with her son about twelve years old. As soon as the boy perceived this French lady he was seized with a violent colic. His mother, with some evident anxiety, asked what ailed him. He answered, 'I do not know, but as soon as I have seen that lady down below, I have been seized with a strong internal pain.' This was very likely a sign to the mother to make his real character known to the French lady, to whom she manifested that her *son was Antichrist!!!*"

CHAPTER XL.

CONCLUDING REMARKS.

WHAT we have collected together in the last chapter, as well as many other detached historical facts, visions, revelations, and private opinions, may be considered straws by some worldly wise men. We also believe them to be straws floating and drifted on the ever-swelling bosom of the wide and deep river of patristic, ecclesiastical, and human tradition. We could have condensed in this book about eighty different previsions and predictions, but we have preferred to select from different books, published in various countries and languages, those predictions and visions which, to the best of our judgment, appeared more strongly supported both by internal evidence and by external human authority.

Will they all be considered illusions? Then all those eminent saints, St. Remigius, St. Cesarius, St. Hildegarde, St. Bridget, St. Francis di Paola, Venerable Bartholomew Holzhauser, Venerable Anna Maria Taigi, Venerable Elizabeth Mora, the Venerable Viannay Curé d'Ars, Father Necktou, Sister Mary Lataste, Sister Rose Colomba, Palma Maria Addolorata Matarelli, the most wonderful living saint of the present age, etc., etc., etc., — all these and all the rest must then be considered persons under the illusion of the Evil Spirit! Equally illuded and deceived have therefore been the hundreds of learned, grave, and pious authors, who have written the biographies of these great servants of God; illuded then all the hundreds of thousands of witnesses who have conversed with them and admired the holiness of their lives. Only a man who has lost his reason can believe that millions of other men have lost it.

To those who have no common faith with these servants of God and with us Catholics, we may remark that, admitting the morally impossible absurdity of illusion, this very supposed illusion can be used as an argument to prove the real existence of these ideas in the human mind; for how could such statements be made by hundreds of persons almost in every age and country, be believed and proclaimed by hundreds of thousands, except they found a corresponding echo in the human soul? Moreover, as these so flippantly called illusions are daily multiplying, we must conclude that Satan himself is doing all in his power to announce through hundreds of his supposed agents, but in reality his most determined enemies, the approach of Antichrist, and of the general judgment and the end of this world. We Catholics prefer to believe, however, that these salutary warnings come from God, and not from the Devil; that they are mercifully intended for our instruction, for our conversion and edification, and not for our illusion and for our mockery. All the efforts of Satan are directed and intended to prevent men from ever thinking about the coming of Antichrist, and more especially about the approach of the general judgment and the end of this world, which affords to him such abundant harvest of souls for hell. The end of humanity will extinguish the dominion of Satan over men upon earth, and will confine him with his companions and followers in the fiery prison of hell during a never-ending eternity of woe. The Devil dreads this increase of misery even more than the reprobates themselves.

Let us be serious; let us think and reason and speak like men and like Christians. Let us be persuaded that the end of the world cannot be very far. Scripture, tradition, the Fathers of the Church, most learned, grave, and pious authors, older and more modern saints, and innumerable servants of God of every age, class, and condition in life, belonging to almost every country upon earth, announce its approach. Famine and pestilence, seditions, revolutions, rebellions, wars, schisms, heresies, the frightful increase of vice and crime in society, charity cooling, iniquity abounding upon earth, earthquakes, destructive conflagrations, terrible accidents on land, shipwrecks on the ocean, sudden deaths, increasing mortality, visions in the sky, disorder in the seasons, spots on the sun, — all nature, in short, announce the pangs of dissolution. But the majority of men affect to be incredulous. This, as we saw above, is an additional sign of the end of the world foretold by our Divine Saviour. Let us then believe and act like sincere and devout Christians. Let us place our treasure in heaven and our heart with our treasure. If we are poor in earthly goods, let us rejoice, for we shall leave behind fewer materials as fuel for the universal conflagration.

Piety with sufficiency is great gain. For we brought nothing into this world, and certainly we can carry nothing out. But, having food and wherewith to be covered, with these we are content. (1 Tim. vi. 6.) The less we possess on earth, the more ardently we shall as Christians covet the eternal riches of heaven.

The end of the world cannot cause much regret to the blessed poor in spirit. *Blessed are the poor in spirit, for theirs is the kingdom of heaven.* (St. Matt. v. 3.)

Let rich Christians take the wholesome advice of our Divine Master, and with the mammon of iniquity make to themselves many friends in the persons of Christ's poor, who will receive them into the eternal mansions. *If riches abound,* the holy King David said, *do not allow your heart to be attached to them.* (Ps. lxi. 11.) *For they who would become rich fall into temptation, and into the snare of the devil, and into many unprofitable and hurtful desires, which drown men into destruction and perdition.* (1. Tim. vi. 9.) *We have the poor with us,* we have orphans, we have widows, we have the sick; we need hospitals, and schools, and seminaries, and some convents and monasteries, because, more than ever, we stand in great need of truly pious and holy religious, learned and zealous priests and fervent missionaries, to convert a sinful world, and prepare humanity for the awful general judgment. Many children already born will very likely witness the final destruction of the large estates and wealth left to them by their incredulous parents. Both then, but in vain, shall bitterly regret not to have acted on the advice which they may have read in this book. O rich Christians, help now, that you can do so to your spiritual advantage at a hundredfold interest! help struggling priests and religious, who sacrifice themselves in promoting the welfare of souls, the glory of God, and the honor of our holy Catholic religion. Restore your riches voluntarily to God, and through your generous alms atone for your past indolence and sins, and secure heaven with your wealth, which, in spite of avarice, shall soon be burnt away by fire, together with your body and soul, if they unhappily are found attached to it. These are plain and strong words, which you are not accustomed to hear; but they are words of truth and charity, from your best friend and well-wisher, who is without human fear or human hope. He is a poor pellegrino pilgrim upon this miserable earth. You will see him on the day of general judgment, where he hopes to be with you at the right hand of the Divine Judge. Pious souls, happy elect of God, you have nothing to fear, but everything to hope at the approach of the universal judgment. Lift up your humble head, your redemption is at hand; you will be exalted and glorified during a blessed eternity. Pray that the writer may be with you. *Come, Lord Jesus,* and delay not.

FINIS.

PRINTED BY RICHARDSON AND SONS, DERBY.

PUBLISHED BY RICHARDSON AND SONS,
26, Paternoster Row, London; and Derby.

Now Ready, cloth, price 1s.

Spiritual Works of
SAINT FRANCIS BORGIA.

THIS DAY, Foolscap 8vo, Price 2s. 6d.

A CATECHISM
FOR THE RIGHT UNDERSTANDING OF
THE SACRIFICE AND LITURGY OF THE MASS,
FOR THE USE OF SCHOOLS.

Compiled at the request of Authority,

BY MRS. STUART LAIDLAW.

From a Work by the Rev. JOHN MACDONALD,
Priest of the Catholic Church.

This day, post 8vo, Superfine Cloth, price 4s. 6d.

FATHER EUDES,
APOSTOLIC MISSIONARY,
AND HIS FOUNDATIONS.
1601-1874.
BY M. CH. DE MONTZEY.

With a Brief of approval addressed to the Author by
HIS HOLINESS POPE PIUS IX.

MEDIÆVAL LIBRARY OF MYSTICAL AND
ASCETICAL WORKS.

NOW READY, Superfine Cloth, post 8vo, price 6s.

MEDITATIONS ON THE
Life and Passion of Our Lord Jesus Christ.

BY DR. JOHN TAULER, DOMINICAN FRIAR.
TRANSLATED from the LATIN by a SECULAR PRIEST.

PUBLISHED BY RICHARDSON AND SONS,
26, Paternoster Row, London; and Derby.

NOW READY, price 4s. 6d.

Spiritual Letters of
FATHER SURIN, S.J.

FIRST SERIES.
TRANSLATED BY SISTER M. CHRISTOPHER,
Order of S. Francis.
WITH A PREFACE BY FATHER FRANCIS GOLDIE, S.J.
EDITED BY THE REV. H. COLLINS.

These most beautiful Letters, addressed to Religious, and to devout people living in the world, are a golden treasury of maxims and instructions for the spiritual life.

NOW READY, price 3s. 6d.

Revelations of St. Bridget,

PRINCESS OF SWEDEN. With a Preface by His Grace the Archbishop of Westminster.

JUST PUBLISHED, price 5s.

The History of the Miraculous Sanctuary of

OUR LADY OF LOURDES.

Translated by

THE REV. FATHER IGNATIUS SISK, O.C.,

Of St. Bernard's Abbey, Leicestershire, from the French of Henry Lasserre, with his special permission. A work honoured through 25 Editions, with a Brief of Approval addressed to the Author by Pope Pius IX.

Printed Wrapper, 1s. 6d. Superfine Cloth, gilt edges, 2s.

The Holy Mountain of La Salette:
A PILGRIMAGE OF THE YEAR 1854.
BY THE RIGHT REV. BISHOP ULLATHORNE.

Louise Lateau, the Ecstatica of Bois d'Haine; her Life, Stigmata, and Ecstasies, by Dr. Lefebvre, translated from the French by J. S. Shepard, with a brief sketch of several former cases of the same nature, 2s.

The Sincere Christian instructed in the FAITH OF CHRIST, FROM THE WRITTEN WORD, by the Right Rev. Dr. George Hay, 2 vols, cloth lettered, price 2s. And may be had in various styles of binding.

PUBLISHED BY RICHARDSON AND SONS,
26, Paternoster Row, London; and Derby.

Life and Martyrdom of the Blessed Andrew Bobola, of the Company of Jesus.

In Two Books, translated from the Original Italian of Father Philip Monaci, of the same Company, with a beautiful portrait of the Saint, 8vo., printed wrapper, 2s.—cloth lettered, 2s. 6d.

Large Royal 32mo, printed wrapper, 1s.—Cloth, plain edges, 1s. 3d.—Cloth, gilt edges, 1s. 6d.

LIFE OF ANNA MARIA TAIGI,
A HOLY WOMAN

Who attained, in the MARRIED STATE, and amidst the cares of a Family, and the trials of poverty, to such EMINENT SANCTITY, that the process of HER CANONIZATION is now going on at Rome; She died in 1837. Translated from the French and Italian lives written by the Rt. Rev. Dr. Luquet, Bishop of Hesebon,

BY A SISTER OF PROVIDENCE.

EDITED BY THE VERY REV. DR. FABER.
ORATORIAN LIVES OF THE SAINTS.
Translated from various languages for spiritual reading, with Prefaces, post 8vo. cloth lettered, price 4s. per volume.

ORATORIAN LIVES OF THE SAINTS.

Now Ready, complete in One Volume. Price 5s.
THE LIFE OF THE
B. Margaret Mary Alacoque,
Religious of the Visitation of St. Mary,
Who died in the Odour of Sanctity at Paray-le-Monial in Burgundy.

Complete in Five Vols. price £1.
The Life of St. Alphonsus Liguori.

THIS DAY, in 2 Vols., price 8s.
Life of St. Francis de Sales,
Bishop and Prince of Geneva.

THIS DAY, IN ONE VOLUME, PRICE 4s.
THE LIVES OF
S. ROSE OF LIMA, B. COLOMBA OF RIETI, AND S. JULIANA FALCONIERI.

LIFE OF ST. PHILIP NERI,
Apostle of Rome, and Founder of the Congregation of the Oratory, complete in one volume, price 5s.

PUBLISHED BY RICHARDSON AND SONS.
26, Paternoster Row, London; and Derby.

Just Published, Demy 18mo, handsomely bound in cloth,
PRICE **6d.** EACH.

CATHOLIC TALES FOR THE YOUNG.

MORNING AND EVENING STAR.
CHRISTMAS DINNER.
HAWTHORN BUSH.
PEARL LOST & FOUND.

THE HOLY HOUSE.
A TALE OF THE CRUSADERS.
MAURICE'S TRIAL.
CARRY'S TRIALS.

☞ Will be followed by others uniform in type and binding.

ONLY ONE SHILLING PER VOL.
With the approbation of
HIS EMINENCE CARDINAL WISEMAN.

BUTLER'S LIVES OF THE SAINTS.

Neat Pocket Edition, illustrated with portraits and vignettes engraved on steel, complete in 12 volumes.

This Day, small 8vo. superfine cloth, price 4s.

SPIRITUAL CONSOLATION,
OR A TREATISE ON THE PEACE OF THE SOUL,
From the French of Pere Lomber,
Interspersed with various Instructions necessary for promoting the practice of Solid Piety,

BY THE AUTHORESS OF "THE URSULINE MANUAL."

THIS DAY, price 4s.

The Mistress of Novices
Instructed in her Duties:
Or, a Method of Direction for the use of Persons charged with the Training of Souls in Christian and Religious Perfection.

Translated from the Second Edition
BY THE REV. F. IGNATIUS SISK,
Of Mount St. Bernard's Abbey.

www.ingramcontent.com/pod-product-compliance
Lightning Source LLC
Chambersburg PA
CBHW032048230426
43672CB00009B/1523